W9-BDY-446

6 HO RAILROADS YOU CAN BUILD

MODEL RAILROAD HANDBOOK NO. 38

FROM **Model Railroader** MAGAZINE

MODULAR PROJECTS

LAYOUT PROJECTS

KALMBACH BOOKS

Dedicated to the memory of Gordon Odegard, who established the tradition of step-by-step layout projects in MODEL RAILROADER

Selected by Bob Hayden
Editorial Intern: Jennifer Kamke Black
Cover Design: Lawrence Luser

The material in this book first appeared as articles in MODEL RAILROADER magazine. They are reprinted in their entirety with the exception of associated special features with the Washita & Santa Fe series (listed below) which were not reproduced due to space limitations. They are available as photocopies from Kalmbach Publishing Co. for a nominal fee.

W&SF articles not included:

Dolese Sand & Gravel (MR August 1984, pp. 63-67)
Scratchbuilding Pauls Valley Station (MR June 1983, pp. 80-87)
Structures for W&SF (MR June 1983, pp. 74-79)

Library of Congress Cataloging-in-Publication Data

6 HO railroads you can build / from Model Railroader magazine.
     p.   cm. -- (Model railroad handbook : no. 38)
   ISBN 0-89024-189-9
   1. Railroads--Models. I. Title: Six HO railroads you can build.
II. Series.
TF197.A13   1993
625.1'9--dc20   93-28560
                                              CIP

Modular Railroading

The first two layouts in this book are HO modules: portable railroad sections that are built to standard dimensions and can be connected to other modules to form an extended model railroad. This is a great way to share your interest with other model railroaders, turning what is often a lone endeavor into a social activity.

When the first N scale modules were built in California in 1973 and displayed in 1974, word spread quickly about this new twist in model railroading — and clubs across the country started building their own modules. So popular was N scale modular railroading that a national organization was formed to ensure uniformity among the hundreds of modules being built. This organization, run by the California group that pioneered the idea in 1973, became know as Ntrak, and the standards it set have taken root. If you're interested in building an N scale module, contact Ntrak for a set of its standards. Almost all N scale modules are built to Ntrak specifications, so it makes tons of sense to obtain its standards and adhere to them. Ntrak also publishes a bimonthly newsletter. Write to it at Ntrak, 2424 Alturas Road, Atascadero, CA 93422.

While N scale modular railroading evolved smoothly, with a firm set of standards, other scales have experienced more fitful efforts to establish national standards. There's no question that HO modular railroading is growing in popularity (as it is in all scales). Recognizing this, the National Model Railroad Association (NMRA) introduced a set of HO module standards a few years ago, and today many HO modules are built to these standards. Splinter groups, however, have formed throughout the country, subverting attempts to form a national set of HO module standards. So before you start building your HO module contact the group you plan on operating with and get a set of its standards. Or create your own with a new group of modelers. To receive the NMRA's standards for HO modules write to it at 4121 Cromwell Road, Chattanooga, TN 37421.

Introducing F&S Junction

Contemporary railroading in a 2 x 4-foot space

BY MICHAEL TYLICK
PHOTOS BY THE AUTHOR

MODULAR RAILROADING is popular for a number of reasons. For those modelers who don't have enough space for a layout, building a module is an obvious choice. It's also a good way to try out techniques for a new layout. Finally, constructing a module is a great excuse for experimenting with a different scale, type of scenery, or era.

I built F&S Junction, an HO scale module depicting contemporary railroading, as a change of pace from my home layout, the 1930s-era Fitchburg & Southbridge. [That layout was featured in the September 1985 issue of MODEL RAILROADER. — *Ed.*] Because of frequent railfanning trips with my son Jimmy, I wanted to try my hand at modeling Conrail operations in our area. See fig. 1.

The F&S Jct. module is part of a setup on which we run prototypically long freight trains. Besides being a pleasant break from the F&S, working on this module has been a good way to enjoy the hobby with other people. Another advantage is that a module can be incorporated into a home layout between shows, something I plan to try soon with O scale.

When I began, there was no universal standard for HO scale modules. I built mine according to guidelines used by a local modular group, the Amherst Railway Society, which are identical to those of the Mt. Claire (Baltimore) Division of the National Model Railroad Association. The methods outlined here can be adapted to any module.

By the way, the NMRA has since established official HO modular standards. Consequently, clubs that built modular layouts before that time must group their modules together, then use special "adapter" sections to fit them into a larger layout. [The sidebar on page 10 describes these standards.]

Left: In this Joseph Snopek photo three Erie Lackawanna units pass the abandoned tower at F&S Junction as a Lehigh Valley train waits on the branch line.

Above: The inspiration for the module came from the author's visits to the local Conrail line with his son. Here he's captured that trackside perspective.

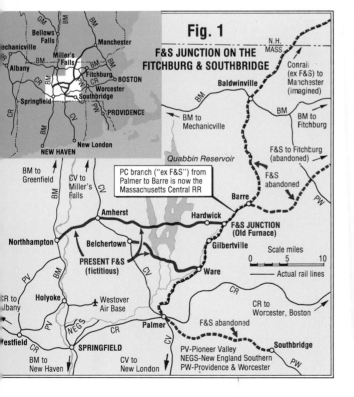

Fig. 1

F&S JUNCTION ON THE FITCHBURG & SOUTHBRIDGE

N.H. MASS.

Conrail (ex F&S) to Manchester (imagined)

Baldwinville

BM to Mechanicville

BM

BM to Fitchburg

BM

F&S to Fitchburg (abandoned)

Quabbin Reservoir

F&S abandoned

PC branch ("ex F&S") from Palmer to Barre is now the Massachusetts Central RR

Barre

BM to Greenfield

CV to Miller's Falls

CV

Amherst

Hardwick

F&S JUNCTION (Old Furnace)

Northampton

Belchertown

Gilbertville

Scale miles

0   5   10

PRESENT F&S (fictitious)

CV

Ware

Actual rail lines

CR

CR to Worcester, Boston

Holyoke

Westover Air Base

PV

BM

NEGS

CR

Palmer

F&S abandoned

CR to Albany

Westfield

CV

SPRINGFIELD

CV to New London

Southbridge

PV-Pioneer Valley
NEGS-New England Southern
PW-Providence & Worcester

PW

BM to New Haven

Bellows Falls

GM

BM

BM

Manchester

Mechanicville

Miller's Falls

BM

Albany

BM

CR

Fitchburg

BM

BOSTON

Springfield

Southbridge

Worcester

CR

CV

PW

PROVIDENCE

BM

New London

NEW HAVEN

The author, Mike Tylick, holds up his son Jimmy to give him a better view of trains approaching F&S Junction at a recent Bedford Boomers Train Show.

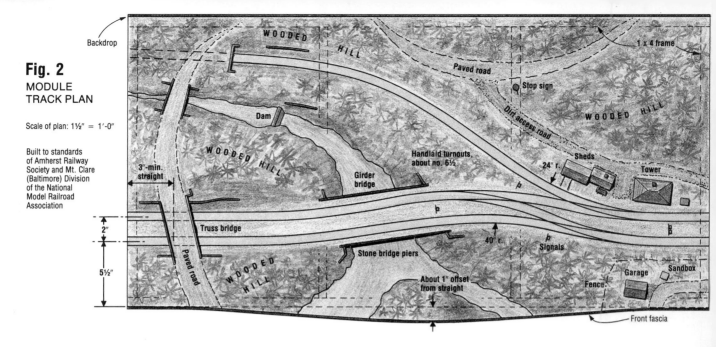

Fig. 2
MODULE
TRACK PLAN

Scale of plan: 1½″ = 1′-0″

Built to standards
of Amherst Railway
Society and Mt. Clare
(Baltimore) Division
of the National
Model Railroad
Association

Backdrop

WOODED HILL

Paved road

1 x 4 frame

Stop sign

Dirt access road

WOODED HILL

Dam

WOODED HILL

Handlaid turnouts,
about no. 6½

24″ r.

Sheds

Tower

3″-min.
straight

Girder
bridge

Truss bridge

Paved road

Stone bridge piers

WOODED HILL

About 1″ offset
from straight

40″ r.

Signals

Garage

Sandbox

Fence

2″

5½″

Front fascia

DESIGN CONSIDERATIONS

With the need to have a small, transportable section that will mate with other units, modules tend to be mechanical looking. The plywood top needed for strength becomes the scenery, and the short lengths of track tend to run straight and parallel to the front edge. I wanted to avoid this, so I offset the track inwards about an inch on a long S curve (the 40″ radius prevents any operating problems) and offset the front about as much outwards to break up the uniformity. See fig. 2.

I also wanted to construct a river below the track grade (rarely seen in modules)

as the lower elevation makes the distant hills seem higher. I designed what I call "inverted benchwork." The plywood is still needed for rigidity, though the track is built in an open-grid fashion. See fig. 3. These methods helped to avoid the mechanical look and made my module look longer than 4 feet.

I wanted the scenery to be mostly woodlands, but felt a center of interest was needed. I added a dummy branch and interlocking plant, the fiction being that the branch was the remnant of the F&S, which wasn't absorbed into Conrail and now operates as an independent short line. While the name F&S Junction was obvious, the location (Old Furnace)

came from Jimmy, who decided that the scenery looked like the area around this tiny nearby village, which was the site of a Revolutionary War cannon foundry. See fig. 1.

BENCHWORK

The inverted benchwork took more lumber and time than the standard version, but the work went quickly thanks to a tip from Bob Oakley. Instead of drilling holes and driving screws by hand, I used wallboard screws, which I could drive easily with an old, single-speed drill. I used Elmer's glue to strengthen the joints.

I had to cut holes in the plyscore (no

This is the completed F&S Junction module. It's amazing how many nicely detailed scenes the author has been able to work into a 2 x 4-foot space.

F & S JCT.
OLD FURNACE MA

MICHAEL TYLICK

need to use finished wood that will be hidden) to allow clearance for the clamps that attach to the next module. (I had the lumberyard cut the base piece as they have the tools for square, accurate cutting of large pieces.) The lag-screw floor levelers proved a blessing when I was moving the module around my garage and working on it in different locations.

Building this framework would be good practice for a new layout builder, as the pieces are small and easy to move.

ROADBED

I drew the final track plan full size on a piece of leftover newsprint. I find it easier to think in full size, and the drawing isn't too large to lay out on the floor. I added ¾" to each side of the center line; then I cut out the pattern and traced it on the subroadbed, which is made from ½"-thick plyscore. A jigsaw made short work of cutting this material. Scraps of 1 x 4 from the framework were used as risers. I lowered the branch line ¼" (about a 2 percent grade) to separate it from the main line, as shown in fig. 4.

Although I'd used cork and Homasote roadbed in the past, I was impressed by the white pine roadbed Jim Woodard was using on his home layout. Jim got the idea from Paul Mallery's *Trackwork Handbook for Model Railroads*. Purchased as ¼"-thick lattice stock, clear pine actually costs less than cork or precut Homasote (about 16 cents per foot). Be sure to use clear pine, as the spikes will follow the grain or imperfections in lesser grades, pulling the track out of gauge. Also, remember that spikes driven into clear pine are there forever.

Lattice stock is sold in 1" widths. That's perfect for straight track, but curves require cutting it into splines as shown in fig. 4. Half-inch widths (ripped on a table saw) can be bent easily to the 40"-radius curves. I had to rip the pine into ¼" widths to flex it enough to go around the 24"-radius branchline curves. I used clamps and small brads to hold the roadbed in place while the Elmer's glue dried. The first piece forms the track center line, and the flex of the wood gives a natural easement to horizontal and vertical curves.

I used Durham's Water Putty to fill rough spots in the roadbed and an automotive sanding block to smooth and level everything. The tapered ballast edges were also made with water putty. A 30-degree angle is about right, but keep the slope irregular to avoid monotony. Don't worry about little imperfections as the ballast will cover them.

I laid the roadbed over the bridge cutout in the plyscore to maintain smooth, level curves. (A ballasted deck bridge is much easier to build and much stronger for a portable layout.) I didn't feel comfortable with just ¼"-thick wood, so I cut a piece of ⅛" Plexiglas to reinforce the bottom. After painting the underside black to hide the lack of detail, I glued the plastic reinforcement underneath the roadbed with Duco Cement, which made a strong support. I painted the finished roadbed with a medium gray latex paint to hide holidays in the ballast.

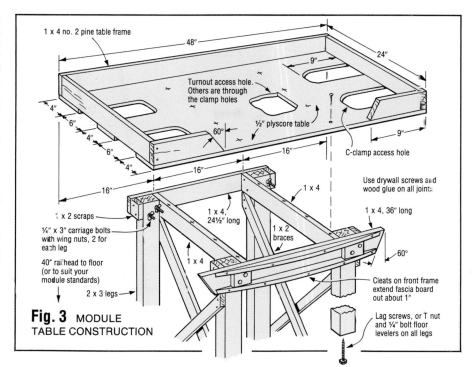

Fig. 3 MODULE TABLE CONSTRUCTION

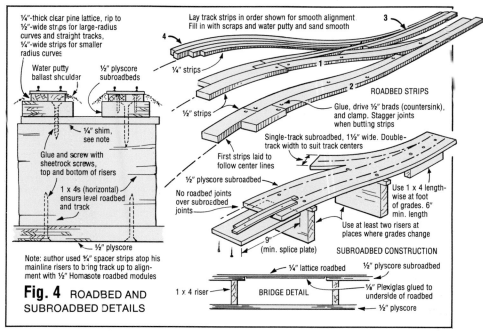

Fig. 4 ROADBED AND SUBROADBED DETAILS

TRACKWORK

While most modules are built with commercial trackwork, there are advantages to laying your own. It's really not difficult, nor does it take much longer, especially if you consider the tedious hours spent adjusting commercial switches and cutting them to fit unusual situations. I could never have built the graceful curved crossover with commercial components.

Best of all, you can lay track and build switches where you want them, without regard to frog numbers, just like the prototype. Handlaid track is also less expensive, particularly where turnouts are involved. While I may not be adept with mechanical things, I know that my scratchbuilt switches are more dependable than any manufactured product.

Although some people do an excellent job of painting and weathering prefab pieces, handlaid track still looks better. Besides being fun, laying your own track allows you to become more intimately involved with the layout and make it more of yourself.

I stained Campbell's ties using a method described in "Track Is a Model Too," an article in the out-of-print January 1955 MR. I put several ties in a "leg" from an old pair of panty hose and dipped them alternately into a can of dark oak stain and thinned gray enamel porch paint. Some batches would go the stain first, others the paint. None were left in for the same time. Some batches went in one or both baths several times. After all the ties were dried on newspaper, I mixed them together until I had a

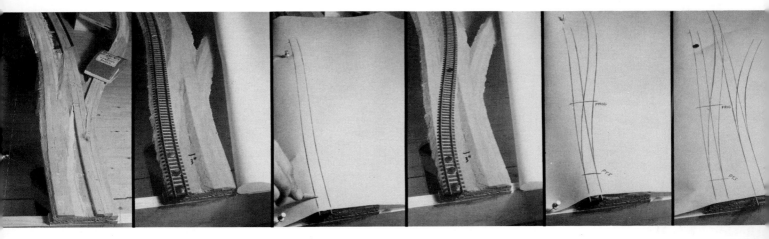

This sequence of photos shows step by step how the author made full-size templates for the module's turnouts. For further information, see fig. 5, below.

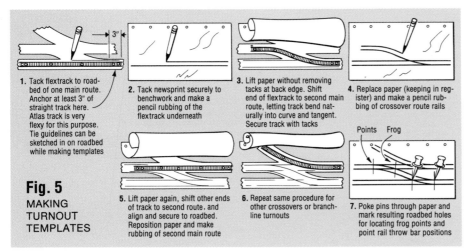

Fig. 5
MAKING TURNOUT TEMPLATES

1. Tack flextrack to roadbed of one main route. Anchor at least 3" of straight track here. Atlas track is very flexy for this purpose. Tie guidelines can be sketched in on roadbed while making templates

2. Tack newsprint securely to benchwork and make a pencil rubbing of the flextrack underneath

3. Lift paper without removing tacks at back edge. Shift end of flextrack to second main route, letting track bend naturally into curve and tangent. Secure track with tacks

4. Replace paper (keeping in register) and make a pencil rubbing of crossover route rails

5. Lift paper again, shift other ends of track to second route, and align and secure to roadbed. Reposition paper and make rubbing of second main route

6. Repeat same procedure for other crossovers or branch-line turnouts

7. Poke pins through paper and mark resulting roadbed holes for locating frog points and point rail throw bar positions

random collection that ranged in color from dark brown to mottled gray with everything in between.

To determine the tie locations on the roadbed, I loosely tacked down a piece of Atlas flextrack and traced the outside of the ties as shown in fig. 5. Allowing the track to form its own curve results in a very smooth flowing track. I determined the switch locations and templates by forming the track to the different routes and making a progressive rubbing of each route. In this case all the switches were on one piece of paper.

The ties were glued in place with Elmer's and held down with heavy metal weights until dry. In my opinion, a jig spaces the ties too uniformly, so I simply spaced them by eye and didn't worry about even placement. I think that irregularities add to the appearance; just don't overdo it.

The switch ties were laid in place full length. When the glue dried I trimmed the ends to the correct size using a razor blade. I then dabbed a little oak stain on the raw tie ends. Save the ends because long ones can be used for other switches and short ones for abandoned ties along the roadbed.

Since a turnout determines the position of two tracks, this is the place to start laying rail. One switch determines the location of the others, so there is an order in which to build them (fig. 6). Although I would have preferred a smaller rail for appearance, the Amherst group requires code 100 rail for dependable operation of varied equipment and a 2½" track center, which makes the crossover extremely long.

The methods I used to fabricate turnouts were based on those described by John Lukesh in the March 1977 MR. I started by building and laying the frog and guardrails first. Refer to fig. 7. Building the frog over the template right side up and filling everything with solder assures much better rail alignment. A hacksaw blade cuts out a perfect-width flangeway in short order. Keep checking the depth with an NMRA gauge. If the frog and guardrail relationships are done carefully and the points are filed well, building a switch is almost foolproof.

I found it easier to paint the rail before spiking. I brush-painted a coat of Polly S Grimy Black followed by a thin wash of Rust. This gives a nice uneven weathered brown effect.

Lay the track by spiking one rail first, making sure to keep a smooth curve a proper distance from the tie ends (the Kadee gauge has a mark for this). Although the white pine seems like it will hold the spikes forever, I like to glue each rail in place with Pliobond first. I think this also makes spiking easier.

I use a Walthers spike tool, and while the spikes take a little longer to drive (and I may bend a few more) in the white pine than they might in Homasote, I'm not worried about having to go back and regauge them. Code 70 spikes are less expensive and look better with their smaller heads. They have a sharper point, which is easier to drive. Their only drawback is that they bend more easily.

The Kadee three-point gauge makes short work of laying the second rail in perfect alignment. By spiking the rail between the finished section and the track gauge, I've found I need only one gauge to keep the rail in alignment. A pair of spikes every five ties or so is plenty. Spike each rail on a different tie for appearance and to avoid splitting the wood, but always put one spike on each side of the same rail to avoid kinks. I put spikes in every tie at the module

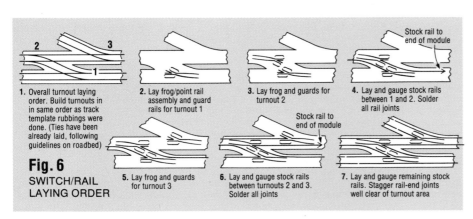

Fig. 6
SWITCH/RAIL LAYING ORDER

1. Overall turnout laying order. Build turnouts in in same order as track template rubbings were done. (Ties have been already laid, following guidelines on roadbed)

2. Lay frog/point rail assembly and guard rails for turnout 1

3. Lay frog and guards for turnout 2

4. Lay and gauge stock rails between 1 and 2. Solder all rail joints

Stock rail to end of module

5. Lay frog and guards for turnout 3

6. Lay and gauge stock rails between turnouts 2 and 3. Solder all joints

Stock rail to end of module

7. Lay and gauge remaining stock rails. Stagger rail-end joints well clear of turnout area

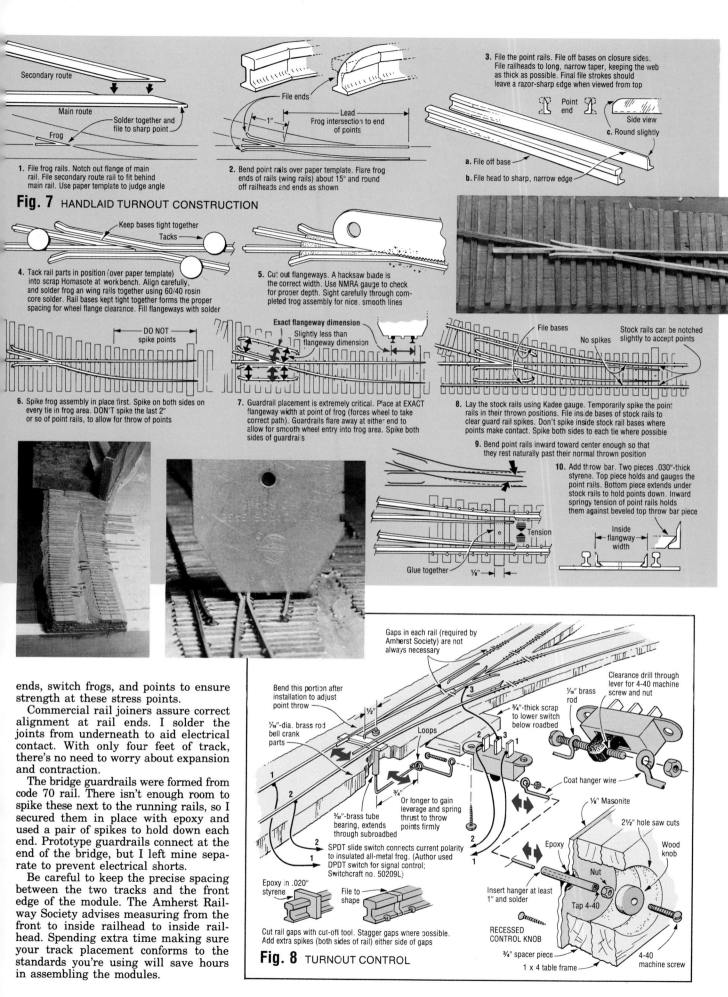

Fig. 7 HANDLAID TURNOUT CONSTRUCTION

Secondary route

Main route

Solder together and file to sharp point

Frog

1. File frog rails. Notch out flange of main rail. File secondary route rail to fit behind main rail. Use paper template to judge angle

File ends

1"

Lead — Frog intersection to end of points

2. Bend point rails over paper template. Flare frog ends of rails (wing rails) about 15° and round off railheads and ends as shown

3. File the point rails. File off bases on closure sides. File railheads to long, narrow taper, keeping the web as thick as possible. Final file strokes should leave a razor-sharp edge when viewed from top

Point end

Side view

a. File off base

b. File head to sharp, narrow edge

c. Round slightly

Keep bases tight together

Tacks

4. Tack rail parts in position (over paper template) into scrap Homasote at workbench. Align carefully, and solder frog an wing rails together using 60/40 rosin core solder. Rail bases kept tight together forms the proper spacing for wheel flange clearance. Fill flangeways with solder

5. Cut out flangeways. A hacksaw blade is the correct width. Use NMRA gauge to check for proper depth. Sight carefully through completed frog assembly for nice, smooth lines

DO NOT spike points

6. Spike frog assembly in place first. Spike on both sides on every tie in frog area. DON'T spike the last 2" or so of point rails, to allow for throw of points

Exact flangeway dimension

Slightly less than flangeway dimension

7. Guardrail placement is extremely critical. Place at EXACT flangeway width at point of frog (forces wheel to take correct path). Guardrails flare away at either end to allow for smooth wheel entry into frog area. Spike both sides of guardrails

File bases

No spikes

Stock rails can be notched slightly to accept points

8. Lay the stock rails using Kadee gauge. Temporarily spike the point rails in their thrown positions. File inside bases of stock rails to clear guard rail spikes. Don't spike inside stock rail bases where points make contact. Spike both sides to each tie where possible

9. Bend point rails inward toward center enough so that they rest naturally past their normal thrown position

10. Add throw bar. Two pieces .030"-thick styrene. Top piece holds and gauges the point rails. Bottom piece extends under stock rails to hold points down. Inward springy tension of point rails holds them against beveled top throw bar piece

Tension

Glue together

⅛"

Inside flangway width

ends, switch frogs, and points to ensure strength at these stress points.

Commercial rail joiners assure correct alignment at rail ends. I solder the joints from underneath to aid electrical contact. With only four feet of track, there's no need to worry about expansion and contraction.

The bridge guardrails were formed from code 70 rail. There isn't enough room to spike these next to the running rails, so I secured them in place with epoxy and used a pair of spikes to hold down each end. Prototype guardrails connect at the end of the bridge, but I left mine separate to prevent electrical shorts.

Be careful to keep the precise spacing between the two tracks and the front edge of the module. The Amherst Railway Society advises measuring from the front to inside railhead to inside railhead. Spending extra time making sure your track placement conforms to the standards you're using will save hours in assembling the modules.

Gaps in each rail (required by Amherst Society) are not always necessary

Bend this portion after installation to adjust point throw

1/16"-dia. brass rod bell crank parts

3/32"-brass tube bearing, extends through subroadbed

¾"

Loops

Or longer to gain leverage and spring thrust to throw points firmly

SPDT slide switch connects current polarity to insulated all-metal frog. (Author used DPDT switch for signal control; Switchcraft no. 50209L)

Epoxy in .020" styrene

File to shape

Cut rail gaps with cut-off tool. Stagger gaps where possible. Add extra spikes (both sides of rail) either side of gaps

1/16" brass rod

¾"-thick scrap to lower switch below roadbed

Clearance drill through lever for 4-40 machine screw and nut

Coat hanger wire

⅛" Masonite

2½" hole saw cuts

Epoxy

Wood knob

Nut

Insert hanger at least 1" and solder

Tap 4-40

RECESSED CONTROL KNOB

¾" spacer piece

1 x 4 table frame

4-40 machine screw

Fig. 8 TURNOUT CONTROL

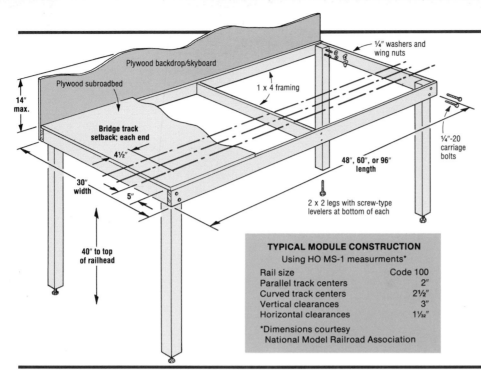

TYPICAL MODULE CONSTRUCTION
Using HO MS-1 measurments*

Rail size	Code 100
Parallel track centers	2″
Curved track centers	2½″
Vertical clearances	3″
Horizontal clearances	1¹⁄₃₂″

*Dimensions courtesy
National Model Railroad Association

NATIONAL MODULAR STANDARDS

Through the years many different modular standards have been developed for various scales and track gauges. Unfortunately, none has been compatible with others in the same grouping.

To solve this problem and arrive at universal standards for all scales and gauges, the National Model Railroad Association has been developing a set of criteria for building interchangeable modules in Z, N, TT, HO, S, and O standard gauge, as well as 24″, 30″, and 36″ narrow gauge in N, HO, S, and O. Special data for traction and electrified railroads are also being considered. All specifications provide for modules 4, 6, and 8 feet in length.

Copies of the existing MS-1 and MRP-1 proposed practices are available free to any NMRA member ($22 annual dues). For more information please write the National Model Railroad Association Inc., 4121 Cromwell Rd., Chattanooga, TN 37421. — *Gordon Odegard* ✿

As you lay track, keep testing the turnouts and track with a pair of trucks and an old freight car. When all the rail is in place, touch up all paint chips and spike heads with washes of Grimy Black and Rust. A little paint on the ties only adds to the appearance.

TURNOUT CONTROL

This is one area in which I departed from the Amherst club's standards. They recommend Caboose Industries ground throws, which I've used and know are excellent. However, I decided on panel-edge control because sooner or later hands reaching for the throws wreck some scenery. Also, with the all-metal frogs provision must be made for power routing as the turnouts are thrown.

The method I've used on my home layout as well as this module is a combination of techniques borrowed from Jeff Boothryd and Jim Woodard. I use slide

switches, which are inexpensive and easy to adjust. They provide a dependable locking throw, and the electrical switch contacts can be used for power routing. See fig. 8. You'll find them at Radio Shack stores or electronics mail order firms. I needed extra contacts for the signal interlocking, so I purchased three double-pole double-throw (DPDT) switches (Switchcraft 50209L) from an electronics supply house. Even at retail, these were only $1.50 each.

I cut recesses for the turnout control knobs with a 2½″ hole saw attachment on my electric drill. Protruding knobs are just begging to be snagged, broken, or accidently thrown. I glued a second piece of 1 x 4 to give sufficient thickness to fully recess the knobs. A piece of Masonite covers the rear of the hole.

The throw bar was patterned after the method used by The Model Railroad Club Inc. It is the least complicated and most dependable throw known to me.

I've found with trackwork and wiring that the simplest approaches usually are the best. If I seem to return to the theme of inexpensive, make-it-yourself components, it's because I started in the hobby as a teenager in the 1950s, when many of the items now available did not exist. Even if they had, I could not have afforded them. Anyway, I still find great joy in making things myself; if I happen to save money in the process, so much the better. The extra time spent is unimportant — I have no deadlines and learn many new skills in the process.

WIRING

The wiring was done to the Amherst group's specifications, except for the live-frog turnouts, which required special wiring. Those specifications have been upgraded to use no. 14 wire and thereby lessen the signal losses over long distances when using the Dynatrol command control system. I also used the carrier voltage to power the signal circuit.

A DPDT switch selects which track to take power from, as one track is often powered with a conventional cab-control setup to accommodate members without receiver-equipped engines. See fig. 9.

I glued and screwed scraps of 1 x 4 above the edge of the clamp holes to provide a base for the terminal strips. Then, with an inexpensive crimping tool, I attached spade lugs to the wire ends. This makes the connections simple and foolproof. Be certain to solder the other joints carefully.

I used color-coded wires and taped a diagram of all wiring to the bottom for troubleshooting. It's easy to forget what you've installed, and with a module other people may have to make repairs.

Using binding twine I laced the wires into a cable, which I attached to the plywood with a staple gun. Do this carefully to avoid hitting the wire with staples.

Next, I ran electrical feeder wires from the terminal strips and soldered them to the bottom of the rails for better appearance. Having terminals at each end made it easier to connect both sides of the gapped sections. I laid the track with no electrical gaps; later, while working on the wiring, I cut the gaps and cemented a small piece of styrene in each to ensure that they wouldn't close up. In addition, put extra spikes near the gaps to keep everything precisely aligned. Make sure to leave some slack in the wires connected to the rail, as any strain on these might break the solder joint or kink the rail.

Now that all the carpentry, mechanical, and electrical work is done, I can turn to the real fun — building scenery, structures, and bridges. Typical construction articles spend most of their time on the mechanics and very little time describing how to make detailed scenery, but this is the part that I find most rewarding. No one is really interested in a neatly constructed, smooth-running plywood table, are they? See you next month. ✿

Fig. 9 MODULE WIRING (Amherst Society)

Optional gap, to keep symetrical for troubleshooting

Female plug, Radio Shack 274-205

Male plug, Radio Shack 274-204

No. 14 stranded wire, Radio Shack 278-1292 or 278-1303

To signal logic

DPDT rocker switch; selects track from which to take constant voltage from Dynatrol

A Conrail freight led by a Canadian National SD50F (being tested on the system) rolls through F&S Junction. The locomotives are custom-painted brass imports owned by Joe Snopek.

A **track gang** watches as a freight with an Erie Lackawanna SDP45 at the point passes under the highway bridge that the author constructed from two Atlas N scale railroad bridges.

Scenery, bridges, and buildings for the F&S Junction

With a little perseverance, scenery building could become your favorite part of the hobby

BY MICHAEL TYLICK

PHOTOS BY THE AUTHOR

WHEN WE left off last month we had assembled the HO scale F&S Junction module, laid the track, and completed the wiring. Unfortunately many model railroaders never get past this point. They're sure they can't build good-looking scenery. Nothing could be farther from the truth. With reasonable care (less than is needed to lay track), common sense, and observation, building scenery isn't difficult.

The methods I'm going to describe are fairly simple and straightforward. I hope I can persuade many of you to try building some scenery. With a little perseverance, this can become one of the most rewarding parts of the hobby.

Being an art teacher, I've been told that this kind of work comes easily to me. That may be true, as I've had some training. Still, the methods I use are based on simple techniques learned from others. I've met many people with no fine arts training who have discovered talents they didn't know they had by building scenery.

HARDSHELL METHODS

Styrofoam scenery is more practical than hardshell for modular layouts because it weighs less and is less apt to be damaged while moving. However, one of the reasons I built this module was to explain the scenery methods I used on my HO home layout, the Fitchburg & Southbridge. Therefore, I employed the same techniques on the module.

The hardshell scenery method I use is based on techniques pioneered by MR's Linn Westcott in the 1960s and included in Bill McClanahan's book *Scenery for Model Railroads* (Kalmbach Publishing Co.). I drape plaster-soaked paper towels over a base of crumpled up newspapers. The towels are industrial-strength ones, commonly used in public washrooms.

About the base — I know that other modelers advocate woven lattices of cardboard, screen wire, or Styrofoam contours because these give a better visualization of the finished scenery. I prefer crumpled newspapers, which may be the most difficult way of forming contours yet give an organic, "living" feeling to them.

I'll admit that I never feel in control when using this method — I just let it do what it wants. Then, while I'm reworking it, a very natural terrain forms. The raw hardshell reminds me of some primeval, volcanic world. Additional layers smooth it out and make it more realistic. Things I'd never planned appear. I keep the good and rebuild the bad.

I find it a good practice to design scenery in only the broadest sense — high here, low there, buildings in this location. I let the hardshell do what it wants. The first coat is always crude looking, but it gives me a sense of what it will eventually look like. Reworking it several times (leave it a day or two for a fresh approach) gradually yields a terrain that I'm willing to accept. I'll never end up with my original plan.

HARDSHELL LANDFORMS

When I built scenery for the first F&S, Hydrocal was difficult to find. The local masonry supply house suggested U. S. Gypsum Special White, a ceiling plaster. Having used it for several layouts, I've found it superior to Hydrocal. Special White is much less expensive and can be purchased at any masonry house (the last 80-pound bag I bought was $9). Since several layers of hardshell are needed to adjust and smooth the terrain, it has more than adequate strength.

Special White takes stains and paints beautifully, can be carved when soft, and has a good set-up time (about 30 minutes). The ratio of water to plaster does not seem critical. I've never had an unsightly plaster chip in all my experiences, including two modules.

Before starting any plaster work, be sure to protect the track. I've had good luck covering the track with a sheet of waxed paper. I use straight pins to hold it in place, then trim the excess waxed paper with a razor blade. The paper will remain until most of the scenery texturing is done. The longer you can keep it in place, the better.

The hardshell work is messy, gooey, and fun. The work isn't precise, so have fun with it and let your imagination go wild.

A large rubber ball, such as an old

children's kickball, cut in half, makes an excellent mixing vessel. When the plaster is dry, the excess can be dumped in the trash by flexing the rubber.

Be sure to wash your hands in a bucket of water and flush the waste down the toilet, as plaster will clog sink drains.

I built the hardshell over the module end. When it had dried I cut the edges even with the ends. The Masonite fascia boards were temporarily screwed in place and traced to match the contour. After removing and cutting the fascia to shape with a jigsaw, I mounted the boards permanently and finished the hardshell to the edge. See fig. 1. Since the fascia boards will be painted, there's no need to mask them or worry about plaster drips.

When the plaster work is done, remove the wet newspaper underneath to aid in drying. Otherwise, it will cause the shell to stay moist for a long time.

ROCKWORK

After I'd made some alterations and applied finishing coats of hardshell, I was ready to add texture to the rock faces. Igneous (volcanic) rock can be simulated by brushing on a coat of thin plaster and jabbing randomly with a large, splayed brush to give a bumpy texture. For sedimentary (water lowering)

rock, apply the same thin mix of plaster and stroke the brush in a more or less horizontal direction to form parallel lines in the rock.

Before doing any of this you'll need to dampen the plaster with "wet water" (water that has a few drops of liquid dishwashing detergent in it). Sometimes I combine igneous and sedimentary rocks in one area, though I tend to use the latter near the edges of water.

Foreground rocks were done with rock molds. Rather than cast them directly on the hardshell, I cast the rocks separately and glue them in place. A filler of Elmer's glue and sawdust takes care of any large gaps at the rear or between rocks. Gaps between rocks are filled by the scenic texturing later.

ADDING COLOR

Coloring the rockwork was next. A gallon of latex paint was mixed to a sand color, using a sample of highway sand as a guide. I thinned this to about a 10:1 ratio with wet water. Black and brown Universal Tinting Colors (available at paint stores) were added until I had eight shades of gray and brown.

After heavily spraying the plaster with wet water from a plant mister, I applied colors one at a time. The paint

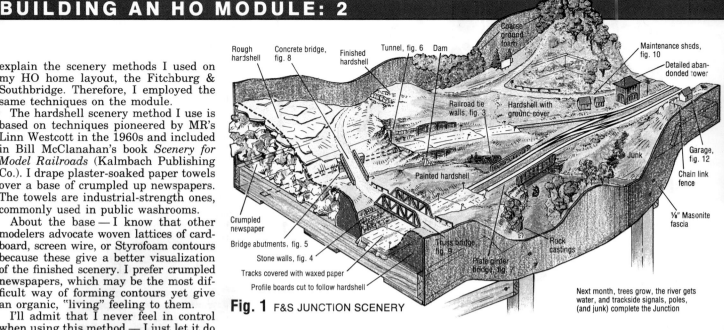

Fig. 1 F&S JUNCTION SCENERY

Rough hardshell
Concrete bridge, fig. 8
Finished hardshell
Tunnel, fig. 6
Dam
Coarse ground foam
Maintenance sheds, fig. 10
Detailed abandoned tower
Railroad tie walls, fig. 3
Hardshell with ground cover
Painted hardshell
Junk
Garage, fig. 12
Chain link fence
Crumpled newspaper
Bridge abutments, fig. 5
Stone walls, fig. 4
Tracks covered with waxed paper
Profile boards cut to follow hardshell
Truss bridge, fig. 9
Plate girder bridge, fig. 7
Rock castings
⅛" Masonite fascia

Next month, trees grow, the river gets water, and trackside signals, poles, (and junk) complete the Junction

Fig. 2. The painted hardshell, left, doesn't look very realistic. But after the ground cover is added, right, the transformation is quite dramatic. The author used real dirt and a variety of ground foams.

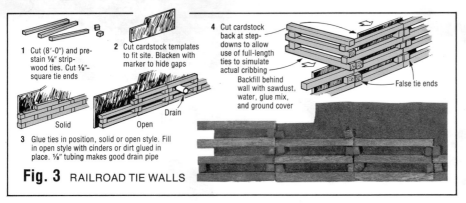

Fig. 3 RAILROAD TIE WALLS

1 Cut (8'-0") and pre-stain ⅛" strip-wood ties. Cut ⅛"-square tie ends

2 Cut cardstock templates to fit site. Blacken with marker to hide gaps

3 Glue ties in position, solid or open style. Fill in open style with cinders or dirt glued in place. ⅛" tubing makes good drain pipe

Solid

Open

Drain

4 Cut cardstock back at step-downs to allow use of full-length ties to simulate actual cribbing

Backfill behind wall with sawdust, water, glue mix, and ground cover

False tie ends

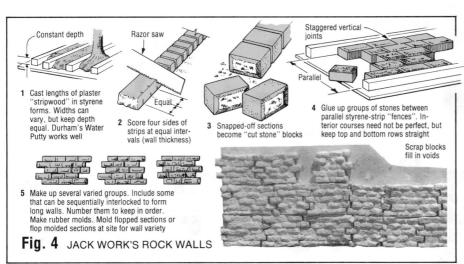

Fig. 4 JACK WORK'S ROCK WALLS

Constant depth

Razor saw

Staggered vertical joints

Parallel

1 Cast lengths of plaster "stripwood" in styrene forms. Widths can vary, but keep depth equal. Durham's Water Putty works well

Equal

2 Score four sides of strips at equal intervals (wall thickness)

3 Snapped-off sections become "cut stone" blocks

4 Glue up groups of stones between parallel styrene-strip "fences". Interior courses need not be perfect, but keep top and bottom rows straight

Scrap blocks fill in voids

5 Make up several varied groups. Include some that can be sequentially interlocked to form long walls. Number them to keep in order. Make rubber molds. Mold flopped sections or flop molded sections at site for wall variety

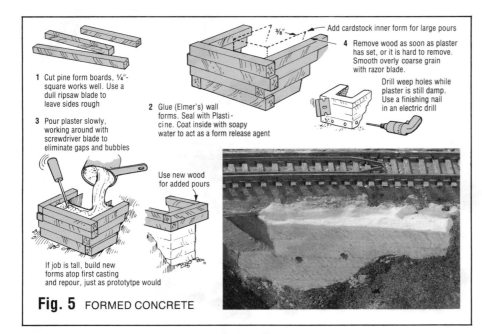

Fig. 5 FORMED CONCRETE

1 Cut pine form boards, ¼"-square works well. Use a dull ripsaw blade to leave sides rough

2 Glue (Elmer's) wall forms. Seal with Plasticine. Coat inside with soapy water to act as a form release agent

3 Pour plaster slowly, working around with screwdriver blade to eliminate gaps and bubbles

Use new wood for added pours

If job is tall, build new forms atop first casting and repour, just as prototype would

3/8"

Add cardstock inner form for large pours

4 Remove wood as soon as plaster has set, or it is hard to remove. Smooth overly coarse grain with razor blade.

Drill weep holes while plaster is still damp. Use a finishing nail in an electric drill

looks much darker when wet, so let each color dry before applying the next coat. I'd apply a coat in the morning before going to work and one when I got home.

I ended up applying seven "washes" of various shades. I began with the latex earth to remove the stark white. Then came a very dark gray to highlight cracks and crevices. A coat of very light gray alters the rock from a brown to a gray tone, while an earth latex tinted with burnt sienna gives the color depth. A final coat of medium gray blends everything.

Finding the rocks too dark for my taste (I always seem to overdo it), I sprayed a very thin coat of earth color to lighten everything. A thin wash of India ink darkened the recesses in the rock. Although the rocks seem to lighten over a few weeks, I'm impatient and so usually finish with a sparse drybrush coat of light gray (which is too stark looking)

after the ground cover is in place. There's no need to paint all the plaster that will be covered, and the texturing also alters the color slightly.

GROUND COVER

As fig. 2 shows, the scenery doesn't look very good at this point. The contours are too extreme and monochromatic. Ground cover will finish the landforms and soften the jagged edges considerably. Real dirt looks better than any substitute, but local topsoil is too dark. I've settled on road sand, which gives a pleasing color. I collect a bucket in the spring when the salt's washed out.

After removing the large rocks (smaller ones add to the effect), I throw handfuls of the sand on the scenery, covering everything. Then I spray lots of water down from the higher elevations. Gentle slopes fill in, and talus and gullies form at bottoms of the steeper cliffs. This method, also learned from Linn Westcott, comes closest to duplicating natural erosion. If too much dirt is washed away, more is added. Along the track and riverbeds I scoop away the excess.

When I've repeated this process a few times and am satisfied with the effect, I spray several coats of dilute glue (don't forget the dishwashing detergent) to fix everything. As this dries over several days I look at it and make changes. The eroded sand really turns the crumpled hardshell into a convincing replica of nature. And why not? Much of it was done in the same way as happens outdoors.

Additional color improves the effect, which is the reason I use a variety of textures and colors of ground foam. I like the kinds sold by Architectural Model Supply (AMSI) and Woodland Scenics. I start with the finest grades and work up to the coarsest. After each application I erode some of it with a generous spray of water and secure it with glue. I add two or three shades a day, going over it at least seven or eight times.

Before reworking the sand or ground foam I look carefully at what I have and determine where I can make improvements. I stress this idea of reworking because I think it's crucial to good scenery. Always work from high to low, and you'll get beautiful cliff bottoms, weeds in the cracks, and realistic riverbeds.

The distant hills were cut from Masonite and covered with coarse ground foam. I overpaint them with thinned latex earth and sky blue colors to add aerial perspective (depth) to the scene.

After the rough scenery work was done, I removed the waxed paper from the track, cleaned up the little spills that always happen, and started to add the retaining walls, bridges, and structures that bring the scene to life.

RETAINING WALLS AND ABUTMENTS

New England abounds in retaining walls. The terrain is rugged enough to require many earth cuts, but generally not rocky enough to allow many places to be a sheer cliff. Retaining walls are also good for gaining height in scenery, and that's important considering the space compression required in the small areas we have.

Fig. 6. The author cast this tunnel portal from a master he made for portals on his home layout.

Bridges must also have abutments, usually with retaining walls to hold back the earth fill used to keep the bridge as short as possible.

If clearances allow, the walls can be glued in place in front of the hardshell. If not, the plaster should be cut away with an old steak knife. Always check clearances with an NMRA gauge.

Places where my rockwork or hills were too close were good candidates for retaining walls. I backfill with a mixture of sawdust, Elmer's glue, and water. I try to give this fill a gradual slope, suggesting a more gentle hill than would really exist. Foliage will also help to hide the exaggerated steepness of my hills. Spreading dirt and ground foam over this blends everything.

I try to use as many types of construction of walls as possible. Doing so adds interest

and gives a feeling of greater distance. Nothing looks worse than a layout on which every retaining wall and abutment has been done the same way.

Railroad tie walls are probably the simplest to make (fig. 3). As for the stone walls, some are commercial castings, though my favorites are made from a method described by Jack Work in the first issue of *Mainline Modeler*. Jack fashioned a number of rocks from lengths of plaster "stripwood" that he scored and snapped to give a rock face. Molds of about 30 of these rocks were made. The stones were glued between horizontal spacers to form a series of interlocking pieces. This method, illustrated in fig. 4, makes beautiful random stone walls, and the molds may be used for other stone structures.

Poured concrete has been used since the turn of the century and is a natural for the abutments of the concrete highway bridge. My procedure for simulating poured concrete walls is shown in fig. 5. A rarely modeled improvement to many prototype railroad bridges is either reinforcing or raising stone bridge abutments with poured concrete.

To add scenic interest and have enough space along the branchline track for a stream, the water must change levels. I'd toyed with modeling a waterfall, but since I haven't had much success with that in the past I decided a dam would be better. The wall is a commercial N scale casting from AIM Products. Holes were bored for drain pipes that were made from 3/8" plastic tubing.

THE TUNNEL

I decided the best way to end the branch line was in a tunnel. This avoids an abrupt end to the track and allows the mountain in the corner to be larger and high enough to continue the roadway across it. The tunnel portal, fig. 6, is made from a rubber mold I used for the F&S. The stones come from the

molds used for the retaining walls, though they're glued on one by one to make a master.

Pieces of mat board were stapled to the side of the roadbed to simulate a tunnel liner. To obtain a blasted rock effect, I crumpled plaster-soaked paper towels that I'd stained a very dark gray to help darken the tunnel and hide the lack of detail. I left the last 6" of the wall open for access, but thumbtacked black paper over the opening to prevent light from shining through.

BRIDGES

While there are many excellent commercial bridges, I prefer to build my own. Besides the fact that I enjoy designing and constructing models, I can never find a commercial structure that's exactly the right type or length. I aim to build bridges to fit the gaps, rather than the other way around.

Railroad plate girder bridge. To avoid complications on the curved track, I made this structure without a center girder. The taller panels hide the added depth of the roadbed. Figure 7 shows how I built this bridge from sheet styrene, a material that is easy to work and, when painted, resembles metal.

For the rivets I used a Vintage Reproductions riveting wheel. Even though few people will ever see the bottom of the bridge, I built a simplified underframe to satisfy the curious and because the lack of detail might show in photos. The underframe was glued to the bottom of the Plexiglas with Duco cement.

Concrete highway bridge. I built this structure from wood and cardboard laminations (fig. 8). It may look spindly and complicated, but actually took less time than the railroad bridge. A stippled skim coat of water putty gave the material the correct texture.

Truss highway bridge. I was going to scratchbuild this structure after local Boston & Albany prototypes, especially

The concrete addition on top of the old stone plate girder bridge abutment is prototypical and indicates the track has been raised.

Fig. 7 PLATE GIRDER BRIDGE CONSTRUCTION

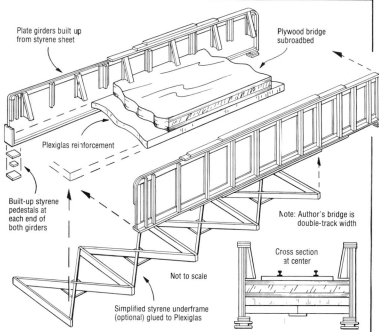

Plate girders built up from styrene sheet

Plywood bridge subroadbed

Plexiglas reinforcement

Built-up styrene pedestals at each end of both girders

Note: Author's bridge is double-track width

Cross section at center

Not to scale

Simplified styrene underframe (optional) glued to Plexiglas

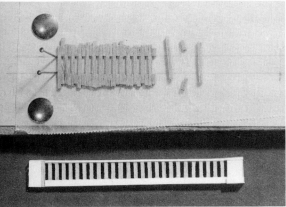

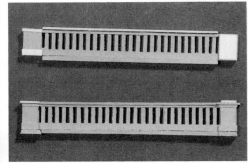

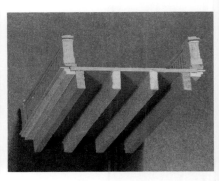

Fig. 8. The steps in building the concrete highway bridge are illustrated in this sequence of photos, left to right. The jig, left, helped accurately place the bridge railing pattern pieces. The completed bridge, made of wood and cardboard, was given a coat of thinned water putty to simulate concrete.

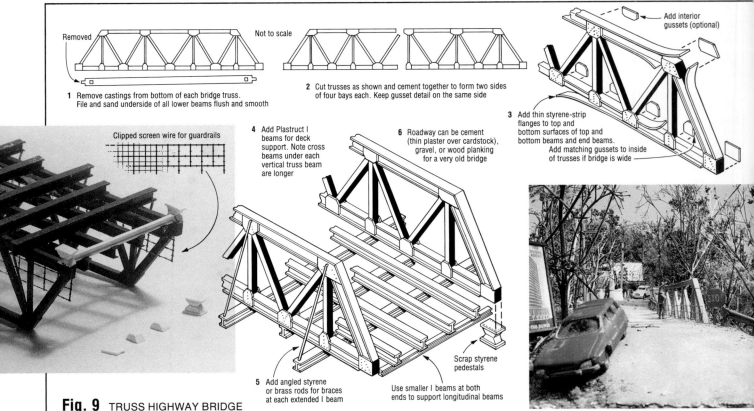

Removed Not to scale Add interior gussets (optional)

1 Remove castings from bottom of each bridge truss. File and sand underside of all lower beams flush and smooth

2 Cut trusses as shown and cement together to form two sides of four bays each. Keep gusset detail on the same side

3 Add thin styrene-strip flanges to top and bottom surfaces of top and bottom beams and end beams. Add matching gussets to inside of trusses if bridge is wide

Clipped screen wire for guardrails

4 Add Plastruct I beams for deck support. Note cross beams under each vertical truss beam are longer

6 Roadway can be cement (thin plaster over cardstock), gravel, or wood planking for a very old bridge

5 Add angled styrene or brass rods for braces at each extended I beam

Use smaller I beams at both ends to support longitudinal beams

Scrap styrene pedestals

Fig. 9 TRUSS HIGHWAY BRIDGE

The author used two Atlas N scale railroad bridges to kitbash this one-lane highway bridge. The girders were spliced and a new deck added.

The color photo shows how the bridge looks from the top side after the scenery was completed. A thin mix of plaster was used for the road.

since these bridges are fast disappearing as Conrail raises clearances to permit double-stack containers. What changed my mind was Rod Guthrie's giving me two Atlas (no. 2547) N scale railroad bridges he had lying around.

The N scale girders are about the right weight for an HO highway bridge and have good detail on one side. One truss wasn't long enough, so I spliced two to get the correct length. After removing the track, I added flanges and gussets for greater detail, which is needed with the wider bridge (fig. 9). I also constructed a new deck to accommodate highway traffic.

A one-lane bridge is ideal for the site. It makes the bridge look longer, and many of the local bridges were built in the horse-and-buggy days. Another reason for the replacement of these bridges (aside from their age) is the traffic hazards caused by sharp turns and narrow bridges. This also offers an excuse to add modern details like Creative Screen Process stop signs and Pikestuff guardrails.

ROADS

After the bridge was painted and glued in place, I paved the road with a thin mixture of plaster. I've never liked the flat wood or cardstock approach to building roads. Mine may be somewhat bumpy (see fig. 8), but I think they look better than roads that are too flat.

To simulate asphalt pavement, which quickly loses its dark hue, I mixed a light gray from white latex and black tinting dye. A thin wash gives the road an uneven coloring and a bit of weathering. The lines were painted with a fine brush. I avoid using chart tape because it's too mechanical and perfect looking. Nothing in real life is that neat.

I built the dirt access road at the same time. George Sellios recommended a mixture of Durham's Water Putty and dirt from a baseball diamond. The local field has plain topsoil, so I tried something different, mixing the putty with fine ash from my wood stove. I sculpted this mixture in place, remembering to add ruts with an old automobile while it was wet. Then I painted it with earth latex and Polly S Dirt until it had a good, dusty feeling. Most access roads to the tracks are either dirt or gravel, and

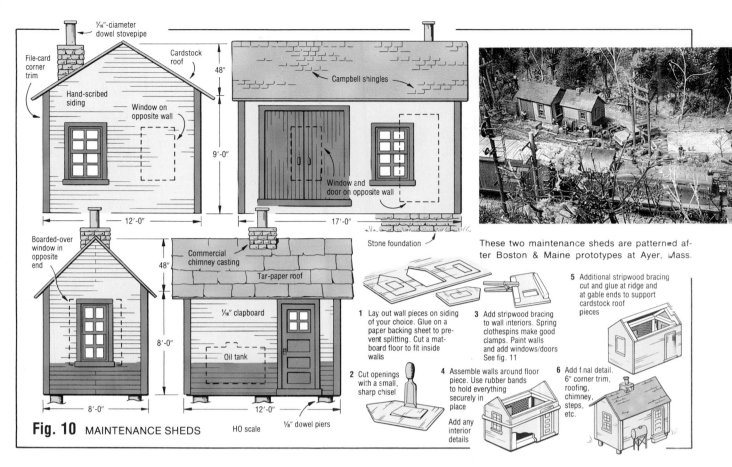

Fig. 10 MAINTENANCE SHEDS   HO scale

1/16"-diameter dowel stovepipe

File-card corner trim

Hand-scribed siding

Cardstock roof

Window on opposite wall

48"

9'-0"

12'-0"

Campbell shingles

Window and door on opposite wall

Stone foundation

17'-0"

Boarded-over window in opposite end

Commercial chimney casting

Tar-paper roof

1/16" clapboard

Oil tank

48"

8'-0"

8'-0"

12'-0"

1/8" dowel piers

These two maintenance sheds are patterned after Boston & Maine prototypes at Ayer, Mass.

1 Lay out wall pieces on siding of your choice. Glue on a paper backing sheet to prevent splitting. Cut a mat-board floor to fit inside walls

2 Cut openings with a small, sharp chisel

3 Add stripwood bracing to wall interiors. Spring clothespins make good clamps. Paint walls and add windows/doors See fig. 11

4 Assemble walls around floor piece. Use rubber bands to hold everything securely in place

Add any interior details

5 Additional stripwood bracing cut and glue at ridge and at gable ends to support cardstock roof pieces

6 Add final detail. 6" corner trim, roofing, chimney, steps, etc.

there are more dirt roads still around in the mountains than you might think.

STRUCTURES

Since the F&S Junction module was supposed to represent a rural scene, I didn't want a lot of buildings. Still, I knew a focal point was necessary. The interlocking plant was a logical choice.

Maintenance sheds. I began by building the maintenance sheds (fig. 10), as I was uncertain about what kind of interlocking tower to include. The sheds were copied from structures at Ayer, Mass., along the Boston & Maine. I didn't have measurements, but was able to draw a set of plans from photos using a known measurement (the 6'-8" height of the door).

Generic buildings like these are often more successful than exact copies. Some people recognize the prototype, while others are reminded of structures they're familiar with. Part of the visual success of a model railroad is the conjuring up of recollections in the minds of viewers.

I also adjusted the shed sizes to fit my location, as I believe it's easier to redesign a building to fit a site than cut out a mountain (one reason I dislike kits with their fixed dimensions) or build the scenery around it.

The beautiful window and door castings most modelers use weren't available years ago when I started scratchbuilding, and old habits die hard. I fabricated my own castings, which saves money and enables me to make any style or size exactly. The step-by-step photos in fig. 11 illustrate the sequence of construction.

The garage. Jim Woodard suggested that the foreground would be an excellent place for a backyard. The house would be

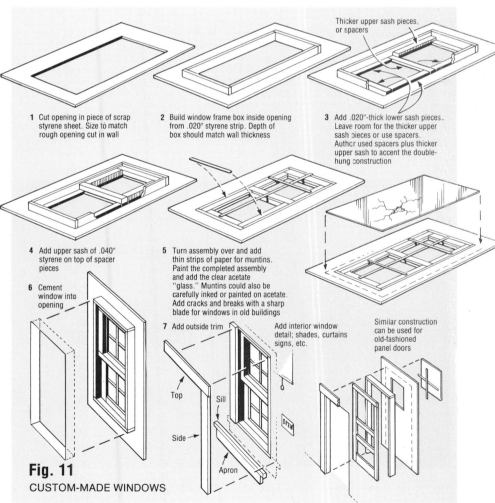

1 Cut opening in piece of scrap styrene sheet. Size to match rough opening cut in wall

2 Build window frame box inside opening from .020" styrene strip. Depth of box should match wall thickness

3 Add .020"-thick lower sash pieces. Leave room for the thicker upper sash pieces or use spacers. Author used spacers plus thicker upper sash to accent the double-hung construction

Thicker upper sash pieces, or spacers

4 Add upper sash of .040" styrene on top of spacer pieces

5 Turn assembly over and add thin strips of paper for muntins. Paint the completed assembly and add the clear acetate "glass." Muntins could also be carefully inked or painted on acetate. Add cracks and breaks with a sharp blade for windows in old buildings

6 Cement window into opening

7 Add outside trim

Add interior window detail; shades, curtains signs, etc.

Similar construction can be used for old-fashioned panel doors

Top

Sill

Side

Apron

OPEN

Fig. 11 CUSTOM-MADE WINDOWS

The author scratchbuilt this garage and used it as part of a backyard for a house that is off the module. He drew tools and garden equipment on the walls using fine-point markers.

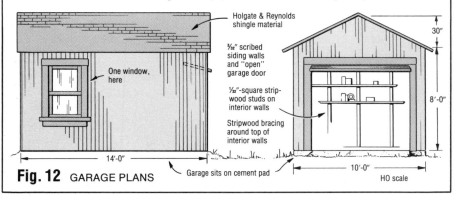

Fig. 12 GARAGE PLANS

(diagram labels:) Holgate & Reynolds shingle material; ³⁄₃₂″ scribed siding walls and "open" garage door; ¹⁄₃₂″-square strip-wood studs on interior walls; Stripwood bracing around top of interior walls; One window, here; Garage sits on cement pad; 14'-0"; 10'-0"; 30"; 8'-0"; HO scale

off the module and only implied. New England is sufficiently developed that many people are fortunate (or unfortunate, depending on their taste) enough to have tracks running behind their homes.

Anyway, I discovered I had room for a garage and built that structure in a manner similar to what I'd used for the maintenance sheds. But instead of bracing with heavy stock, I used ¹⁄₃₂″-square stripwood and framed the inside to resemble a stud system. Bits of wood were glued in place for shelves, with little pieces of wire insulation and colored cardboard simulating the junk that accumulates in every garage. Tools and garden equipment were drawn on the walls with fine-point markers (fig. 12). I decided to leave the door open to show off the detail. The interior is dark enough, though, that only a suggestion of detail was necessary.

Common sense dictates that a fence would be erected to protect small children (the sandbox was built of styrene). I made one using wedding veil material (netting). The pipe frame of .020″ brass wire was soldered over a template drawn to fit the terrain. The netting was glued in place with Elmer's. I use white glue often as I've found I can make very neat joints that are quite strong, even if this isn't the correct glue for the material. I sprayed the completed fence aluminum-color and washed some Grimy Black and Rust over this to help kill the newness.

The interlocking tower. Modern signal and communications practices have rendered most interlocking towers obsolete, so the module seemed like a good place to include an abandoned one.

I'd planned to scratchbuild a model of the one at Ayer, but again Rod Guthrie changed things. This time he passed along some pilot epoxy castings of the walls for a concrete New Haven tower.

The polyester castings went together rapidly using five-minute epoxy, but painting them to resemble old concrete was a challenge. I primed the structure with flat white spray paint and tried to apply my water putty texturing, but the mixture wouldn't adhere to the castings. However, a very thin wash of yellow oxide Universal Tinting Dye and burnt umber watercolor gave a correct color to everything. Various washes of black, brown, and white watercolor followed until the structure looked old enough.

The window frames on the castings were damaged; I added a few dents of my own and some stripwood window mullions to suggest second-story windows that had long since been destroyed. The first-floor windows and doors were covered with thin wood to suggest plywood covers to keep out intruders.

I inserted clear plastic in the window frames to suggest broken glass. Next I littered the interior with a pile of scrap stripwood that I'd sprinkled with white plaster to resemble a collapsed ceiling. Graffiti aren't that common in rural areas, but I added some with typewriter correction tape to further the illusion of an abandoned structure. Stairs weren't necessary, as the railroad would have removed them long ago to prevent second-story access. A few streaks of Rust indicated where they had been.

The roof is a Crow River Products casting. I scraped away a few tiles where they might have been broken and painted the exposed wood a muddy gray to simulate rot. The Spanish tiles were painted Reefer Orange, with washes of brown, black, and white watercolor to add age. Pieces of Plastruct channel and rod added detail in the form of broken gutters and drain pipes.

I popped the completed tower in place and then used ground cover to hide the gaps. This abandoned structure, shown in fig. 13, helped to place the scene in the 1980s and added visual interest.

Well, that's all there is to it. A fair amount of work, though nothing too complicated or time-consuming, has transformed F&S Junction into a real place. Next month I'll describe how to add signals and trees, along with other details that are needed to finish the project. ✪

Fig. 13. The abandoned interlocking tower at F&S Junction, based on a New Haven prototype, is a major focal point of scenic interest and helps set the module in the contemporary time frame.

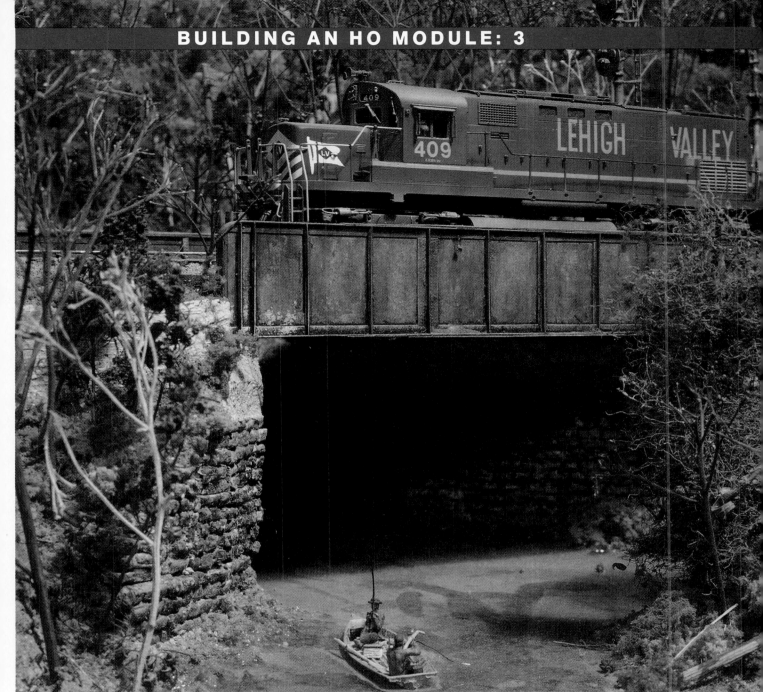

On this beautiful autumn day these two fishermen seem oblivious to the rumbling overhead as Lehigh Valley no. 409, an Alco C-420, leads westbound TV-9A across the Ware River.

Trees, signals, and details complete the project

Tips and techniques on detailing scenes authentically and inexpensively

BY MICHAEL TYLICK
PHOTOS BY THE AUTHOR

READERS OF the first two articles on the HO scale F&S Junction module know how far we've come. The terrain's been formed, and most of the bridges and buildings are in place. Even so, everything looks barren and uninhabited.

What we need are some trees and land cover, along with signs that people live and work here.

This time we'll add some of the details and modeling touches that will transform this module into a convincing scale replica of a railroading scene. I'll explain how to model and install trees, then how to add signals, telephone poles, and signs, all of which are vital to most railroads. Finally, I'll describe the vehicles, figures, and junk that make this module come to life.

Fig. 1 USING TREES TO ADD DEPTH

Foam-covered backdrop

Transition to backdrop made with coarse foam

Building flats

Road ends in trees, covered by their foliage

Trees blend full-scale building flats into foam-covered backdrop

Forced perspective by using N or other small scale structures

Trees get gradually smaller to help forced perspective

Trees hide access joints (or flaws)

Use curved roads and gradually narrow them to force perspective

Trees hide exaggerated vertical cliffs, walls

Trees in valleys shed leaves earlier than those on mountains — luckily, railroads also run in valleys

Trees add a feeling of detail to a bare scene

Bare trees between layout edge, track, and structures add depth, but allow good visibility

A little foliage here and there helps effect

FALL AT F&S JCT.

No matter which region or locality you model, it's important that you become familiar with its land and vegetation. Rural New England, the setting for F&S Junction, is covered with pine, birch, and hardwood forests. Once it was heavily cultivated, but over the last century, as land wore out and farmers moved to more fertile areas farther west, the hills and valleys reverted to forest.

Those forests are especially striking in the autumn, a season that is rarely modeled. That surprises me because having a layout set in the fall has some advantages. First, the beautiful colors of autumn foliage make any scene stand out. Second, placing bare trees in front of tracks and structures creates an impression of real depth in a scene. Those leafless trees also allow easy viewing of the points of interest.

Foliage has no easily discernible scale, and that also has benefits. For example, you can plant smaller trees in the background and make the foliage opaque enough to hide perspective distortions. All of a sudden steep hillsides look natural. The addition of short, bare trees

gives a great feeling of detail to rocky areas and retaining walls (fig. 1).

MODELING DECIDUOUS AND EVERGREEN TREES

To be honest, I don't think that my trees are excellent models in themselves. It's more important to me that they look good when planted in groups. So I've settled on techniques for making individual trees fairly quickly and inexpensively. That's made modeling large forests practical. The great number and variety of trees on the module create an effect that viewers like. Their compliments make me forget that modeling trees can be tedious.

To make deciduous trees I use dried weeds gathered in the fall in swampy fields along railroad and highway embankments. A good way to select tree frames (weeds) is to go out when the leaves have fallen and pick a few of everything. Leave them at home for a few days before you examine them. Many weeds will make beautiful trees if you remove their seeds or trim their tips. I haven't needed to preserve the weeds.

I've begun trading weeds with friends in California. Every part of the country has its own types of weeds, and the more

you can select from the better your modeling will be. Don't make the common mistake of using the same kind of weed for everything. After all, real forests contain many varieties of trees.

While some trees of each type were left bare (birches were stuck in a Styrofoam block and spray-painted white), others were covered with foliage. I've had good luck with ground foam from Architectural Model Supply (AMSI) and Woodland Scenics. The more diverse the colors and textures, the better your scene will look. See fig. 2.

The Woodland Scenics foam comes on a foliage matrix, so you just stretch and drape the foliage over the skeleton. The AMSI foam requires a separate netting material, which they also sell.

You can make your own foliage netting. I had excellent results using steel wool pulled very thin. The only reason I gave up this method was that I afraid of getting steel wool into locomotive mechanisms.

Tufts of rug yarn work well for modeling grass; the fuzz left after combing out the yarn makes a good foliage matrix. Use yarn that's about the same color as the foliage. I attach the foam with spray adhesive. Work over a large sheet of paper so you can save excess ground foam.

Most evergreen trees in central New England have been taken over by hardwood forests. Since it's unusual to find a freestanding pine in the wilds, I didn't have to spend the time on them that western modelers might. Mine are tufts of dark green floor buffer pads impaled on straight twigs. Don't cut these pads with scissors, as they'll look too neat. Rip and shred small pieces with your hands. Triangles of this material also make excellent background trees. I've glued ground foam to my pines, but still think eastern white pine is best simulated with the plain buffer pad material. See fig. 2.

PLANTING TREES

Tree planting goes rapidly, thanks to some useful tools and methods of installation. First I use a motor tool with a finishing nail as a bit to drill holes for the trees (plaster will destroy drills). Next I start filling in those holes with trees, dipping the trunk of each in Elmer's white glue before inserting it. If more trees are needed after I've filled all the holes, I just push them down in place — the other trees hold them up.

Here are a few tips for planting trees:
• Plant rapidly and trust your instincts.
• Put larger trees in front, smaller ones in the rear. (At the backdrop, some trees are only an inch high.)
• Mix types of trees, colors of foliage, and sizes. Put some very small trees under large, foreground ones.
• Use foliage where you want to hide exaggerated scenery or flaws, bare trees where you want to show what's behind.
• Put some foliage near bare trees and have a few bare trees sticking out above foliated areas.
• Above all, *look at what you're doing!* If, after a few days, you're not satisfied, judiciously remove and replant until you have the effect you want.

When all the trees are in place, I add a final coat of ground foam, making sure to cover any bare holes or unsightly trunk mountings. Extra tree ends and twigs are scattered on the ground to represent the dead growth that litters every forest. I fix everything in place by spraying the area with water and diluted white glue.

In a shallow scene such as this module, roads must end at the backdrop. Foliage hides the fact that they go nowhere. The trees get closer together until the end of the road can't be seen. A curve in the road towards the back improves the effect and breaks up another mechanical straight line. Another "trick" involves making the roads full width at the front and gradually narrowing them as they get farther away.

SIGNALS

Nothing adds more life to a scene than working signals. My signals were modeled after those Conrail recently installed near my home after single-tracking the old Boston & Albany line. I scratchbuilt them from brass, styrene, and Radio Shack components (fig. 3). The signal bridge was patterned after an older Conrail prototype, which has had new signal heads installed. No measurements were made — I worked from memory and think they came out pretty close.

Light-emitting diodes (LEDs) are great for illuminating signals. Besides being less expensive than light bulbs, the components will never burn out if the correct limiting resistor is used. They also give a realistic light that's easily seen from a wide angle.

I made electrical connections using a wire-wrap tool. This is a solderless connection method in which special wire is wrapped around the terminals. This way I can get the wire right up to the LEDs without risking heat damage. The no. 30 wires are available in different colors, and I've snaked as many as ten through a 1/16" brass tube with no problems.

Unfortunately, the signals aren't fully functional yet. Tom Laroche (one of the modular group's coordinators) offered to figure out a logic circuit. Through a lack of communication, he designed the circuit using negative logic (the positive side is common) while I wired the signals just the opposite.

Many little details like instrument cases, telephones, and battery boxes were built following methods and plans from MODEL RAILROADER's Close-up column. See fig. 4. I'm especially proud of the interlocking plant because at the module's first show an Amtrak signal maintainer looked it over and told me I'd correctly duplicated the prototype down to the last detail.

DETAILS

As we've all heard again and again, details make a model or layout stand out. Small things suggest a railroad's period and locale and catch the attention of viewers. Here are some of the details I added to finish F&S Junction.

Signs. These do so much to set time and place. They also make a monotonous scene look highly detailed and finished. Finding contemporary lettering and advertising was easy compared to finding period signs. I made signs from matchbook

Fig. 2. The author made his trees using inexpensive materials. **Top and middle:** His deciduous trees were made from dried weeds that he gathered in the fall. Foliage netting was stretched and draped over the weeds, as shown in the top center photo, and then various shades of ground foam were sprinkled on. In the middle photo, left, is a weed as picked before the seeds were removed. The author suggests using a variety of weeds for greater realism. **Bottom:** Realistic pine trees can be made quickly by stringing bits of floor buffer pads onto straight sticks and sprinkling on ground foam.

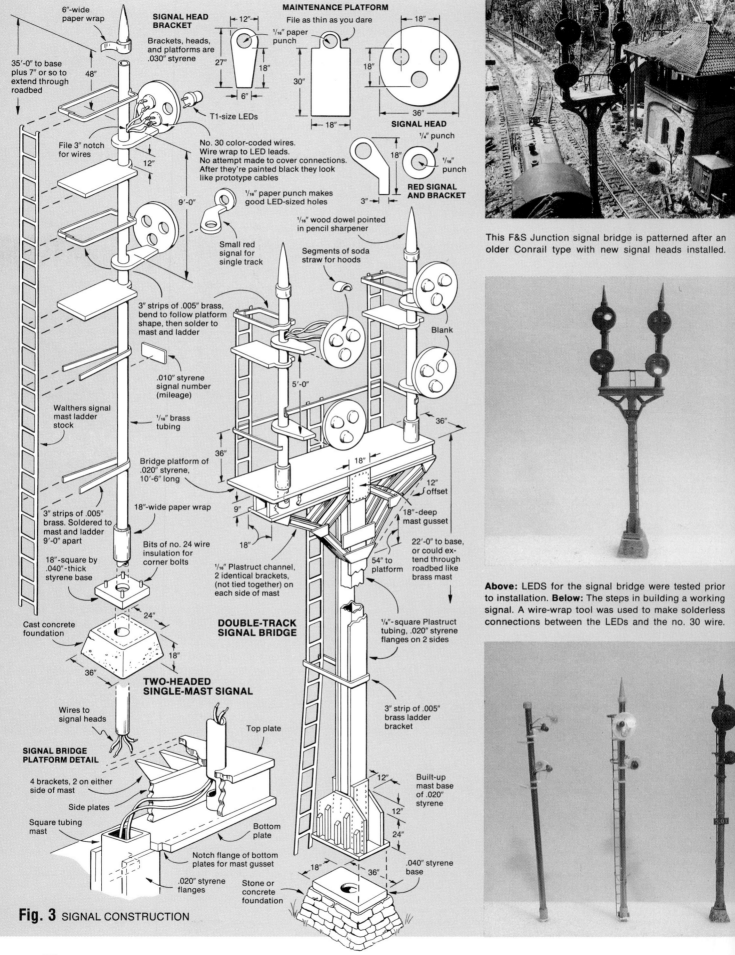

SIGNAL HEAD BRACKET

Brackets, heads, and platforms are .030" styrene

6"-wide paper wrap

35'-0" to base plus 7" or so to extend through roadbed

48"

T1-size LEDs

File 3" notch for wires

12"

9'-0"

No. 30 color-coded wires. Wire wrap to LED leads. No attempt made to cover connections. After they're painted black they look like prototype cables

1/16" paper punch makes good LED-sized holes

Small red signal for single track

3" strips of .005" brass, bend to follow platform shape, then solder to mast and ladder

.010" styrene signal number (mileage)

Walthers signal mast ladder stock

1/16" brass tubing

3" strips of .005" brass. Soldered to mast and ladder 9'-0" apart

18"-wide paper wrap

Bits of no. 24 wire insulation for corner bolts

18"-square by .040"-thick styrene base

24"

Cast concrete foundation

36"

18"

TWO-HEADED SINGLE-MAST SIGNAL

Wires to signal heads

SIGNAL BRIDGE PLATFORM DETAIL

4 brackets, 2 on either side of mast

Side plates

Square tubing mast

Top plate

Bottom plate

Notch flange of bottom plates for mast gusset

.020" styrene flanges

MAINTENANCE PLATFORM

File as thin as you dare

12"

1/16" paper punch

27"

18"

6"

30"

18"

18"

18"

36"

SIGNAL HEAD

1/4" punch

1/16" punch

18"

3"

RED SIGNAL AND BRACKET

1/16" wood dowel pointed in pencil sharpener

Segments of soda straw for hoods

Blank

5'-0"

36"

DOUBLE-TRACK SIGNAL BRIDGE

Bridge platform of .020" styrene, 10'-6" long

36"

18"

9"

18"

1/16" Plastruct channel, 2 identical brackets, (not tied together) on each side of mast

12" offset

18"-deep mast gusset

22'-0" to base, or could extend through roadbed like brass mast

54" to platform

1/8"-square Plastruct tubing, .020" styrene flanges on 2 sides

3" strip of .005" brass ladder bracket

12"

Built-up mast base of .020" styrene

12"

24"

18"

36"

.040" styrene base

Stone or concrete foundation

Fig. 3 SIGNAL CONSTRUCTION

This F&S Junction signal bridge is patterned after an older Conrail type with new signal heads installed.

Above: LEDS for the signal bridge were tested prior to installation. **Below:** The steps in building a working signal. A wire-wrap tool was used to make solderless connections between the LEDs and the no. 30 wire.

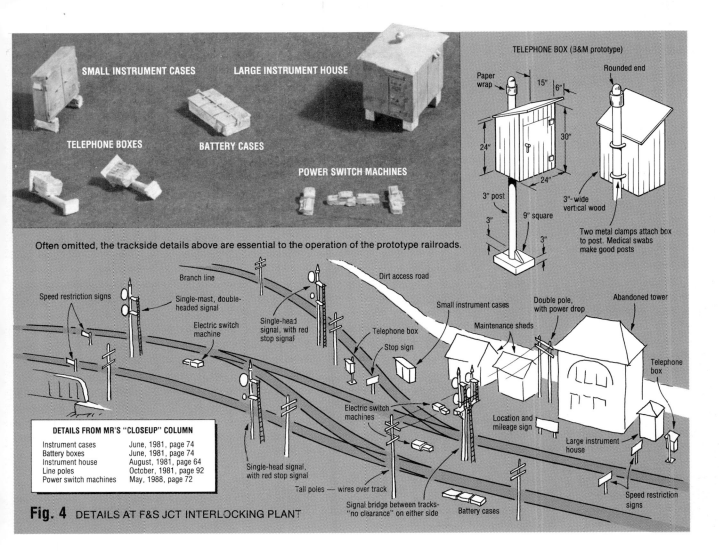

SMALL INSTRUMENT CASES   LARGE INSTRUMENT HOUSE

TELEPHONE BOXES   BATTERY CASES

POWER SWITCH MACHINES

TELEPHONE BOX (3&M prototype)

Paper wrap   15"   6"   Rounded end

24"   30"

24"

3" post   3"-wide vertical wood

3"   9" square   3"

Two metal clamps attach box to post. Medical swabs make good posts

Often omitted, the trackside details above are essential to the operation of the prototype railroads.

Speed restriction signs
Branch line
Single-mast, double-headed signal
Electric switch machine
Single-head signal, with red stop signal
Dirt access road
Telephone box
Stop sign
Small instrument cases
Maintenance sheds
Double pole, with power drop
Abandoned tower
Telephone box
Electric switch machines
Location and mileage sign
Large instrument house
Single-head signal, with red stop signal
Tall poles — wires over track
Signal bridge between tracks- "no clearance" on either side
Battery cases
Speed restriction signs

DETAILS FROM MR'S "CLOSEUP" COLUMN

Instrument cases	June, 1981, page 74
Battery boxes	June, 1981, page 74
Instrument house	August, 1981, page 64
Line poles	October, 1981, page 92
Power switch machines	May, 1988, page 72

Fig. 4 DETAILS AT F&S JCT INTERLOCKING PLANT

covers and magazine ads glued to two thicknesses of tagboard.

The railroad signs are photocopies of a set that appeared in MR years ago. I cut them out and glued them to scraps of rail. The posts and back were painted Grimy Black with a wash of Rust to add age.

The F&S Jct. sign was done with dry transfers on blue cardstock and follows current Conrail practice of displaying the location and mileage. Decals and dry transfers were used to represent the location markers found on every bridge, signal, and instrument box. They're written in hundredths of a mile (e.g., 34.82) and appear all over the place. Numbering the switch machines was another nice touch. (I cast mine from a scratchbuilt master following plans in MR, though Alexander Scale Models sells excellent castings for the interlocking apparatus.)

Billboards. I framed these with various sizes of stripwood. They follow no particular prototype. I painted them different shades of dark green and brown, followed by a coat of Polly S Flat Finish to dull the shine on the signs. Washes of black, brown, and white watercolors make the billboards look like they need replacing (they don't look new for long in New England) and blend them into the scenery.

Vehicles. No detail's better at establishing the time frame of a scene. Just about everyone is familiar enough with automobiles to place them in time —

generally speaking, there aren't very many really old ones around.

I used some nice Wiking autos from a hobby shop. They follow European prototypes, but with so many imported cars in this country that wasn't a problem. If I wanted a large parking lot on the module, I'd include a few American-made cars.

More troublesome, however, is the fact that the colors of these vehicles aren't convincing and the raw plastic castings look just like what they are. I disassembled and repainted them with flat colors. Real cars may be shiny, but the gloss looks awful on a model. I used a pinhead to paint the hubcaps, chrome trim, and lights.

For the trucks that are typically found at railroad maintenance centers I used Life-Like pickup trucks. I made new back covers and tool racks from styrene (fig. 5); then I painted the trucks bright yellow and weathered them with chalks. A small F&S herald was simulated with a scrap of decal film painted black. With a small paper punch I cut out the center circle, then trimmed the outside to a diamond shape to duplicate my old-style Erie-inspired herald. I numbered the trucks with alphabet decals.

Telephone poles. While there are excellent commercial poles, I prefer to build my own. I use wood, which resembles wood better than plastic or metal does. Also, I can tailor each pole to the location, just as the prototype does.

I used 1/8" dowels for the poles. Make sure to cut the top at a slant to shed water. Telephone poles are usually quite tall, but railroad line poles tend to be shorter, often at a level with the cars, and rising only when they have to clear something. The crossarms are made from 1/16" x 3/32" stripwood. I file a notch in the pole to accept the crossarm, then stain everything with a mix of cigarette ashes and brown watercolor.

While they're wet I glue and pin the crossarms in place. The damp wood lets me drive sequin pins through the dowels and stripwood without drilling holes. For insulators I use tiny craft beads (Indian beads), which I secure with white glue. I put transparent green beads on the railroad poles and black ones on the utility poles. Strips of cardstock simulate crossarm braces. After painting the metal pieces with Grimy Black and a wash of Rust, I drill holes and "plant" the poles with a dab of white glue on the end. See fig. 6.

Junk. Since litter piles up everywhere around modern railroads, I placed lots of it along my right-of-way, particularly around structures. Jim Woodard suggested dumping a pile down the side of the riverbank as shown in fig. 7.

Some of the debris — barrels, drums, and crates — are commercial castings. However, like any experienced modeler, I have plenty of old scrap that's right for

Most any model scene should include a few vehicles. The author used the Wiking van and car at right, and modified some Life-Like pickup trucks into maintenance vehicles as shown below.

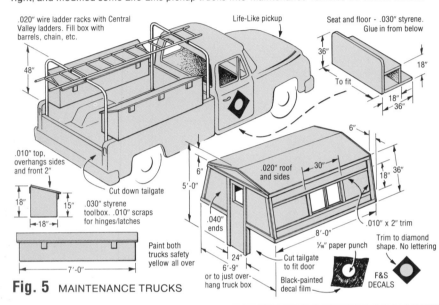

.020" wire ladder racks with Central Valley ladders. Fill box with barrels, chain, etc.

Life-Like pickup

Seat and floor - .030" styrene. Glue in from below

48"

36"

18"

To fit

18"

36"

.010" top, overhangs sides and front 2"

Cut down tailgate

6'

6"

.020" roof and sides

30"

18"

36"

.010" x 2" trim

18"

15"

.030" styrene toolbox. .010" scraps for hinges/latches

18"

5'-0"

6"

.040" ends

8'-0"

1/16" paper punch

Trim to diamond shape. No lettering

Paint both trucks safety yellow all over

24"

6'-9"
or to just overhang truck box

Cut tailgate to fit door

Black-painted decal film

F&S DECALS

7'-0"

Fig. 5 MAINTENANCE TRUCKS

this. So my clutter includes pieces of Plastruct shapes, old sprues and broken parts from plastic models, bits of Athearn underframes, clock gears — anything that looks like it could be painted with rust and dumped.

People. Before putting figures in a scene, think about what they're supposed to be doing and why. By having scale people "tell a story," you'll make each scene more realistic and more fun. I never get over how much interest little everyday scenes generate when visitors see my module or layout.

Though factory-painted figures are common, why not try unpainted ones? Preiser's

are great bargains. Buy all 5 of their sets of 120 unpainted figures — a model railroad can never have too many people!

Painting these tiny castings seems forbidding, but I've learned several tricks to make the task manageable. Towards the end of a project, when I have an idea of which people may fit the scenes, I go through my sets and pick out about a dozen figures. Any that aren't used go back into the box painted and are available for photos.

Water-soluble paints (Polly S and Tamiya) work best for painting figures. Leave on the sprues, so it's easier to hold them. Use a small brush (no. 1) and load it with paint to prevent running out in the middle of an edge. I start by painting the shirts or coats, doing each figure's in a different color. The bottles stay open so I can mix colors on waxed paper.

I'll paint one coat on each figure at each session and let them dry. Working just a few minutes two or three times a day, I'll have all the figures done in less than a week. I don't mind if the colors don't cover completely; the lightened high spots emphasize the details. I also apply a thin wash of watercolor paints over entire figures. The paints settle into the cracks to bring out the detail. A coat of Polly S Flat Finish removes any lingering shine.

WATER

I leave modeling water to the very end. It's too easy to spill glue or paint and mar the surface, which should be as smooth and shiny as a mirror.

To start, you need a flat, level surface for the riverbed. I used scrap 1/2" plyscore and carefully sealed the edges with hardshell, including the Masonite front, which was cut about 3/8" higher than the riverbed. If the edges aren't sealed carefully the "water" will leak on the floor.

Most articles suggest using paint to simulate the riverbed. That's never worked for me: The earth-colored shore doesn't seem right, and the black center always looks black. Nor have I had much luck blending the two colors. So I carry the hardshell, paint, and the ground cover

Fig. 6. Among the many details in this scene are the telephone poles. They were scratchbuilt from 1/8" dowels with stripwood crossarms and craft-bead insulators.

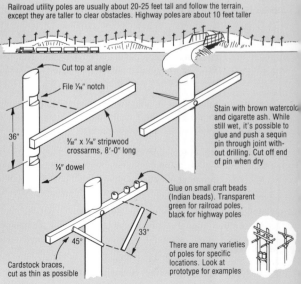

Railroad utility poles are usually about 20-25 feet tall and follow the terrain, except they are taller to clear obstacles. Highway poles are about 10 feet taller

Cut top at angle

File 1/16" notch

36"

3/32" x 1/8" stripwood crossarms, 8'-0" long

1/8" dowel

Stain with brown watercolor and cigarette ash. While still wet, it's possible to glue and push a sequin pin through joint without drilling. Cut off end of pin when dry

Glue on small craft beads (Indian beads). Transparent green for railroad poles, black for highway poles

33"

45°

Cardstock braces, cut as thin as possible

There are many varieties of poles for specific locations. Look at prototype examples

over the riverbed as though it wasn't there. The small rocks that end up tumbling to the lowest level only add to the effect of a rocky New England river.

After securing everything with dilute Elmer's white glue, I brush on several coats of acrylic gloss medium to seal the bottom. This time I modeled the water with Enviro-Tex, an odorless material that's mixed with equal parts of resin and hardener. The use of casting resin has been covered many times; remember to follow the directions carefully.

Capillary action causes a little "water" to creep up the riverbanks. When everything had dried I touched up problem areas with Polly S Flat Finish and ground cover. The boat is flat-bottomed, so it was glued in place with Duco Cement.

PROTECTIVE COVER

Moving this heavy module and possibly damaging some of the fragile details had me worried. I mentioned this to some members of Ntrak at the Minuteman '86 NMRA convention, and they advised using a "coffin," or protective cover. They had built plywood versions, which were strong but very heavy. I modified their ideas to come up with the lightweight, inexpensive cover in fig. 8.

Wallboard corner bead seemed like an inexpensive lightweight angle stock to use for a support. It was easy to cut and bend. I screwed everything together, putting a wood screw at each corner to hold the support in place. My wife kindly sewed a dust cover from heavy plastic tablecloth material. Turning the cover inside out prevents the fabric from snagging trees.

The cover has proven a great success. The module is several years old and has been to a half-dozen public shows, several houses for photo sessions, and a school fair, yet the damage has been minimal. It's stayed nice and clean.

CONCLUSIONS

As my articles have suggested, I really enjoyed building F&S Junction. It was constructed at a time when, because of a potential new model railroad space, I was uncertain what to do with my permanent layout, the Fitchburg & Southbridge. As such, the module was a good break from the layout and sent me back to it with a fresh outlook.

While I think building a module is worthwhile for those in the hobby desiring a break from a home layout, a change of scales or era, or the fellowship of other model railroaders, I especially recommend it to anyone who wants to build a layout but doesn't have the space. A 2 x 4-foot module fits almost anywhere and can be moved long distances with ease. Best of all, it's small enough to let you take the time to do things carefully and completely.

The next time you attend a train show, stop and talk with members of the modular groups and obtain copies of their specifications. They'll be happy to help someone who's open to their way of modeling and may sometime join their group or club. I will be pleased if this series gets a few of you out of your armchairs and into modular railroading. ✿

Fig. 7. In the real world litter seems to be everywhere. Here the author has realistically scattered some junk down the riverbank. It's a combination of commercial castings and old scrap pieces.

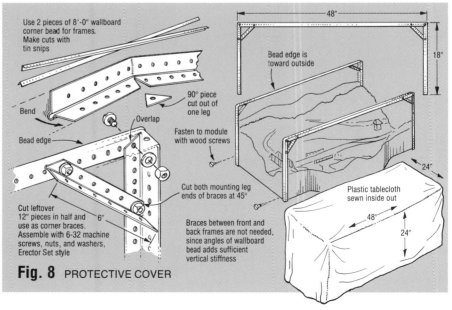

Use 2 pieces of 8'-0" wallboard corner bead for frames. Make cuts with tin snips

Bend

Bead edge

90° piece cut out of one leg

Overlap

Bead edge is toward outside

48"

18"

Fasten to module with wood screws

Cut leftover 12" pieces in half and use as corner braces. Assemble with 6-32 machine screws, nuts, and washers, Erector Set style

6"

Cut both mounting leg ends of braces at 45°

Braces between front and back frames are not needed, since angles of wallboard bead adds sufficient vertical stiffness

24"

Plastic tablecloth sewn inside out

48"

24"

Fig. 8 PROTECTIVE COVER

Port of Los Angeles project railroad: 1

The trains were running on this HO module after just two weekends of building

BY ROBERT SMAUS
PHOTOS BY THE AUTHOR

WHEN I called MODEL RAILROADER to say that I was finished with our project layout, there was silence on the other end of the line. "Finished?" they finally asked, "Already?" Compared to some of MR's project railroads, this one might seem a little simple, and it was certainly quick to build, but that's the idea. I used the most basic, the most tried-and-true construction methods, and trains were running on the module after only two weekends of work, though admittedly, they can't run very far.

Since this might bother the E. H. Harrimans, Commodore Vanderbilts, and other empire builders in the crowd, let me point out that this is a module. That means you can add to it anytime you like, or you can join a modular group and let others participate in the expansion.

In the meantime, you can run a switch engine back and forth, moving a variety of cars here and there, which sure beats looking at them gathering dust on a shelf! After a few months of this, you can add loops to either end if you like watching trains run in circles, or incorporate it into a more complicated plan. So, no more excuses guys, this layout is easy to build and it's so small it will fit in some people's closets (though I keep it in the garage).

If you're not sold yet, let me say that it's also one heck of a great backdrop for photography. I had as much fun photographing my models on this module as I had building it. I even got brave and finally tried a pinhole lens I had purchased a few years back. I could hardly wait for the weekend! Part of the spare look, however, is not for simplicity's sake.

A GE 44-tonner switches some tank cars at the bulk oil terminal. This Bachmann model handles most of the switching chores.

ft: Robert Smaus has captured the flavor of a big port terminal on this 2½ x 6-foot module.
ove: The California Terminal container crane is the focal point of our project HO scale module.

Modern rail facilities, especially terminals, are big, open, tidy spaces. Big, so semis 50 feet and longer can maneuver; tidy, because you don't leave junk around anymore unless you're looking for a lawsuit or an environmental fine of some kind. This is modern railroading, set in the 1990s.

The module is easy to build because the benchwork is no more than a simple box, and the trackwork is "out of the box" with only minor modifications. There are no grades — it's as flat as a pancake — and wiring is practically nonexistent, yet you have walk-around control, which lets you enjoy the admittedly limited action from every angle. The scenery is as plain as dirt and asphalt, and almost all the structures are built from kits.

Using the same techniques, you can construct something bigger, but starting small instills confidence and, after building a module like this, you're less apt to be terrified of layouts and layout construction. You'll see that it's really easy!

WHY THE PORT OF LOS ANGELES?

This project models the Port of Los Angeles, one of the world's largest and busiest. This may seem an unlikely candidate for a layout that's only 6 feet long and 30 inches wide, but ports are one place you find lots of track running in every direction in a relatively small space. There's also a great mix of stuff, which gives you more to model — old factories, new warehouses, little docks, huge refineries, not to mention freight cars of all kinds.

Something else to remember is that ports are places where trainloads originate or terminate. They are a source for the freight that goes on flatcars and in gondolas, covered hoppers, and even boxcars. This brings a touch of realism to any model railroad. You have customers with goods that need loading and moving.

Finally, ports are where the latest thing in railroading begins or ends — double-stack container trains. They will be the center of activity on our HO project railroad.

Container terminals dominate today's ports, and they make dramatic models. Huge cranes tower over the scene, and there are stacks of containers everywhere. Those containers are every bit as colorful as the beloved boxcar. There are lots of trucks and people, and all of this is easily modeled because there are kits or ready-built models of everything from the cranes to the container chassis.

Clustered around the container terminal on this module are other typical port industries, including a bulk liquid

terminal, where tank cars can be unloaded or loaded; a dockside warehouse, where a variety of goods can originate (I made it a banana terminal where refrigerator cars can be "spotted" or put); and a cotton transfer dock, where good old boxcars can bring in loads of cotton destined (here's a switch) for Japan.

In all, there are four industries on this tiny module, where four different kinds of freight cars can be spotted. If you plan to join a modular group, that's quite a contribution to their freight revenue. If you yourself add to this module, you're already off to a most profitable start.

PLANNING

Feel free to copy the plan shown in fig. 1 exactly. First, though, let me explain how it came to be, and perhaps you can come up with your own modular track plan that more closely models an area nearby. "Nearby" is an important consideration since it's much easier to model something you can actually see and photograph, which is how I began this project.

I made several trips to the L. A. harbor and took lots of pictures of whatever caught my attention. I photographed tracks weaving through paving and manicured main lines. I found industries that looked like they could be modeled using kits I was sure existed somewhere in the Walthers catalog. I photographed interesting details, such as the special racks made to hold the container chassis. If you don't live near a port, you may choose to model a nearby industrial area.

This research is fun as long as you stay out of the way of people trying to get their work done and don't go where you don't belong. I had prints made from slides of scenes I especially liked, then started thumbing through the Walthers catalog looking for kits that resembled the real thing (modelers refer to what actually exists as a "prototype").

I wrote down the models' dimensions given in the catalog so I could use these when planning. I found only a few kits that could be used out-of-the-box, so I spent some enjoyable evenings making crude sketches of how I could modify stock kits to make them look more like what I saw at the docks. I even bought a few kits and started building them, so that when it came time to lay track I would have some actual structures to work around.

Be sure to include books in your research. I found several that were useful, in particular, *The Port of Los Angeles, From Wilderness to World Port,* published by the Los Angeles Harbor Department. Most ports have books that boast of them. When in Baltimore last summer, I read *Baltimore Harbor, A Picture History,* by Robert C. Keith

Above: This dramatic shot captures some of the action at this busy port as a double-stack container train is being loaded.

Right: Here's the completed module mounted on the base with wheels and storage shelves that the author made for home use.

Fig. 1
PORT OF LOS ANGELES MODULE

Scale of plan: 3/4" = 1'-0"

"Well wash" bulk oil terminal

Cotton transfer dock

No. 6 turnouts are code 100, others are code 83

Leads beyond switches are 13" minimum (switcher and 1 50' car)

Wiring is common ground, no blocks, handheld throttle control

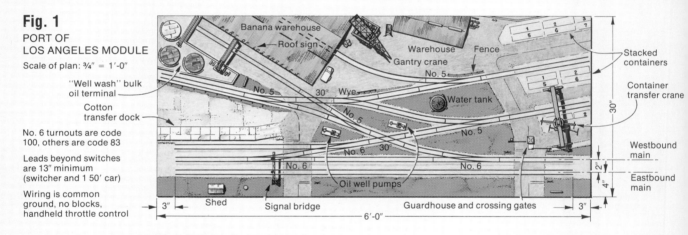

Banana warehouse
Roof sign
Warehouse
Gantry crane
No. 5
No. 5
30°
Wye
No. 5
Water tank
No. 5
No. 6
30°
No. 6
Oil well pumps
Shed
Signal bridge
Guardhouse and crossing gates
Fence
Stacked containers
Container transfer crane
Westbound main
Eastbound main
30"
2"
4"
3"
3"
6'-0"

Below: The action includes a semi waiting for the container train to clear the crossing, oil pumps working, and a lift truck loading a trailer.

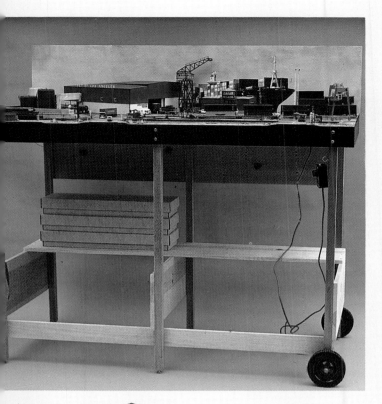

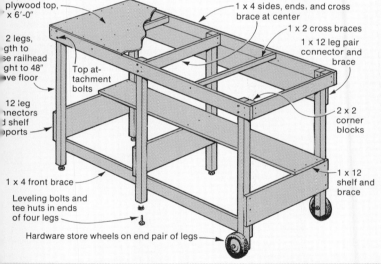

plywood top, x 6'-0"

2 legs, gth to se railhead ght to 48" ve floor

Top attachment bolts

12 leg nnectors d shelf pports

1 x 4 front brace

Leveling bolts and tee nuts in ends of four legs

1 x 4 sides, ends, and cross brace at center

1 x 2 cross braces

1 x 12 leg pair connector and brace

2 x 2 corner blocks

1 x 12 shelf and brace

Hardware store wheels on end pair of legs

A PERSONAL (AND PERHAPS OPINIONATED) CHECKLIST FOR LAYOUT PLANNING

☐ Know the length of the shortest "train" (in this case an engine and one car). This determines the length of the shortest siding.

☐ Plan paving so it doesn't interfere with the point end of turnouts or their throws.

☐ Know the dimensions of all buildings and structures, so you can leave room for their "footprints."

☐ Decide which structures can be kitbashed or cut at odd angles, and save those for difficult spots on your plan.

☐ Pay attention to height. It really helps to have a few tall structures as focal points.

☐ Don't use too many small structures. Have at least one huge one to set a realistic sense of scale.

☐ Watch out for buildings that are at right angles to the edge of the layout, or you'll see too much backdrop.

☐ Plan for color. Make a color sketch of the layout and its structures, and see how it looks.

☐ Control color. Don't use too many colors. Pick prototypes that blend with each other, then let one or two stand out from the rest.

☐ In general, you want the tallest structures at the back of the layout so they don't get bumped. Still, put a few in front too — they add a sense of distance and perspective.

☐ Plan for small things too — where to put signs and other accessories. They can fill odd spots on your plans.

☐ Don't overdo detail. Most modern industrial and rail facilities have a spare look to them — lots of empty space and little clutter.

(Ocean World Publishing, 1985), and nearly switched ports of call.

But try to model some place you can get to and photograph because it will help you out of a lot of tight spots. When you're building that tank farm and can't remember exactly how those pipes got across the street, you can go back and take another photo. It's so easy if you have the real thing to refer to.

With all my ideas, notes, photos, and books nearby, I started drawing track plans that might work. I measured the lengths of different model switch engines coupled to various freight cars to learn how long to make the sidings (to make sure they would fit!). I even measured a double-stack train someone

had built for a local train store, to see if it would fit inside my proposed container facility. Nope, didn't fit, so I used modeler's license and came up with a four-car double-stack (normally five-car sets).

I had already decided to use Walthers code 83 track for the branch lines and spurs, and code 100 is required by most modular clubs for the main lines. I tore out the page from the Walthers catalog that has little ¾" scale turnout templates and made a bunch of copies. These I cut apart, then I pasted the drawings of turnouts and crossovers to my layout plan. This enabled me to see what the layout would actually look like and learn whether I was trying to

cram too much onto it. Just playing around with these cutouts turned up some new possibilities.

I tried to make the plan as busy as possible since that's what I saw at the docks — lots of turnouts, sidings going every which way, and many crossings. I could do just about whatever I wanted because only the two main lines are specified by modular group guidelines. One of these had to be 4" from the front edge, while the other had to be 6" (measuring from the track center line).

I even managed to come up with a runaround track so the switcher could couple to either end of a car. Runarounds are useful in switching since they enable you to get the freight car

Fig. 2. Here's the happy builder with a roof full of materials: ¼" plywood cut to size at the lumberyard, 1 x 4 and 1 x 2 framing, and pieces of tempered hardboard for the backdrop.

Fig. 3. All cuts were made with a saber saw and a square. **Fig. 4.** Smaus drilled pilot holes for the drywall screws to avoid splitting the wood; then he countersank them slightly.

Fig. 5. Left: The corners were joined together with a block of 2 x 2. The idea is to keep the screws away from the edges of the framing so they don't split it. Clamps helped hold everything in place. However, the author decided that both were a bit of overkill — simply butting the pieces together using glue and screws would work about as well. **Fig. 6. Below:** Bob used a rechargeable drill and screwdriver bit to install the drywall screws. By working on top of the plywood he managed to keep everything square. **Fig. 7. Right:** Next, he flipped the frame over and fastened the plywood top using glue and 1" drywall screws. He removed the screws when the glue had set.

on the proper end of the train so the switcher doesn't get stuck inside a dead-end siding.

The most important spurs, the ones leading into the container facility, are angled so a mainline train can back straight in and pick up its cars. Most modular groups consider the inner main line the westbound track (trains move to the left) and the outer the eastbound.

BENCHWORK

Enough background, let's get building! It really did take but two weekends to get trains running on this project railroad, though they were long days and the kids had to watch *Star Trek, The Next Generation* by themselves at night.

The first step was a visit to the local lumberyard to purchase the necessary materials, which I hauled home on the roof of my car! See fig. 2. The first weekend was spent building the benchwork; the second was spent laying track and hooking up the few wires. The benchwork, if that term even applies to such a simple project, is no more than four pine 1 x 4s screwed and glued together to make a box, with three extra pieces in between for additional support. See fig. 1. It's a pretty flimsy affair until you screw the plywood on top; then it's as solid as a rock.

I've seen some very clever modules at club layouts, made out of just about everything, but this 1 x 4 construction is the standard adopted by the NMRA and most clubs, probably because it's simple and provides flush ends so modules can be butted together.

I followed West Coast module practices, which differ slightly from the new NMRA standards and those used on the East Coast. Specifically, I used the excellent *Los Angeles HO Modular Group Handbook* as a guide, and members of that group have kindly volunteered to send any interested party a copy for $5 (write to Wayne Hallowell, 3136 Las Olivos Ln., La Crescenta, CA 91214).

A LABOR-SAVING STEP

To make sure everything would end up square, I had the lumberyard cut a piece of ¼"-thick, A/B fir plywood to size — 6 feet long and 30 inches wide. They have the saw for the job, but I stood there and checked their measurements.

This is an important step as it ensures that everything will be square and exactly the right width and length. You can almost build it from here without a tape measure, cutting the 1 x 4 pine members to fit. I made all my cuts with a saber saw, using a square to keep them true as shown in fig. 3. Then I drilled pilot holes for the drywall screws and countersank each hole to keep the wood from splitting.

If you haven't discovered drywall screws, you're in for a pleasant surprise. Available at building supply and hardware stores, they slice into wood like that proverbial hot knife through butter. They can be driven by hand, but the best investment you'll ever make is a rechargeable, variable-speed, reversible drill to use as a drywall screwdriver (fig. 6). It makes assembling benchwork a piece of cake. Be sure to drill pilot holes and countersink them. (Pilot bits with countersinks are available at hardware stores.) Fig. 4 shows me countersinking a hole for a drywall screw.

I also used wood glue and clamps, but the clamps weren't necessary since I worked on top of the piece of plywood and that kept everything square. I confess to being overly cautious, because this was an MR project railroad! I didn't drive the 2" drywall screws into the ends of the 1 x 4s, but into blocks of 2 x 2 lumber in each corner (fig. 5).

It would have worked just as well to simply glue and screw directly into the ends and forget the blocks of wood. I know this because I have since built more benchwork that way.

The plywood top is what really makes this construction strong. Just drive the screws in straight so they don't burst out of the sides of the 1 x 4s, or make pilot holes as guides. Refer to fig. 7.

I centered another 1 x 4 between the ends, then centered a 1 x 2 between the center and each end for more support. I

Fig. 8. Two of the legs for the permanent base were marked and holes drilled for an axle so wheels could be attached later on.
Fig. 9. Right: The 1 x 12 is attached to the legs to add some bracing and also to support the two storage shelves to be added.

used 1 x 2s for the same reason I chose ¼" plywood — to keep the weight down. Remember that you have to pick up this module, and the weight increases quickly. If you don't plan to move it, use ½" plywood, which is the standard for regular layout construction.

The plywood top is fastened to the frame with wood glue and 1" drywall screws spaced about every 4" (fig. 7). After the glue had set, I took out most of the screws and filled the holes with spackling paste.

LEGS

Next I built a base for the module. For

modular club layouts all you need are two sets of 2 x 2 legs that are removable for transport. I built these but also made a more permanent base with three sets of legs so I could put storage shelves underneath (the 1 x 12 pine shelves will span only about 3 feet). I added wheels so I could move the layout around, even taking it outside for photography. See figs. 8 and 12. When it's at home, the layout rests on this base, but should it ever venture forth to a modular meet, I have the other legs standing by.

The legs on the at-home base are longer than those used at modular meets. They make the layout 4 feet tall,

Fig. 10. The module base nears completion. The 1 x 12 being installed gives the base added strength and supports the top. Bolts also hold the completed top to the base.

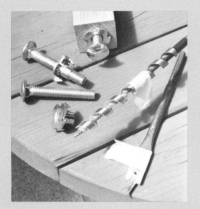

Fig. 11. The four legs without wheels have carriage bolts installed in the ends so the height can be adjusted. The pieces of tape wrapped around the bits were meant to keep the author from drilling too deep. **Fig. 12. Middle:** Slip the wheels on their axles, and the module is ready to roll. **Fig. 13.** At this point Bob tested the accuracy of his track plan by assembling the track on the plywood.

which is a comfortable height for me (40″ from the floor to the top of the rails is the standard height for club modules). Each pair of legs is joined together with a piece of 1 x 12 pine. These add a little cross bracing and serve as shelf supports. See fig. 9. This type of construction does wobble a little, but not objectionably (trains won't fall off the track) and only if you give it a hard push.

These three sets of legs were attached to another 1 x 12, which the module rests on in back, and a 1 x 4 that crossbraces the base in front and makes a handy footrest. The base is just sturdy enough to stand alone, but gets quite sturdy once the module is slipped on top. The plywood on the module rests on top of the legs, and the 1 x 4 frame sits on the 1 x 12 brace. The module is held in place by sets of bolts so it can be taken on and off. See fig. 10.

To make the height adjustable for an uneven floor, I used a bolt in a tee nut in the bottom of four of the legs. See fig. 11. (The portable legs also have these tee nuts, usually required by modular clubs so the various modules can be precisely aligned when they are all connected.) To install, you drill a hole up into the leg that is a little larger in diameter than the bolt and then pound in the tee nut (available at hardware stores). Screw

the bolt into the nut, and you'll have about an inch of adjustment.

The end set of legs got wheels instead of adjustable bolts. Again, these are fairly common at hardware stores. Just drill a hole for the axle, and attach the wheels with the special fasteners that come with them.

TRACK CHECK AND A HOMASOTE TOPPING

I put the module on its legs and started laying out track, following my track plan (fig. 13). I also put the models I had already built on top of the module. Everything seemed to fit. I spotted only one possible kink but thought it acceptable.

Be sure to sight down all the track to look for kinks. This is your last chance to straighten things out.

Satisfied, I moved on, adding a ¼″ Homasote topping to the plywood. It took me years to find a source for Homasote on the West Coast, but I'm a real admirer now of its ability to hold nails and spikes and its sound-deadening qualities. It makes a perfect base for laying rail on, or paving over, or whatever.

For this project, I used the 24″ x 32″ sheets of ¼″ Homasote sold by B. O. Manufacturing (mail orders are accepted; write to RD 7, Box 363-B, Kingston, NY 12401). Two full sheets

and a partial one were needed to cover most of the layout. I also used several sections of their contoured ¼″ Homa-Bed roadbed for the main lines (fig. 14).

I fastened the sheets with wood glue, but temporarily drove more 1″ wood drywall screws to hold them in place while the glue set up (see fig. 15). Then I removed the screws and filled the holes and gaps between sheets with spackling paste as shown in fig. 16. (The Homa-Bed main line was nailed down with small brads while the glue set up.)

When the glue and spackling paste had dried, I sanded the tops of the roadbeds and the sheets with sandpaper. Be sure to do this sanding — and any cutting — outdoors since Homasote makes its own unique kind of sawdust that gets all over the place (it's worse than cat hair). At least have the vacuum standing by.

As a finishing touch, I borrowed my neighbor's belt sander and smoothed the sides of the module after first recessing and puttying the screw holes. I was now ready to lay track, but that would have to wait for another weekend. I'll cover that in the next installment, as well as how I kitbashed a number of buildings to look like what I had seen down at the docks. ⛯

Fig. 14. Next the Homasote was fastened to the plywood with wood glue. Sheets of Homasote fill most of the module, though the main lines are made of Homa-Bed. **Fig. 15.** Hold the Homasote in place with more 1″ drywall screws until it sets; then remove them. **Fig. 16.** Fill any cracks or holes with spackle paste. After it has dried, sand the top of the Homasote so it's as flat as possible.

Here's an even better view of the crane, which is loading a container onto a truck chassis for transport to a point unknown. Starting on page 40 you'll find out how to build this impressive structure.

This month Bob Smaus tells how he did such a nice job of laying track on the Port of Los Angeles HO module, a 2½ x 6-foot project that was introduced in the December MR.

Port of Los Angeles project railroad: 2

Module construction continues with tracklaying and street paving

BY ROBERT SMAUS
PHOTOS BY THE AUTHOR

FOR ME, laying track is perhaps the most challenging part of building a layout. Mess up here, and things will never run right. Cars pop off the track, while locomotives surge and hesitate, or just stall. But, let me quickly add, laying track is also exciting work, because as you progress you can see a railroad unfolding in front of your eyes. Your models in the closet seem to holler, "Lay track!" You know it won't be long now before you can watch them run over that vast prairie of Homasote.

On this project layout, those models admittedly can't run too far, but I managed to cram a lot of track and industries onto the Port of Los Angeles module by cutting out-of-the-box track and turnouts to fit my busy plan. This sounds tricky, and I confess I was terrified when I made the first few cuts — turnouts are expensive and I didn't want to ruin even one — but it turned out to be a piece of cake. It was also a valuable lesson because learning to fit track and turnouts to your plan makes all sorts of interesting arrangements possible.

I wanted as many destinations for a switch engine as possible because switching is fun if you're using one of today's models that run so well. In this case "well" means slow and sure. Many of today's HO switch engines, including the Bachmann 44-tonner I chose, will really creep along, like the real ones do, going oh-so-slow around the tight curves that often lead to industrial sidings. They are realistic enough to make you think you hear the clang of couplers and the creaking of metal wheels on the curved track.

In this case, I was able to fit five spurs serving four different industrial customers, along with two mainline tracks and a branch line leading somewhere, someday (it dead-ends at the moment), all on a layout measuring only 2½ x 6 feet. To do this I had to use two crossings and cut switches short so they wouldn't take up as much space.

Study fig. 1, and you'll see how all these turnouts and crossings fit together. Note that the switcher is just finishing a "runaround," a maneuver that puts it at the other end of a boxcar. If you think there are too many sidings, too many turnouts, and too many crossings, visit a harbor and you'll see that I haven't exaggerated the complexity that much.

TURNOUT TERROR

If cutting track really terrifies you, look into the Peco brand of track and turnouts. Their proportions are a little odd, but the turnouts are already cut short, so fitting is a little easier (you may be able to just cut the flextrack and not the turnouts). I used Walthers code 83 track and turnouts for all the industrial track and Shinohara code 100 for the main lines. Cutting them to size isn't difficult, and perfect fits aren't necessary or even desirable. Metal wheels make a nice clickety-clack when they bump over gaps in the rails. And those gaps soak up rail expansion on hot days. So screw up your courage, and let's lay track!

Set out all the track on top of the module one more time, and mark the track center lines with a pen or pencil. Make little dashes between the ties, centered between the rails, then pick up the track and connect these marks with straight or curving lines. They will be your guides.

THE FIRST TURNOUT

I suggest you plunge in by beginning with the important set of turnouts that connects the main line with the sidings. See fig. 2. Note that the end of the turnout (the point end) is 17" in from the end of the module, so there is enough room for an Athearn switcher and one 50-foot boxcar. Also note that there is no track at all on the main line until you are 3" in from the edge. This empty space is where connecting tracks go when modules are joined together.

This arrangement doesn't conform with module standards recently set by the NMRA; they suggest that the main line be 4½" from the end. However, it does conform to West Coast standards. Similarly, though the NMRA specifies

Fig. 2. After laying out the track and marking the center lines, begin with the two code 100 no. 6 turnouts off the westbound main line. To get the adjoining tracks 2" apart, some of each turnout must be cut off. Align them, one on top of the other.

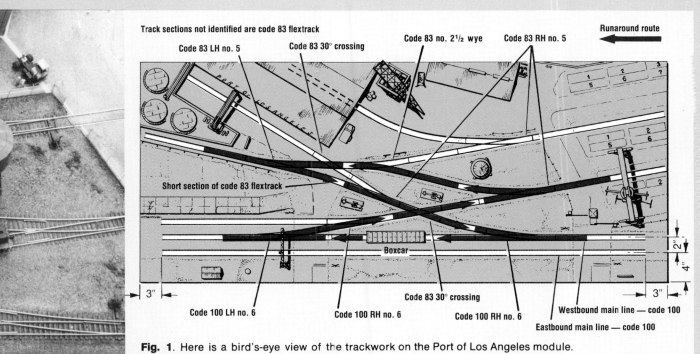

Track sections not identified are code 83 flextrack

Code 83 LH no. 5

Code 83 30° crossing

Code 83 no. 2½ wye

Code 83 RH no. 5

Runaround route

Short section of code 83 flextrack

Boxcar

2"

4"

3"

3"

Code 100 LH no. 6

Code 100 RH no. 6

Code 100 RH no. 6

Code 83 30° crossing

Westbound main line — code 100

Eastbound main line — code 100

Fig. 1. Here is a bird's-eye view of the trackwork on the Port of Los Angeles module. The colored line shows the route taken by a switcher when it "runs around" a boxcar

Fig. 3. Above left: Make your cut marks on the turnouts. **Middle:** Cut the ties that join the two sets of rails with a chisel blade. **Above right:** Cut the rails with a pair of rail nippers as shown, and then file the ends flat and remove any burrs on the sides of rails.

that the track nearest the front of the layout should be 5″ from the front edge (measuring to the track center line) and the next track should be 7″ in, clubs out here generally go with 4″ and 6″. Obviously, if you plan to join a club later on, find out what standards they are using.

The NMRA and West Coast clubs do agree on various other track standards for modules. Both specify that mainline track must be code 100, track centers (center lines) have to be 2″ apart, and turnouts off the main line must be no. 6s.

In recognition of these standards, the turnouts off my main line are code 100 no. 6, made by Shinohara (most clubs don't allow Atlas turnouts, though Peco is okay). To get the westbound main line (second one in from the edge) and the cotton transfer dock siding

only 2″ apart, the turnouts must be shortened for them to line up properly — so the adjoining track center lines are spaced 2″ apart.

TURNOUT BASHING

Lay one turnout on top of the other, and make marks where you plan to cut — about halfway between where they overlap — on the uppermost turnout as shown in fig. 3. Now it's time to cut. First slice away the ties that join the two sets of rail, using a chisel-blade in your hobby knife. Now make the cuts with a razor saw or a pair of rail nippers.

Regardless of which tool you use — but especially the nippers — be sure to file the ends of the rail flat after cutting. A good, new file really helps when laying track — I use a short Nicholson

mill bastard — because you can remove excess metal from the rail end quickly to even things up. Be sure to run the file over the bottom, top, and sides of the cut, to knock off any burrs. That way the rail joiners will slide on easily.

Now lay this turnout back on top of the other, and make another set of marks on the other turnout. Cut away the ties, and make your cuts in the rail. Now see how they fit. Better that they fit a little tight at first because you can always file away extra rail. Whenever you make cuts, remember the carpenters' old adage: You can always make a board shorter, but it's darn hard to make it longer.

Figures 4 and 5 illustrate how to handle some special tracklaying situations.

In this case the turnouts face into

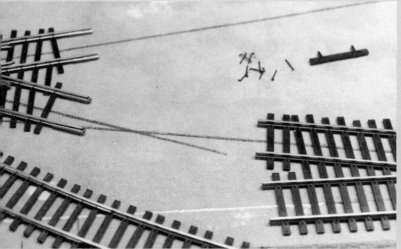

Fig. 4. Left: When joining two turnouts with a short section of track, the track center lines should cross as shown. The point where the center lines cross marks the middle of the curve. **Right:** Curve the flextrack and mark where to cut the track as shown. Then cut enough ties from one of the turnouts so you can slide a joiner all the way on, then slide it back over the section just added.

each other (the frog ends — where the rails cross — face each other), so there must be an insulated gap, or the rails will short when they're electrified. Most modular groups don't allow "air gaps" because if a metal wheel ends up sitting on a gap it will bridge the gap and short out the layout. It doesn't do much for the wheels that are sitting on the gap either, and I've seen plastic trucks melt from the heat generated by metal wheels sitting on an air gap.

The solution is to fill the gap with a piece of styrene held in place with epoxy and then filed to the contour of the rail. Now if a wheel is sitting on a gap, it's sitting on plastic. Put the turnouts in place, then cement the bits of styrene (they can be as thin as you like) to one turnout and slide the other up against it, dabbing on more epoxy. See fig. 6. Now spike it in place, and sight down the rails one last time to make sure everything is aligned.

There's one other code 100 no. 6 turnout in the westbound main. Otherwise, the remainder of the track is code 83.

TRANSITION TRACK

I tried two techniques where the taller code 100 rail joined the code 83. One was the old standby — flatten one half of a rail joiner and solder the shorter rail on top of the resulting flange. I also tried Walthers new transition track — one half of this is code 100, the other code 83. Both worked, though the older method takes up less space and, frankly, is more fun. See fig. 7.

All the other joints use conventional track joiners. Any joints that occur on a curve are soldered; the rest are left loose so the track can expand in the heat of my garage.

After joining the code 83 crossing to the code 100 turnout, I installed the third code 100 turnout and connected it to the crossing. Then I built on from the crossing toward the various sidings.

If you study the photos and the plan, you'll see that I actually cut all the turnouts shorter so I could begin curves closer to the frog for a smoother transition from turnout to curve. The only turnout I didn't cut is the "wye," that Y-shaped turnout near the center of the layout. Many of these turnouts face each other and must be insulated (see the track plan).

There's a lot of cutting and joining of track, but it took only a weekend to do the whole module, including hooking up the electrical wire. Most of it followed the procedure just outlined — align the track and turnouts, cut it, file it, join it (or insulate it), spike it.

ONE-MINUTE WIRING

Each module club has its own wiring standards so the various modules can be connected. All the wires are color-coded, and each club seems to use a different connector. As a result, I made no attempt to wire this for club use, figuring I'd add those wires under the supervision of a club when I got to that point.

The wiring on my module is therefore simplicity itself. A red wire and a black one run from the power source to the end of the layout. Short wires connect the tracks to these. That's it. Takes about a minute.

The power source is a Rix handheld throttle (fig. 8), perhaps the most commonly available of the walkaround controllers and one I had experience with. It's easy to wire, though you need to buy a transformer for it (I used a 16-volt Radio Shack unit as Rix recommends).

All of this is fastened to the inside edge of the layout, at the back.

SEVERAL SWITCH STANDS LATER

With a handheld throttle, it's easy to throw turnouts by hand; I used Caboose Industries switch stands (the tall ones) and ground throws (the low ones). These are a breeze to install, and even though they aren't to scale, the feel is right and they actually count as part of the scenery instead of being something you have to hide. Besides, it's more fun to throw your own turnouts, especially the tall switch stands since you can watch the targets turn.

Some people don't like the tall switch stands, and I have found that they do

Fig. 5. Use the same "mark and cut" technique for these facing turnouts and crossing.

Fig. 6. **Above left:** To make an insulated "airless" gap between the facing turnouts, first glue down ties where the turnouts meet so there is something to rest the styrene pieces on. **Right:** Then glue two scraps of styrene to the rails of one turnout, slide the other up against it, and spike it in place. Recheck alignment by sighting down the tracks.

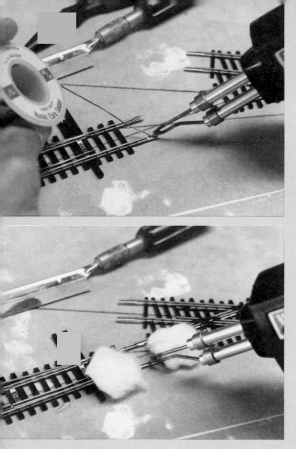

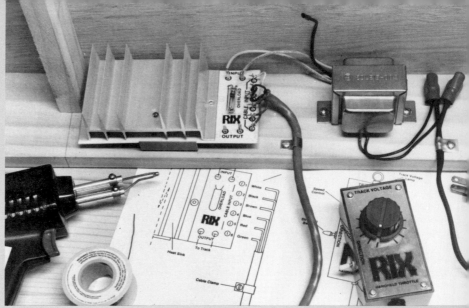

Fig. 8. The author installed the circuit board for his Rix handheld throttle under the layout's inside edge and powered it with the Radio Shack 16-volt transformer that's recommended.

Fig. 7. **Top:** To join code 100 to code 83 track, flatten a rail joiner already attached to the higher code 100. Flow some solder onto the flattened side. **Above:** Now solder the code 83 to it, using wet cotton balls to soak up heat that might deform nearby plastic ties. **Below:** File the top and sides flat and smooth. **Bottom:** Slide ties under the empty spot, and glue them down.

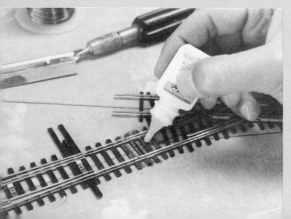

stick sometimes. However, most people don't know that they are easy to snap apart, fix or lubricate, and put back together. Although they look delicate, I've never broken one (the ground level throws are so tough they could probably survive a nuclear blast).

You'll notice in fig. 9 that you must use pieces of cardboard to center the points of the turnout while installing the throw or stand. I sprayed them with Testor's Dullcote (which helps paint stick to the engineering plastic) and then gave them a light coating of rust paint and rust-colored chalk.

One throw had to be mounted across the track, so I just used a piece of brass rod to extend the reach of the throw bar as shown in fig. 10.

When all the track and the throws were installed, I pulled the module outside and sprayed the rails, ties, and throws with a can of Floquil Roof Brown. I did this at about 3 p.m. on Sunday. After sanding off the paint from the top of the rails, I had trains running that night.

I hope I haven't zipped through this too quickly, but I don't want the telling to be longer than the doing. As I've mentioned, it really did take only a weekend to get all the track down and wired. Then I prepared to do a little paving.

AN ASPHALT JUNGLE

The ground around the harbor in Los Angeles is about half dirt and half asphalt but it's the asphalt you notice — acres of the stuff. How was I to do this quickly without making too much of a mess? A product named Sculptamold (made by American Art Clay Co.) saved the day. It's commonly available at artist's supply stores, and some hobby shops also carry it.

Sculptamold is like a mix of papier-

Fig. 9. Use bits of cardboard to center the points in the turnout when installing the ground throws from Caboose Industries.

Fig. 10. You can cut off the long ties that hold the switch stands and move them to the other side of the turnout. Sometimes, however, even that doesn't work. Here a piece of brass rod makes the long reach.

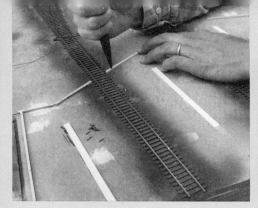
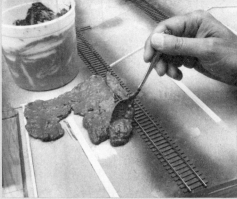

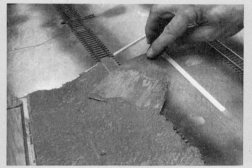
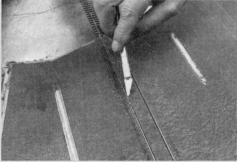

Fig. 11. To pave an area with Sculptamold, you need to first install guides or forms for the trowel to slide along the top of. **Top left:** Here, the styrene gutters (already in place), the rails themselves, and strips of balsa tacked down will do the job. They serve as the forms. **Top right:** Spoon the Sculptamold onto the layout. When wet it looks darker than it will end up. **Below left:** Spread it out with a wide trowel. **Below right:** While the Sculptamold is still wet (you have lots of time with it), clean out a groove for the wheel flanges with a hobby knife. Bob did one section at a time and used the previous sections (after they had set hard) as his form board, adding others where necessary. **Right:** This access road would have been paved separately in the real world.

mache and plaster, but without the mess. It does take a while to set up, but once Sculptamold has dried you can easily scrape, cut, or sand it and don't have to worry about any obnoxious dust, as with plaster. Sculptamold takes colors perfectly. It can take a little flexing should the layout bend — don't forget that this is a portable layout. Does it sound like I love the stuff?

The paving is planned so it doesn't interfere with any of the turnouts, though it does take advantage of some of the turnouts' guardrails and the spaces between facing turnouts where I could never hope to add any scenery or structures. Note how the access roads go between or very near to turnouts. The paving procedure is shown in fig. 11.

TRACK IN PAVEMENT

I was surprised that the track which cuts through the paving at the harbor is not the fancy girder rail used on city streets. It's plain track, sometimes with a board set next to it to keep the paving from the rails, but usually just surrounded with paving as if the whole thing were paved over and then a train run over it so the wheels could cut their own grooves. This is pretty much how I did it, too, but I used a hobby knife to scrape away the Sculptamold from the rails as it set up. See fig. 12.

Though I paved right over the track, I did hold the Sculptamold in place everywhere else with strips of balsa tacked down to the Homasote. I used a drywall trowel to smooth and flatten it, then I worked it until the surface looked as I desired. I left the Sculptamold rough in some spots, while in others I troweled it longer and floated a nice flat finish. Still elsewhere I waited until the Sculptamold

Fig. 12. Don't panic when you pave over all these turnouts and crossings. Just protect the turnout throw bars and points with masking tape, then slop on the Sculptamold, scraping it out for the wheel flanges.

had dried completely (about a week, though it sets up in an hour or less) and then sanded it flat.

I used equal parts Sculptamold and water and added 2 teaspoons of India ink to each cup to get the faded asphalt color. However, be sure to test this mixture as I found that various brands of India ink were darker or lighter than others. When wet the India-ink-colored Sculptamold looks much darker than it ends up, so let your tests dry for several days. Two cups of the Sculptamold mix did the area in front of the small building. It took between six and eight cups to do all the paving.

I even added some drainage channels made of flat styrene strips propped up near their edges with other bits of styrene so they would slope inward. These were later painted a concrete color. These strips, along with the rails and the form boards around the edge, act as guides for the trowel to slide across. This ensures that the surface is flat, though not level (if it were to rain on this layout, the water would drain properly).

I began by paving the roads and the container area and didn't pave the rest until the foundations for the buildings were in place. The next installment of this series will look at the other structures and scenicking, if that word applies to an industrial area like the Port of Los Angeles! ⌀

Port of Los Angeles project railroad: 3

Structures and the "setting" bring the module to life

BY ROBERT SMAUS

PHOTOS BY THE AUTHOR

SOME model railroaders like the scenery as much as the trains that run through it. I confess that I sometimes rush through benchwork and tracklaying to get to the scenery and structures, though "setting" may better describe industrial areas like the one modeled here than does "scenery."

Scenery sounds like hills and trees and other pretty things, while setting is simply what surrounds the railroad. On the 2½ x 6-foot HO scale Port of Los Angeles module, that's more likely to be industrial structures or drainage ditches, chain link fences, and oil wells. Like the American artist Edward Hopper, you must find beauty in the starkness of utilitarian, man-made objects.

Setting also hints at the purpose of scenery on a model railroad. Like the setting surrounding a precious stone,

the setting is the stage on which your trains perform. It gives them scale and purpose, and it shows them off. Sure, you can enjoy just the train — just as many railfans enjoy looking at photos that show only a locomotive — but wouldn't you rather see that locomotive in its context, so you know why it's there and can guess at what it's doing? I, for one, like the bigger picture.

While planning this module, I spent the most time and had the most fun designing the setting — figuring out which structures best said "Port of Los Angeles." (I made one literally spell it out so there would be no question!) I had to decide what building would fit where or how I could kitbash them into place. Then I went ahead and filled the odd corner with signs, fences, and other details.

I also tried to make the structures part of the backdrop, tilting them at odd angles, making them tall, or doing whatever was necessary to hide the back edge of the layout. When I sent in

my first plan to the editors at MODEL RAILROADER, they were concerned that too much of the layout edge showed. They were right, it did look like the world before Christopher Columbus. I tilted and twisted and sliced the structures even more, until there was no edge left on my little world.

While I built the benchwork and laid the track in two weekends, I spent about two months on the setting, in particular, the buildings and the freight cars that frequent them. Also, several structures were complete long before the module was even begun, because I needed to know how much space to allow for them.

THE STRADDLE CARRIER

On any layout, but particularly on a small one like the Port of Los Angeles module, it is important to know how big some of the buildings and other structures are going to be before getting too far into the actual construction

ft: This month the author explains how
added the structures and the scenery,
ich he calls the "setting," to the Port of
s Angeles module. This HO project rail-
ad was introduced in the December MR.

Right: The straddle crane is the focal point
for the whole layout, so it was painted
bright yellow and lettered like a billboard.

of the layout. In this case, I had to
know how wide the straddle carrier
would be, so I would know how far
apart to space the tracks inside my container terminal. That's why I built it
early on, not trusting the dimensions
given on the model box.

Container ships are unloaded by
huge container gantry cranes. Straddle
carriers are smaller cranes that cart
the containers around the facility, piling them in stacks or loading them
onto railcars or (more often) trucks.
Modeling one of the towering gantry
cranes was tempting, but it would have
been several feet tall in HO scale, so I
settled for a straddle carrier.

Because it's probably the most important model on the layout — a "sig-
nature model" that instantly states,
"This is a port facility serving double-
stack container trains" — it had to fit.
The model ended up being 10¼" wide,
and that determined the spacing of the
tracks inside the container terminal. I
wanted enough room under the carrier
for two rows of stacked containers, an
aisleway for trucks, and a section of
track, and they all fit.

Vollmer makes a nice model of a contemporary straddle crane (no. 5624),
and I built it pretty much as called for.
However, most straddle carriers do not
run on tracks, but are free to roam on
huge rubber tires. For that reason, I
used Lego toy wheels and rubber tires
(abandoned by my growing children) in
place of the railroad-type wheels that
come with the model. See fig. 1. I also
added some landing gear bits and
pieces that were salvaged from an air-
craft kit (also abandoned by my kids) to
represent the various struts and shocks
that control the wheels.

I built the carrier in several subassemblies (fig. 1) so I could individ-
ually paint and letter various parts. I
wanted it to stand out, which is why I
used Floquil Railbox Yellow. I left the
finish flat, enabling me to add dry-
transfer lettering. The big "California
Terminal" leaves no doubt where or
what this layout is about! I'm not one for
being subtle, but neither are most industries — their lettering is also very large.

I painted the control cab white and
added Pikestuff Smoke Tinted Windows
(no. 1003), so no one would notice the
lack of an operator. After it was built I

Fig. 1. Here are the subassemblies for the straddle carrier, with some of the dry-transfer
type that's used to letter it and a piece of the smoked glass added to the control cab.

Fig. 2. To get two containers for the price of one, pop the sides off a Con-Cor container (above) and cut it in half (right).

Fig. 3. Two modes of container conveyance: A simple truck chassis in the foreground (a model no longer in production) and a Thrall well car being shoved into place by a Geep.

Fig. 4. Any size wall can be made by joining Pikestuff kit sections together with strips of styrene. Long styrene strips keep walls from flexing too much. Fig. 5. To make the warehouse taller, plain styrene was used below the Pikestuff walls. Here you can see both how the huge doors were framed with styrene lengths and which pieces make up the front wall.

was surprised and delighted to discover that it would actually hold the containers made by A-Line. Surprises like this are another good reason to build some of the key models before getting too far along on the layout construction. They might change your layout ideas.

CONTAINERS

Containers are the center of attention at any modern port. Nearly everything arrives or departs in them, and they come in a variety of sizes from 20 feet to 53 feet. There are refrigerated containers and containers equipped with tanks to hold liquids. Almost all are available as models, though I pretty much used the standard 40-foot containers made by A-Line and Con-Cor.

I bought enough to pile them high in the terminal — high enough to act as part of my background. To save money I popped apart the Con-Cor containers and cut them in half lengthwise (fig. 2), putting them at the bottom of the stack where their partial nature would not be noticed. That way I got two for the price of one.

Since my fictitious California Terminal handles containers from a variety of companies, I painted them a variety of colors, but let red dominate so they would not be too much of a hodgepodge. Microscale makes lots of decals for containers, and I used a number of them, though I'm still not finished decaling all my containers.

Most containers are loaded onto special chassis and then trucked to a rail head or their final destination. There are a few terminals that load directly onto railcars like the one I've modeled (fig. 3) and more are planned. Unfortunately, there are no accurate models of these chassis. I used the presumably European chassis made by Con-Cor and the American tractors that come with them, repainting them all. A friend also gave me a more accurate chassis that's no longer being made, and examples appear in some of the photos. The chassis are so simple they could be scratchbuilt, and I'm sure a proper model will be forthcoming.

Inside the terminal, special tractors haul the chassis around, and these are available as white-metal kits from The Wheel Works. They're so neat I made three. You can see two of them parked inside the terminal in the lead photo. They add a nice touch to the scene.

Many of the containers end up on trains, and the special cars that carry them are easy to model because A-Line makes two of the most common types — the Thrall well cars and the more elaborate Gunderson cars. Both are fun kits to assemble, and I did nothing special to either. I did make unprototypically short strings of them so they would fit inside my terminal.

Fig. 6. Far left: The author used a carpenter's square and blocks of weighted wood to keep everything at right angles as the cement set. **Fig. 7. Left:** To make the oddly angled roof, he set the walls on a sheet of styrene and traced the outline. A triangle of styrene braces the corner of the walls. **Fig. 8. Above:** Here the terminal is in place, though it's still roofless. Note the supporting rafters and the back wall. The tracks leading into the warehouse had to be moved from their planned location as indicated by pencil lines on the Homasote.

I plan to make more and then model some of the hotshot locomotives that pull them, particularly the Dash 8s used by the Southern Pacific. In the meantime, my trusty old SD40T-2 tunnel motors do the job.

ONE BIG BUILDING

The next structure I built had to wait for most of the track to be laid because this one was kitbashed to fit the site. It is a loose representation of a modern warehouse that handles what is called "break-bulk" cargo, which is anything that doesn't come in a container, though it's usually loaded on pallets.

Actually, most of these warehouses at the Port of Los Angeles are pretty old, and I considered building one from scratch so I could have this feeling of two eras — the modern container facility and the old stevedoring facility. However, I settled for one that looks more recent because I couldn't resist playing with the Pikestuff line of modern industrial buildings.

For a very few bucks, you can buy several of their kits and use the walls and roof sections to make all sorts of buildings, even a very oddly shaped, to-fit structure like I put together.

I made my warehouse a banana terminal because I already had a nice modern fleet of Pacific Fruit Express reefers, and presumably this is how bananas are transported to other cities. I say presumably because in the labyrinth that is the Port of Los Angeles, I never did find the banana terminal, although I know one is there because I've seen photos of it in books. Mine, however, is pure conjecture.

Dockside warehouses are huge structures, and all of them have tracks that run alongside or even inside, which is where I put mine. That way you can't

see the end of the track (a friend suggested I go one step further and put a mirror at the end, inside the warehouse, to make it appear endless).

A SENSE OF SCALE

Because the terminal is so big, it brings a believable sense of scale to the layout. It also hides a lot of the layout's edge, one reason it's oddly tilted. I couldn't figure out how to plan such a building so I designed it on the spot. I used two of Pikestuff's Distribution Center kits (no. 10), laying out the wall sections on the layout and cutting them to fit as shown in fig. 4.

To make the warehouse taller and save a few bucks, I made the bottom of the walls out of plain .030" styrene (to represent plastered walls or concrete). See fig. 5. The various sections are held together with .030" strips of styrene on the back side, and additional strips were cemented on to act as bracing so the wall wouldn't flex too much. When the walls were assembled, I shoved them against a carpenter's square to make sure they were at right angles as shown in fig. 6.

After the cement had set, I put the walls on top of several big pieces of styrene and traced out a roof. See fig. 7. More plain styrene makes a back for the warehouse, and again I simply laid the model against it and trimmed to fit. I added the back and some rafters of styrene (fig. 8), then cemented on the roof.

I wanted to model the "Port of Los Angeles" lettering that's on the roof of actual warehouses. Inspiration struck one day while reading the notice board at church — use those plastic letters! Well, actually, I went out and bought my own. They work perfectly, even having little bases that make cementing them to the roof easy. See fig. 9.

I had enough wall and roof sections left from the Pikestuff Distribution Center kits to put together another little building. It neatly hid more of the layout edge, where I had planned to stack up more containers. See fig. 10. I built this the same way — to fit — but tilted it at a slightly different angle to suggest that it was at the end of a slip.

MORE PAVING

When I was done with the warehouse, I discovered I had to move the track leading into it a little. I did so and then spiked it down. Though I had already paved the container yard and the streets that cross the tracks, I was now ready to pave around my buildings.

I glued down lengths of styrene for the building foundations (fig. 11) and used those as well as more strips of balsa as a guide for my trowel. The floor of the big warehouse is asphalt paving (Sculptamold), but the small

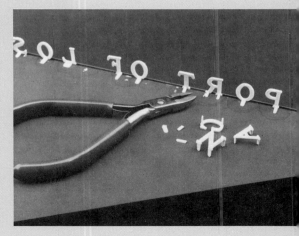

Fig. 9. The author found these plastic bulletin board letters at an artist's supply shop for the big "Port of Los Angeles" sign.

Fig. 10. The small building was made from wall and roof sections left over after building the warehouse. **Above, left to right:** The walls were assembled, then the roof and back wall were cut out and trimmed to fit. Short blocks of styrene hold them in place.

Fig. 11. Strips of styrene make a foundation for the warehouse and serve as a guide for the trowel when paving with Sculptamold.

building has its own concrete (styrene) floor. More height needed!

Between these two buildings was a little gap where I wanted to put yet another crane — ports are full of cranes. This would be a "stevedoring crane" to unload break-bulk cargo with hook, net, and pallet. I wanted it to appear to be facing out into the slip, where it could unload ships in the water just beyond the edge of the layout. And, I wanted it to be tall.

There are no mountains at the Port of Los Angeles, so structures would have to give this layout height and drama. The stevedoring crane was the perfect solution. The tallest kit I could find was Faller's gantry crane (no. 162). Like my other crane, this kit is designed to travel on rails, but I trimmed off all that gear and, to make it taller, added pieces of Plastruct I beams and additional ladders and bracing to the bottom.

It still wasn't high enough to clear my warehouse, so I put the whole thing on top of concrete piers made from wood

Fig. 12. Below: This immense Faller gantry crane gives the layout height and drama; even better, it fits nicely between the two buildings.

dowels. See fig. 12. I put short lengths of brass rod in the tops of the dowels, drilled holes up into the I beams I had added to the crane, and slid it on.

EVERYTHING REMOVABLE

This made it possible to lift the crane off its base. In fact, all the structures on the layout are designed that way, including the big warehouse, which just sits on its foundation. I did this partly because I wanted the module to be portable and didn't want to risk breaking off anything while moving it around. In addition, designing the structures to be removable makes cleaning and repairing much, much easier.

All the little figures, most of them made by Preiser, are also removable, held in place the same way the stevedoring crane is — with short lengths of thin brass rod. A hole is drilled in one foot, and a piece of rod cemented in place. Wherever I want a figure I drill a hole in the layout, which is real easy to do on Homasote or in the Sculptamold paving.

Preiser makes all sorts of industrial-type figures wearing hard hats and doing things like climbing ladders and waving directions to some other figure. Some of the most animated looking unfortunately have distinctly European-looking hats, but there is a way to turn these into more American-looking baseball caps: Dab a drop or two of cyanoacrylate adhesive (CA) on top of the flat European hats, as shown in fig. 13, to give them a crown, and then repaint the hat. Otherwise, I did little to the figures, though a few got a total repaint.

Some modelers don't like lots of little plastic people on their layouts, but nothing sets the scale faster than a person standing near something really large like a locomotive or a crane. One tends to forget, for instance, how big a boxcar really is unless there is some sort of comparison standing next to it.

A PLACE FOR BOXCARS

I could put PFE and other refrigerator cars in my warehouse and line up double-stack container cars under the straddle carrier. But where could I put plain old boxcars, which I had a closet full of?

Well, I had to do some hunting to find ordinary boxcars dockside. Covered hoppers? Sure, tons of them, and flatcars, tank cars, and auto racks full of Toyotas. But boxcars?

I finally found some alongside a rather plain-looking loading dock that was standing all by itself in the middle of some vacant land. On the other side of the dock there were rows of those ubiquitous 40-foot boxcars, and forklifts scurried like ants between the two carrying bright yellow bundles of something. On close inspection it turned out to be American cotton, being loaded into containers destined for Japan.

It was being operated by Loaders Unlimited ("Expert Cotton Handling"), and owner Willie Gauff Sr. let me take a few photos of the dock and boxcars. It was an interesting collection of boxcars, many of them quite old. All had wide doors or double doors for the forklifts, and most were from southwestern roads — Cotton Belt, Missouri Pacific, Southern Pacific, Railbox relettered for the SP, Santa Fe, and even a few very dirty Pacific Fruit Express reefers pressed into service.

THE COTTON TRANSFER DOCK

If the warehouse seemed like a complicated project, you'll love the cotton transfer dock. It's just plaster poured into a mold of balsa strips tacked to the Homasote (fig. 14). You'll be done building it before I've finished describing it.

Lines were scribed on the top while the plaster was still damp, and after it had dried I painted it with Floquil Concrete mixed with White, after first driving a model forklift made by Wiking (no. 12659) through some black paint and then over the ramp. After painting over them with light sprays of Concrete, these tire tracks looked like the scuff marks made by rubber tires.

I made some bales of cotton out of cotton (of course) and yellow plastic bags. In addition, I modified the Wiking forklift by removing the lower arms and attaching some new ones to the sides so they could grip the bales.

Protecting one edge of the dock (the rail side) are strips of Plastruct angle. Protecting the other (from bumping by the containers) are strips of stained basswood. When the dock was all done, I rubbed garden dirt over the whole thing to tone it down and then sprayed it with a can of Testor's Dullcote. See fig. 15.

MORE TO COME

This wasn't the end of building at the Port of Los Angeles. The next installment of this series will show how the most elaborate model — the bulk oil storage facility — was modeled. Also, if I can get back on my soapbox, I'll say a few words about "detailing" and throw some dirt and ballast on the layout. ✿

Fig. 13. Above: Applying just a drop of cyanoacrylate adhesive turns a flat European hat into a round-topped American baseball hat. Bits of brass wire set into the feet of figures are used to hold them to the layout. **Fig. 14. Below:** The cotton transfer dock is made of plaster poured into a mold of balsa wood.

Fig. 15. The completed cotton transfer dock includes some scale bales of cotton wrapped in yellow plastic shown here being loaded by a modified Wiking forklift.

Construction of a liquid bulk terminal is the last major project on the HO Port of Los Angeles module, which was introduced in the December 1990 MR. The bridge shown here passes over the road and tracks carrying pipes from one part of the terminal to another.

Port of Los Angeles project railroad: 4

More structures are added, and then lots of details complete the module

BY ROBERT SMAUS
PHOTOS BY THE AUTHOR

IF SOMEONE will hand me a soapbox, I'd like to get up on it and say a few words about "details" on model railroads. Many modelers believe that details can make or break a layout, especially in photographs, but I think there's a tendency to overdo it on modern-era layouts.

Thanks to the value of scrap metal, environmental laws, and Americans' inclination to sue, modern industrial areas are not cluttered with junk. It's dangerous, dirty, and probably worth something, so if you find any at all, it's securely behind fences.

The Port of Los Angeles is particularly clean and tidy. There might be the odd tire in a drainage ditch and a stack of pallets by a warehouse, but the overall look is of wide-open spaces without much clutter. There's plenty of oil-stained asphalt, to be sure, and bits of paper and other rubbish piled against

Fig. 1. The author made this cardboard mock-up of the pipe bridge and moved it around until he found a location where it would block the view of the corner of the layout.

fences where the wind has left them, but even that gets picked up in time.

So, to detail our 2½ x 6-foot HO Port of Los Angeles module, you can't look in the scrap box and toss whatever you find on the layout. Once again you have to look to the prototype for clues because details should be found, not invented.

This reasoning caused me to make yet another trip to the port, with notebook and camera in hand, to look just for details. What I found was that most of the details were attached to something else — the walkways and ladders on cranes and other structures, the signs and fences, the piping that seems to run everywhere. These details bring a sense of delicacy and scale to models. The best example of this was on the last structure I intended to model — the liquid bulk terminal.

THE LIQUID BULK TERMINAL

The Wilmington Liquid Bulk Terminal is a huge facility at the Port of Los Angeles. Big tanks line both sides of every road, and pipes run everywhere. I'm not exactly sure what they store here, but my guess would be anything liquid. I do know that the part I modeled handles oil residues, what they call "well-wash," from oil wells all over Southern California. It arrives in tank trucks and tank cars, and the two can be found side by side in the unloading area. It's stored here while awaiting refinement. I learned this from a trucker who was waiting in line.

I knew that the liquid bulk terminal would make a great model, and I saw it as a way to use an odd corner of the module and to hide the tracks so they don't seem to end so abruptly at the edge of the layout. The key was a bridge that passed over road and tracks carrying pipes from one part of the terminal to another. Early on, I made a cardboard mock-up of this bridge (fig. 1) and moved it around until I found just the right spot, where it would block the view of the corner of the layout.

LOTS OF PIPES

I found the necessary bridge piping in the Kibri kits that also provided the tanks. I bought one Single Storage Tank kit (item no. 9806) and one Double Storage Tank (no. 9808), and the bonus was lots of piping with all sorts of valves and regulators attached. The actual bridge was made of styrene bits and pieces, some of them scribed to represent the metal sheathing on the bridge. To this I added the pipes from the Kibri kits. See fig. 2.

The tanks themselves were actually built earlier because I thought I had room for three in the little triangle of space at the corner of the layout, but wanted to make sure. They were tall enough to become part of the backdrop,

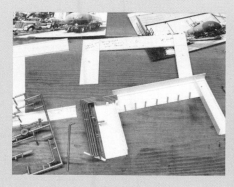

Fig. 2. Above: Here are the bits and pieces that went into the bridge carrying pipes across the road and rails. The piping is from Kibri tank kits. **Fig. 3. Right:** The whole liquid bulk terminal can be lifted off the layout for cleaning and repairing and to avoid damage when the module is moved.

Fig. 4. The tanks were positioned on top of tracing paper, and the area for the terminal was outlined. The outline was used as a guide for cutting the base from ⅛"-thick styrene.

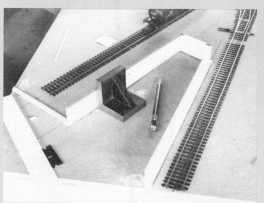
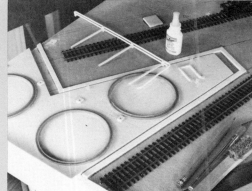

Fig. 5. Above: The author made the block wall around the tank farm like a hollow sandwich of Evergreen scribed styrene sheet and strip styrene. **Fig. 6. Right:** Here's the styrene base with the rings that hold the tanks. It's surrounded by the foundation for the wall.

but also tall enough to knock over. For that reason, I designed the tanks so I could take them off.

IT'S REMOVABLE

I made the entire liquid bulk terminal removable by building it on top of a ⅛"-thick sheet of styrene from a store that sells plastic and Plexiglas. See fig. 3. This was necessary because there were

so many bits and pieces involved — pipes, stairs, ladders, and lights.

First I laid a piece of tracing paper on the layout and drew the outline of the area I planned to cover (fig. 4). This I used as a guide when cutting the thick styrene. Then I put the styrene base on the layout and drew its outline. Along this line I built, out of strip styrene, a foundation for a concrete block wall. The

Fig. 7. The completed liquid bulk facility neatly fills this odd corner of the module.

Fig. 8. A reasonable facsimile of a nifty water tank found at the Port of Los Angeles was kitbashed by the author from a Faller kit. Behind the tank you can see two Wheel Works yellow terminal tractors parked behind an Alloy Forms chain link fence.

Fig. 9. Styrene signs with dry-transfer lettering like this one tell truckers where to go in the terminal. One of Diamond Scale's walking beam oil pumps can be seen in the background.

block wall, fig. 5, uses the scribed styrene Evergreen calls "tile." To build the wall I made a hollow sandwich, with scribed styrene being the "bread" and lengths of strip styrene the "bologna."

These walls, cemented permanently to the Homasote layout top with CA (cyanoacrylate adhesive), hold the styrene base in place and hide its edges. That way no one knows it's unattached. I could pave right up to the wall or mound the soil against it. I also covered it with Microscale graffiti.

The tanks come with their own bases, so with a hand jigsaw I cut off everything but the rings that hold the tanks and cemented these to the styrene base as shown in fig. 6. Then I dug around in the kit boxes and found various pipes and ladders and steps and put them on the base. The final touches were two inexpensive light fixtures made by Life-Like. Their wires go through holes in the base that align with holes in the layout.

More pipes were cemented to a strip of styrene, and these were placed between the rail and the truck loading area; shorter strips of styrene on either side of this collection of nozzles also served as a guide for the trowel when it was time to pave. The completed liquid bulk facility is shown in fig. 7.

DETAILS, DETAILS

After finishing that facility, I had lots of piping left over, so I built some of the pipes that connect the oil wells that dot the harbor area. These come to the surface here and there, perhaps so they can be cleaned, repaired, or just shut off, as there are many regulators and valves attached. They make nice details that easily fit in odd places and are much more realistic than piles of junk.

I also built a couple of the amazing Diamond Scale walking beam oil pumps (no. 401). These can be motorized to rock back and forth. See fig. 9. Some of the ones at the harbor were painted bright blue, and I copied them.

ANOTHER HIGH SPOT

I like tall structures that stick up from the layout. Too often structures end up all about the same size and shape, which gives the layout a flat, toy-like look. To my delight, I found yet another tall tank to model. The prototype no longer seemed connected to the industry it advertised — the California Shipbuilding Co. — because it was sitting all alone amid oil pumps. It was just the thing to fit another odd corner between tracks.

I modeled it using a Faller water tower kit (no. 144), but I built a new base out of Central Valley girders and

Fig. 10. Life-Like lights slide neatly into ⅛" styrene rods to make mast lights for the container yard. Figure 11 shows how the parking lot lines and lettering were made.

brass rod because the base on this kit was too short and bulky.

This tank made a colorful model and shows why you should find prototypes for your models — my unaided imagination would never have come up with the interesting paint scheme that's on this tower (fig. 8).

EUROPEAN KITS

You may have noticed that I've used a lot of European kits on this layout, all of which had to be modified somewhat. But in this international age, that's often all it takes — a little modification — because so many modern structures are similar worldwide. In a port this is especially true because much of the heavy equipment is made elsewhere.

Almost any inexpensive, out-of-the-box model can be made to look completely different by replacing bulky or unrealistic parts with pieces you construct. In this case, I removed the heavy beams that made up the base and replaced them with the delicate Central Valley parts.

SIGNS POINT THE WAY

I'm not terribly fond of signs in real life, so I always surprise myself by adding lots to my layouts. The Port of Los Angeles module is no exception. The water tank is really a big sign with its dry-transfer lettering.

In front of the liquid bulk terminal, I built a little sign out of the same Evergreen styrene used to make the walls. In front of this, I built signs of styrene at the edge of the layout to help truckers find their way into the area (fig. 9). These signs, which copy real ones, were painted with flat Floquil paint and lettered with dry transfers.

I put signs on the warehouse, big numbers on the cranes (all harbor cranes have numbers), and of course, railroad crossing signs by the main line. I even put signs on the paving, an obvious place often overlooked on layouts.

The container facility has painted lines that show the straddle carrier where to stack the containers, and they are lettered by row as shown in fig. 10.

Fig. 11. Use masking tape to make the paving stripes, sealing the edges with Dullcote before spraying them white. Then rub down large dry-transfer letters to identify the rows.

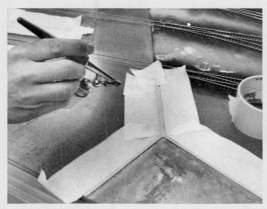

Fig. 12. While the masking tape is out, mask and spray the gutters a concrete color. Then rub dirt on the concrete color to give it a more realistic brown tone as shown above, right.

For these lines and others on the streets, I used masking tape and an airbrush. Before I sprayed the white paint, I sealed the edges of the masking tape by brushing on a thick coat of Testor's Dullcote. See fig. 11. Otherwise, the white paint would have bled under the tape because the Sculptamold paving is so porous. The letters are dry transfers.

By the way, the railroad crossing signs on the street are bigger than you may think. The "X" is a scale 8 feet across and 20 feet high; the "RR" is 2½ x 5 feet.

While you have the masking tape out, mask off the concrete drainage ditches and curbs and spray them a concrete color (I use a mix of Floquil Concrete and White). See fig. 12. Rub dirt on the dry paint to give it a more realistic brownish tint.

Also mask the rails that run through any paving. You'll find that much of the paint has popped off, so they need redoing. Paint them with a rust mixture and then brush some powdered rust-colored chalk into the gaps as shown in fig. 13. Finally, sand the tops of the rails to make sure they're clean.

Fig. 13. The author discovered that when he cleaned the Sculptamold from along the inside of the rail after he did the paving, most of the paint came off too. As a result, he found it necessary to repaint the rail with a mixture of Floquil Rust and Roof Brown (left) and then brush in some chalk for a dry, rusty look (middle). For the final touch, he sanded dirt or paint off the top of the rails.

Fig. 14. Bits of Plastruct angle were used to make this upright storage rack for the container chassis. Note the sea gulls in front.

Fig. 15. The entrance to the container facility is protected by gates, a guardhouse, and a guard. The gates are modified Bachmann grade-crossing gates, while the guardhouse is from AM Models. A chain link fence (made by Alloy Forms) surrounds the entire complex.

LET THERE BE LIGHTS

I put in some light masts made from inexpensive Life-Like lights (fig. 10). Once you've pulled off the toy-like bases, these will slide perfectly into ⅛" styrene tubing. The wires are even long enough to run the length of the styrene tubing, and the tubing slides into holes drilled through the layout top.

CONTAINER CHASSIS RACK

The truck chassis that carry the containers are often stored in a vertical position in special racks, one of which was an obvious detail to model. I used Plastruct angles to build it (fig. 14). I have yet to figure out how the prototypes are stood on end and put into these racks!

CHAIN LINK FENCING, OF COURSE

An obvious detail for any modern layout is chain link fencing, and I used two of the kits made by Alloy Forms (each no. 2009 kit does about 200 feet of fence). After assembling the fencing, I laid it on a piece of cardboard and marked where the posts were going to be placed, then used the cardboard as a guide when drilling my postholes in the tabletop.

I added gates and a guardhouse, and a guard, at the entrance to the container facility (fig. 15). The gates are modified Bachmann grade-crossing gates, and the guardhouse is an AM Models product. AM makes nifty easy-to-assemble-and-paint outbuildings, and I put another

Fig. 16. Left: All the detachable detail parts are stored in boxes to protect them from dust and damage. A-Line makes the nifty boxes for locomotives and freight cars; the other boxes were found at a box store.

Fig. 17. A cheap paintbrush provides material to make lots of long grass. Stick the bristles into slightly dry globs of glue.

and a cantilevered signal bridge (by Oregon Supply) at the front of the layout. The signal bridge is removable, and if it gets bumped it will topple, not snap off. It's tempting to put nothing there since anything is likely to get bumped. However, having something substantial in the foreground does make a layout look deeper.

A ROACH COACH AND MORE DETAILS

Pikestuff makes another nifty detail, a highway guardrails set, that I used behind the cotton transfer dock to keep truckers off the branch line. In a similar vein, I used Plastruct I beams to make bumping posts, painting them yellow and putting them where appropriate.

Nearby is a handy spot for a lunch break. Wiking calls it a Verkaufswagen; we Americans call it a lunch wagon or, unfairly, a "roach coach." Preiser provided the diners and the chef inside.

Not too far away is an item readily found anywhere in industrial America, a Dumpster, or roll-off body, made by Alloy Forms. Near it are piles of pallets from AM Models. These are all legitimate details, and just about the only junk to be found on this layout is paper trash or the occasional tire in the drainage ditch. Everything else is in the Dumpster where it belongs.

Details such as these make nice one-evening projects for those spare moments when there isn't time for bigger projects. If you have them written down in a notebook, you can quickly build them when that spare minute appears.

Since many of the details aren't permanently attached, I take them off and store them in boxes on a shelf under the layout (fig. 16). Proto Power West and A-Line make boxes to hold rolling

Fig. 18. First, sprinkle ballast over the tracks, then add dirt. Next, smooth everything with a soft brush. The final step is to fix everything in place. Using an eyedropper, apply a 50:50 mixture of glue and water between the ties and wherever there is ballast or dirt.

stock and locomotives. You can also try the box stores opening up everywhere; I found plenty of useful ones there.

DIRT AND BALLAST

I like to add dirt last. That way you can push it right up against the edge of the paving or a building foundation and not leave an unrealistic gap or air space.

I made weeds by cutting up some cheap paintbrushes with straw-colored bristles and putting clumps of the bristles in blobs of glue that had dried just a bit. See fig. 17. These represent the dried grasses seen all over the Port of Los Angeles. I clustered them near the tracks to make them very visible when a dark freight car or locomotive goes behind. These weeds are another reminder of scale.

The photos in fig. 18 pretty much show the rest of the process. First I sprinkled on Highball gray ballast and then, using a soft brush, got if off the rails and tops of the ties. Near the turnout throws I carefully applied just a little. Next, I sprinkled on real dirt and smoothed it out with a soft brush.

I use dirt found locally, looking for kinds that are not so fine as to become mud when wet — more like finely ground rock than dirt. I run it through a fine strainer and set aside the coarser material. Then I put down the finely sifted dirt and at the base of slopes add some of the coarser material. On flat areas I scatter the coarser material in drifts, as it might end up when pushed by water during flooding. Study the ground you're modeling, and you'll see that there is probably a natural distribution of materials that can be convincingly modeled.

To create weeds, I scatter at least two different sizes and two slightly varied

colors of ground foam from Architectural Model Supply Inc. Trash (bits of paper) is also added in the appropriate places. Put weeds where they would naturally grow (mostly low spots where water collects) and trash where it generally collects (against fences and walls).

Typically, I put down all these materials then stare at them for a day to make sure I like where they lay. When I'm ready to fix them in place, I first cover buildings with old sheets or newspapers and then fill up a spray bottle with a mixture of 1 part white glue to 4 or 5 parts water, with a few drops of Kodak PhotoFlo (a wetting agent) to make the water "wetter." Shake this mixture real well and then, while standing way back from the layout, aim the bottle slightly up in the air and mist it onto the dirt and ballast.

If you don't stand back or you aim the bottle down, the force of the spray will blow the ground foam away and maybe rearrange your dirt. You'll also be glad that the module can be rolled outside; if yours can't, make sure to cover the floor and everything else you don't want glued down. When the scenery looks good and wet, give the mixture a few minutes to soak in and go at it again. Keep this up until the diluted glue actually puddles and you think, "Now I've put on too much!" You haven't; it will soak in and disappear in short order.

Between the ties and in places where I've put down ground foam or made the dirt or ballast especially thick, I make up a mixture of white glue and water (about half and half, with a drop or two of PhotoFlo) and flow it on gently with an eyedropper. This is my insurance that things are really stuck down.

A BACKDROP FOR THE HARBOR

I was on the home stretch now. With all the dirt down and the glue dry, I sanded the edges of the layout one last time and used a small, throwaway paint roller to put on a coat of black paint.

Now I needed a backdrop. Stealing an idea from MR, I decided to use a poster print of a ship. A friend, Dave Lustig, just happened to have a slide of a container ship that he took from precisely the right angle while he was out fishing or doing something in the harbor.

But first I painted the hardboard backdrop white; then, with an almost dry roller, I put on a thin, bright blue coat so the white showed through and looked like the high, hazy clouds typical of Southern California.

I took the slide down to the photo store and had a Kodak Poster Print made of it. I trimmed the ship from its surroundings, laid it on top of a big piece of paper, traced its outline, and cut along this line (fig. 19). What I ended up with was a mask the exact shape of my ship cutout.

I put this cutout on the piece of tempered hardboard that I had painted, so it covered everything but the place where the ship cutout would go. Then I used a spray adhesive to coat this "shadow" of the ship and the back of the ship photo. I let the adhesive dry, carefully positioned the ship, covered it with waxed paper, and used a flour roller to stick it down.

ONE LAST DETAIL

As I was finishing the Port of Los Angeles, I realized that a little gap left between the stack of containers and the small Pikestuff building stuck out like

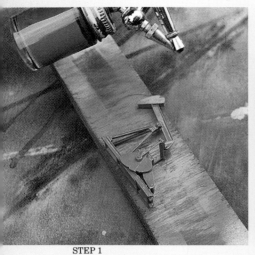

STEP 1 STEP 2

The author's painting and weathering procedure goes like this: **1.** Start by spray-painting on a base color. **2.** Then go ahead and push some powdered chalk onto the wet paint.

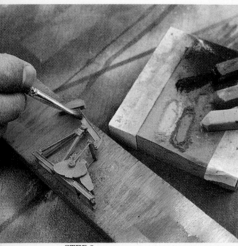

STEP 3 STEP 4

3. After the paint has dried, spread chalk around. **4.** Touch up with base color if needed.

STEP 5 STEP 6

5. Spray on a coat of rust paint, using a mixture of Floquil Rust and Roof Brown, concentrating on those areas that are already covered with chalk. **6.** For a really grimy look, puddle dilute Polly S Oil and push black powdered chalk onto the wet pools of paint.

PAINTING AND WEATHERING

Just about everything on the Port of Los Angeles layout was painted and weathered in a similar fashion. I use an airbrush to apply the basic coat of paint. I believe that an airbrush is the one essential tool needed by a modeler (other than an X-acto knife and scale rule). It's the only way to apply a thin, even coat of paint.

If I'm going to heavily weather what I'm painting (and a lot of machinery is heavily weathered being so near the sea), I immediately brush on powdered chalk, so it sticks to the wet paint. I don't touch the paint with the brush; I just use it to push the chalk off the board.

You can see the colors I use most often in the photos — this is my basic weathering kit. These are plain pastels, not oil chalks; mine happen to be made by Koss. Rubbing them on a piece of sandpaper taped to a block of wood turns them to powder.

When the paint has dried, I use a big, soft brush to spread the powder around. Next, I use the airbrush to spray a mixture of rust-colored paint (a 50:50 blend of Floquil Rust and Roof Brown). This mixture is usually heavily diluted with lacquer thinner, though that depends on how obvious the rust is supposed to be.

This coat of rust from the airbrush blends the chalk with the base coat of paint and helps hold the chalk in place. Here and there I add a touch of undiluted Rust/Roof Brown by hand, with a small, stiff brush. If I overdo the weathering, I touch up with the original base color, again applied with an airbrush.

Not everything is weathered with rust. Some structures get a light dusting of dilute Floquil Grimy Black; others get a coat of dust, using a dilute spray of Floquil Grime or Earth. I always use about 1 part paint to 10 parts thinner and slowly build up the coats with lots of passes from the airbrush.

To make things greasy and oily, I use the same technique I use for rust, but apply everything with a regular brush because I use water-soluble paints: Polly S Oil looks like old oil, Gunze Oil (a Japanese paint) looks very fresh. These paints look wet even after they've dried.

I puddle diluted mixes of these, and while they are still wet I push black powdered chalk onto the puddles. Here and there I use less diluted solutions of these two paints. The effect is so convincing that nobody wants to touch parts of my layout for fear of getting their fingers dirty!

a sore thumb. I decided to add one more detail — a fisherman. Of course he needed company, so I also added some cheering compatriots (one use for all those Preiser figures that have their arms in the air!) and a bunch of sea gulls waiting for something to fall out of the bait bucket.

I made the pole of brass wire, adding guides with drops of CA. The fisherman's really leaning into it because the bonita in the harbor put up one heck of fight, running like tuna. The sea gulls (fig. 20) are English models, ordered from The Engine Shed, BR792, Arundel, West Sussex, BN18 9BR, United Kingdom. I had about given up on finding any birds that looked remotely like gulls when a friend suggested this source. The Engine Shed has three different kinds to choose from! Their list of animals and other figures is impressively long, though they are all OO scale, which is just slightly larger than HO. That's all right because the gulls in L. A.'s harbor are big and fat.

To give my fisherman a little water to fish in, I cut into the layout top just a bit and then hid this edge with pieces of stained basswood. A friend stopped by at this point and suggested the addition of a bollard, those things that ships tie up to. It was modeled using the tops of two pushpins. See fig. 20.

Details such as this miniscene aren't initially noticed, but they reward the patient viewer. The longer he or she looks, the more that's found. Kids especially like these touches, while they hardly notice the handsome models of diesels and freight cars that thrill us modelers.

ADDING ON

Before the module was completed, I knew I would want to add on to it at some point. If you take one last look at the plans, you can see how easy that will be. On the right side, I will simply extend the tracks and the container yard, piling up more stacks of containers for my backdrop. Why, I might even build one of the huge container gantry cranes. The tracks here can easily go another few feet, which would allow me

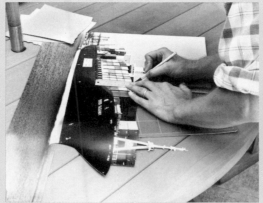
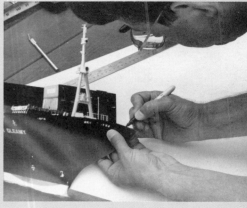

Fig. 19. Above: Cut out the backdrop ship photo. Then use a felt-tip pen to blacken the edges. **Below:** Make a mask that will protect the backdrop when spraying on the mounting adhesive. Simply trace the outline of the ship and then remove that part of the paper. Next, apply spray adhesive to the back of the photo and the area not protected by the mask of paper. Now install the backdrop by carefully positioning the photo and rolling it flat.

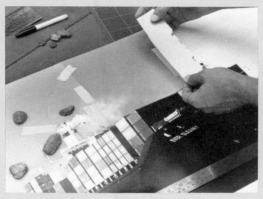

to use full-length strings of double-stack freight cars.

On the left side, the liquid bulk terminal will get more tanks, which will become a backdrop in this direction. The truncated branch line will continue into a small yard. I plan to fit one more industry on this side of the layout — a U. S. Borax facility that handles lots of covered hoppers, the one common freight car I couldn't fit on the original module. At the front of this extension, I'll continue the Cotton Transfer Dock so there's room for more old boxcars.

As I've said before, the telling takes more time than the building. I'm sure

I've spent more time writing about and photographing the Port of Los Angeles module than I did building it. Construction was more fun, though I think it would be worthwhile building a module like this just so you can roll it outside and take pictures of your models on it.

As proof of how simple this module is to build, let me point out that, unlike most project railroad authors who are real experts, I've built only one other layout before this one, and it was pretty small. I think that's why MODEL RAILROADER asked me to build this one, for that amateur viewpoint — they figured if I could do it, *anyone* could. ₪

Fig. 20. Above: The heads of pushpins make fine bollards, those things ships tie up to. **Right:** The fisherman and his buddies and the flock of sea gulls are nice realistic touches for this harbor scene.

Allen Keller puts the Seaboard Central through its paces. The handheld Onboard throttle permits him to go to either side of the layout. A. L. Schmidt photo.

Our Seaboard Central: Part 1

Overcoming the perils of working before a live audience,
we build an HO railroad that grows

BY JIM KELLY

HERE, still redolent with the fragrance of fresh Floquil, is our latest HO scale project railroad, the Seaboard Central. Our MODEL RAILROADER staff built it live before a series of eight audiences during the NMRA's 50th anniversary convention right here in Milwaukee. Three of our most popular writers, Dave Frary, Malcolm Furlow, and John Olson were in town for the festivities, so we called on them for lots of expert help. Three more experts were easy to find. Bob Hayden, Fred Hamilton, and Art Curren all work here at Kalmbach Publishing Co., and we see them every day.

The room at the convention center where we built the layout held upwards of 300 people, and we had no audience smaller than 175. The more popular sessions (those dealing with scenery techniques) were standing-room-only. To our surprise and delight 13 members of the audience attended all eight sessions. Two of these became lucky winners of official MR shop aprons.

The audiences were lively, and their questions and comments helped tremendously in keeping the demonstrations moving. (Try talking nonstop for 20 minutes while several guys are screwing together benchwork.)

We could pretend all the sessions went perfectly, but too many eyewitnesses who know the truth have gone back out into the world. The rock-casting crew — Dick Christianson, Malcolm Furlow, Mike

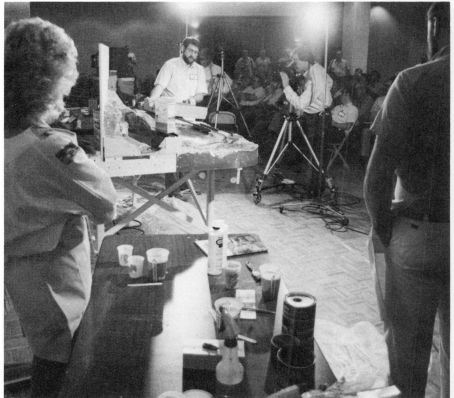

John Olson

Much of the work on the Seaboard Central was done live during the NMRA's national convention. Here's Bob Hayden expounding on modeling water. Vera Savic (left) and Dave Frary (right) also participated in this session. Allen Keller is manning the TV camera. Everyone in the room had the equivalent of a front row seat, as they had good closeup views of the action on two 19″ TV monitors.

Dick Christianson (left) and Allen Keller operate the expanded SC, built by combining the new layout with our earlier Kitty Hawk Central.

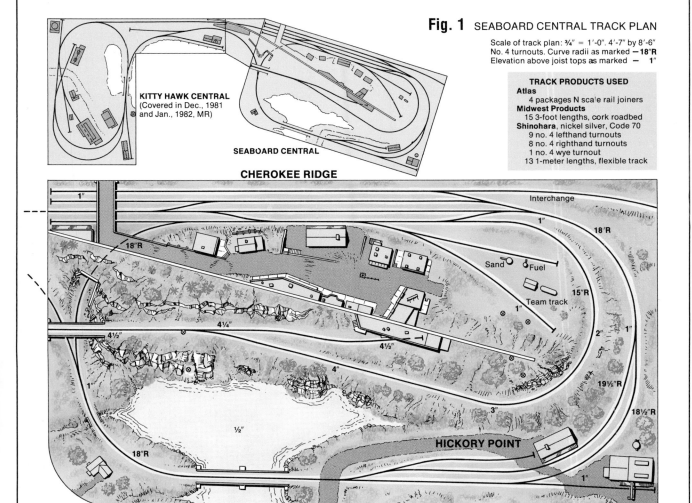

Fig. 1 SEABOARD CENTRAL TRACK PLAN

Scale of track plan: ¾″ = 1′-0″. 4′-7″ by 8′-6″
No. 4 turnouts. Curve radii as marked —**18″R**
Elevation above joist tops as marked — **1″**

KITTY HAWK CENTRAL
(Covered in Dec., 1981
and Jan., 1982, MR)

SEABOARD CENTRAL

CHEROKEE RIDGE

TRACK PRODUCTS USED
Atlas
4 packages N scale rail joiners
Midwest Products
15 3-foot lengths, cork roadbed
Shinohara, nickel silver, Code 70
9 no. 4 lefthand turnouts
8 no. 4 righthand turnouts
1 no. 4 wye turnout
13 1-meter lengths, flexible track

Interchange

18″R

18″R

Sand

Fuel

15″R

Team track

4¼″

4½″

4½″

4″

2″

1″

19½″R

18½″R

3″

½″

HICKORY POINT

18″R

1″

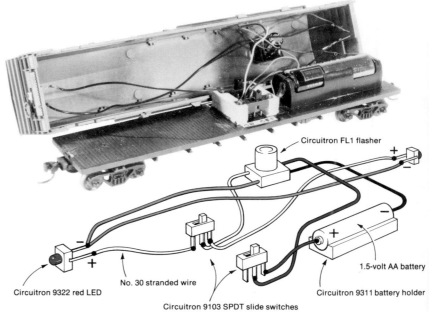

Circuitron FL1 flasher

Circuitron 9322 red LED

No. 30 stranded wire

Circuitron 9103 SPDT slide switches

1.5-volt AA battery

Circuitron 9311 battery holder

Sigmon, and John Olson — had the most trouble. The plaster in their rock molds took 30 minutes to set, and it was beginning to look as if it would never set at all. As John put it, they "tap-danced to beat the band that morning."

The other big snafu came during the final session. For our Grande Finale we carried the Kitty Hawk Central into the room and joined it to the newly built SC. (The Hawk is a 4 x 6½-foot beginner's layout built several years ago and covered in the December 1981 and January 1982 issues of MR.) The big finish was to be a train running entirely around the two layouts, but we just couldn't get it to go. We worked frantically under the layout while Gordon Odegard kept the crowd at bay with a dramatic recitation of "Casey at the Bat." After a few agonizing minutes the train finally rolled.

PLANNING

Many readers will realize that building the SC live was not a new idea. Two summers ago, during our magazine's Fiftieth Anniversary Conference, we had built the Gold Hill Central over a period of 2 days. (The results were featured in the March and April 1984 issues.)

Our six Gold Hill demonstrations had been well-received during the MR conference, so it was only natural that we would have another go during the NMRA's get-together. The convention center was only 3 blocks away, making this a once-in-a-lifetime opportunity.

Adding the Kitty Hawk Central to the new layout would help make this project a little different as well as instantly double the mainline run. It would probably triple the potential for interesting operation. See fig. 1.

We wanted to show that a small beginner's layout can be expanded with little modification, once the builder has the space and the inclination. After all, even a small layout like the Hawk represents a lot of time and expense that might just as well be salvaged. Also, keeping that first small layout around provides something to run on while building the new, bigger layout.

The Seaboard Central's name and locale grew out of the fact that we were planning to join it to the Hawk, a fictitious railroad set on the North Carolina

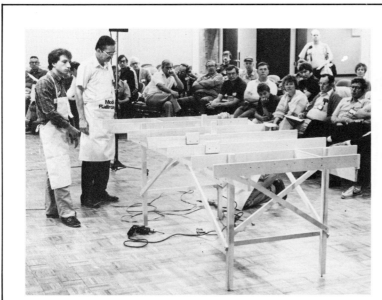

A. L. Schmidt photos

Fig. 3. Left: Marty Oetting, left, and Gordon Odegard survey the benchwork. **Above:** The crew installs the prebuilt plywood roadbed sections. Most of the track had already been laid and painted.

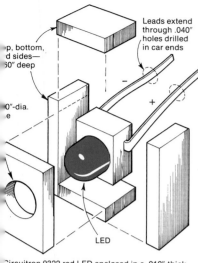

Leads extend through .040" holes drilled in car ends

p, bottom, d sides, 0" deep

0"-dia. e

LED

Circuitron 9322 red LED enclosed in a .010"-thick styrene box. Front face is approximately .125" wide by .156" high

Fig. 2 END-OF-TRAIN DEVICE

IN PLACE of cabooses many contemporary railroads are using end-of-train devices. These are small boxes containing equipment to monitor the train line air pressure and radio it to the locomotive. In many cases the box is equipped with a flashing red or yellow light. Since the Seaboard Central is a contemporary model railroad, I decided to make an EOT monitor. My flasher is a generic design not intended to represent any particular product.

In real life the EOT is portable and is mounted on the coupler of the last car in a train. This would be hard to do in model railroading unless every freight car was equipped with a power supply, a flasher unit, and plug-in sockets. I used one car with an LED at each end.

The flasher car has to be the last car in the train, and to simulate real railroad practice it must be moved just as you would a caboose. Since the model couplers must remain functional, I mounted the flasher boxes just above the couplers rather than on them.

Any small-diameter (no. 30 or 40) stranded wire can be used to wire the flasher car. The small LEDs are enclosed in .010" styrene and the box painted silver. I drilled two no. 60 (.040") holes in each car end for the LED leads and attached the boxes in place with ACC.

All of the parts are from Circuitron, with the exception of the battery, which can be any AA 1.5-volt dry cell. I used ACC to affix the battery case and the FL1 flasher to the floor and roof respectively. Two miniature slide switches are mounted in the doorways. One is an on-off switch, and the other determines which LED will flash. The slide switches are cemented to blocks of styrene cemented to the floor.

I attached a small piece of file card next to each switch, identifying its function. You could also use a Circuitron no. 9101 or no. 9102 magnetic reed switch mounted to the underside of the roof for the on-off slide switch so you don't have to reach inside the car to turn off the circuit. — *Gordon Odegard*

---

coast. The new layout would represent an inland area, perhaps in the North Carolina mountains.

The SC is a contemporary railroad, a new conglomerate along the lines of Seaboard System or Norfolk Southern. Its bright red and blue diesels give the SC a distinctive modern look, and Andy Sperandeo completed some Con-Cor "Fuel Foiler"-type piggyback cars so the SC would be right up to date. Cabooses are a fading memory on the SC, having been replaced by black boxes riding the couplers on the last car in a train. Gordy Odegard built a modern end-of-train device with working flasher. See fig. 2.

Choosing the SC's mascot was easy. No seabird is more common than the gull (we even have them here on Lake Michigan), so we adopted that graceful but boisterous creature. Our art director, George Gloff, designed our lettering and herald; Rail Graphics produced the custom decals.

Lately we've become partial to vertical scenery dividers as a means of making small layouts appear much larger. The main advantage, demonstrated again with Gordon Odegard's design for the SC, is that the scenery on one side need bear no relation to that on the other.

THE BENCHWORK

Figure 3 shows the benchwork. We built it using Linn Westcott's classic L-girder system, as explained in his book *How to Build Model Railroad Benchwork* (Kalmbach Publishing Co.).

Lately readers have been extolling the advantages of building benchwork with drywall screws, so we gave them a try. They worked fine and cost much less than wood screws. A simple drill bit worked fine for a pilot hole (as opposed to the special shaped bit usually used with wood screws). Cheating shamelessly, we built the benchwork before the first demonstration session, then disassembled it and put it back together in front of the crowd.

For the subroadbed we used the basic cookie-cutter method — a cutting diagram is included in fig. 3. With this method smooth grade transitions are virtually guaranteed, as practically all the roadbed is cut in one continuous piece from a single sheet of ½" plywood.

For roadbed we used tried-and-proven cork, attached with Elmer's Carpenter's Glue (a yellow glue) and a few track nails to hold it until the glue set.

TRACK AND WIRING

The SC was conceived as a second or intermediate layout, rather than one for beginners (although many beginners could build it without much difficulty). Generally we associate sectional track with first layouts (as was the case with the Hawk), so here we chose to go flexible Code 70 Shinohara track. Code 70 simply means the rail stands .070" high and is proportionally smaller and closer to scale than the Code 100 (.100" high) rail Atlas uses in their sectional track. With a few alterations you could certainly build the SC with sectional track.

If you build with the same Shinohara track we did, you'll quickly find that none of the turnouts will fit without trimming back the rails at one or both ends. See fig. 4. A lot of modelers hesitate to start whacking away on those beautiful turnouts for which they paid a lot of money, but the performance won't be affected in

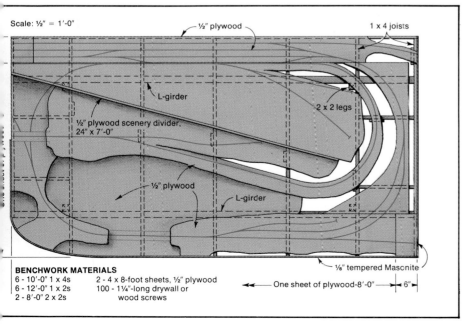

Scale: ½" = 1'-0"

½" plywood

1 x 4 joists

L-girder

½" plywood scenery divider, 24" x 7'-0"

2 x 2 legs

½" plywood

L-girder

⅛" tempered Masonite

BENCHWORK MATERIALS
6 - 10'-0" 1 x 4s
6 - 12'-0" 1 x 2s
2 - 8'-0" 2 x 2s
2 - 4 x 8-foot sheets, ½" plywood
100 - 1¼"-long drywall or wood screws

One sheet of plywood-8'-0" — 6"

A. L. Schmidt

Our city scene was created from inexpensive plastic kits by Art Curren. Part 2 of our story, coming next month, will cover how he built them.

any way. Trimming turnouts is almost always required in building small layouts with compact track arrangements.

Andy Sperandeo wired the SC. Figure 5 shows where he located insulating gaps and soldered on feeder wires. Rather than use insulating joiners Andy prefers to join all the track sections with metal joiners, then cut in the insulating gaps, using a cut-off disk in a Dremel motor tool. He epoxies a small square of styrene in the gap, then trims and files it to shape after the epoxy has cured. The styrene prevents the gap from closing, should the rails ever shift.

Because we were planning to use a command control system, Andy soldered all the rail joints for the best possible electrical continuity. (A command control system relies on encoded electrical signals transmitted through the rails to receivers in the locomotives. Since the rails must conduct not only current but a variety of signals, good electrical continuity is especially important.)

If you elect to install the Keller Engineering Onboard system, as we did, or another system, then we refer you to the literature provided by these manufacturers. Keller offers a very complete handbook that Andy found answered his questions and took him through the hookup process with no glitches. An excellent reference if you wish to wire the layout for traditional two-cab control is Eric Lundberg's All Aboard article in the January 1985 issue of MR.

For our Keller system we used one M4 mixer (with LED indicators added per the instructions), one K116 keypad (handheld throttle), one K220 keypad, three T1 throttles (receivers inside the locomotives), one DS-35K diesel sound unit, and one AM-TX transformer (Stancor P8686). Andy says the T1 receivers were easy to install in the SC's Atlas GP38s and that the sound unit underframe, though meant for an Athearn GP35, required only simple modifications.

Although the initial cost is high (equipment for the SC cost $709), we heartily endorse command control. The freedom to be able to run any locomotive anywhere on the layout without worrying about toggle switches or getting into another locomotive's block is a wonderful thing, *especially* on a small layout like the SC.

We often think of command control as a province of big operators and big layouts, but it makes even better sense for smaller layouts, where running into another train's block is much easier to do, and where the number of locomotives — and therefore the number of receivers required — is far less.

THE AMAZING RS2 SWITCH MACHINE

Straight out of the box, there's no provision on Shinohara turnouts to hold the points to one side or the other. Until some sort of switch machine is attached to the throwbar, they are free to flap in the breeze, a bothersome characteristic as we usually like to start trains running as soon as we've laid a little track.

The less-than-exciting job of attaching a throw of some sort to those 18 turnouts fell to me. Borrowing the idea Peco uses in their turnout design, I built and installed throws as shown in fig. 6. As

Jim Kelly

Fig. 4. Above: We shortened the turnouts so they would fit our track plan. A metal scriber works well for marking where to cut the rail. **Right:** Rail nippers make a good, square cut that needs only a touchup with a file. N scale rail joiners worked better than Shinohara's Code 70 HO joiners.

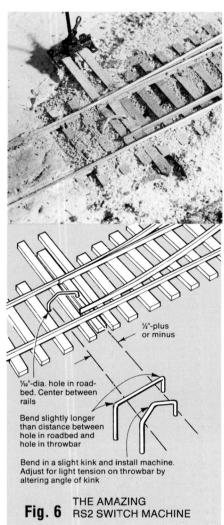

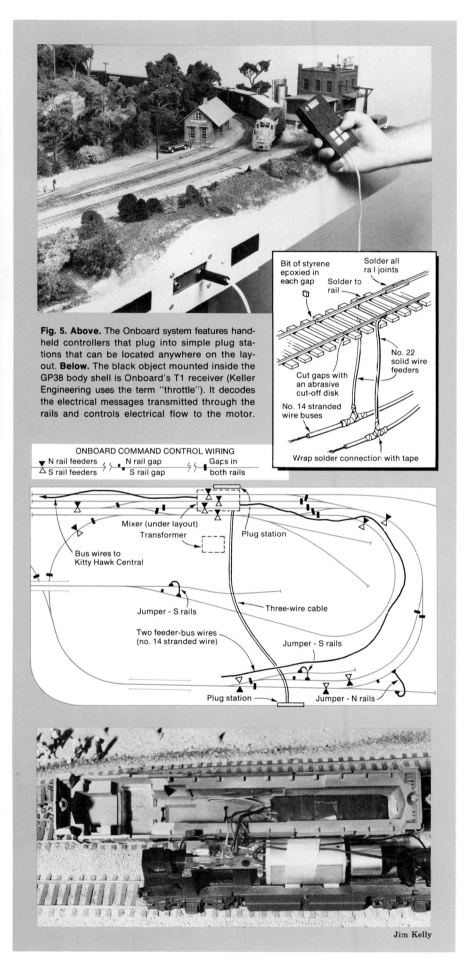

Fig. 5. Above. The Onboard system features hand-held controllers that plug into simple plug stations that can be located anywhere on the layout. **Below.** The black object mounted inside the GP38 body shell is Onboard's T1 receiver (Keller Engineering uses the term "throttle"). It decodes the electrical messages transmitted through the rails and controls electrical flow to the motor.

Bit of styrene epoxied in each gap

Solder all rail joints

Solder to rail

No. 22 solid wire feeders

Cut gaps with an abrasive cut-off disk

No. 14 stranded wire buses

Wrap solder connection with tape

ONBOARD COMMAND CONTROL WIRING
▼ N rail feeders   N rail gap   Gaps in both rails
△ S rail feeders   S rail gap

Mixer (under layout)
Transformer
Plug station
Bus wires to Kitty Hawk Central
Jumper - S rails
Three-wire cable
Two feeder-bus wires (no. 14 stranded wire)
Jumper - S rails
Plug station
Jumper - N rails

Jim Kelly

½"-dia. hole in road-bed. Center between rails

½"-plus or minus

Bend slightly longer than distance between hole in roadbed and hole in throwbar

Bend in a slight kink and install machine. Adjust for light tension on throwbar by altering angle of kink

Fig. 6 THE AMAZING RS2 SWITCH MACHINE

Marty Oetting, our summer editorial intern observed, they were "ridiculously simple," so I labeled them the RS1. Control of the turnouts is digital — you throw the points to one side or the other with your finger. The simple spring holds the points in place.

The spring on the Model 1 was about ¾" long. Dick Christianson was impressed with this invention but thought the spring could be made only half as long. The device would still work and be even less obtrusive. I scoffed at this suggestion and quickly made such a machine, just to prove him wrong. It worked fine, and thus was born the advanced model RS2.

If you try the RS2, I think you'll like it. In only about 2 minutes you can make a turnout operational; you can always come back to install a more sophisticated machine. I see no reason why the device, made with lighter wire, wouldn't also work for N scale turnouts.

We finished off the track by airbrushing it with Floquil's Grimy Black, then covered it with masking tape to protect it from the scenery construction coming in the next session. After all, when Furlow and Olson get together they can stir up an awful lot of dust, as we'll see next month when we complete the tale of the Seaboard Central. ✿

An Atlas GP38 backs two boxcars loaded with fine North Carolina furniture down from the switchback serving Hickory Point Furniture. Jim Kelly photo.

Our Seaboard Central: Conclusion

Furlow, Olson, Hayden, and Frary build scenery; Curren adds structures

BY JIM KELLY

Last month we began our tale of the Seaboard Central, a small HO scale railroad built in 3 days before a live audience. The occasion was the National Model Railroad Association's 50th anniversary convention, held here in Milwaukee last summer.

This month we'll finish the story by telling about the scenery, structures, and final details. We were fortunate to have some of the finest modelers in the country helping us.

BUILDING THE TERRAIN

Allen Keller's crew was faced with 40 square feet of bare plywood and less than an hour to transform it into some semblance of scenery. They built the basic scenic shapes using the cardboard strip method popularized by John Olson in his book, *Building an HO Railroad with Personality* [Kalmbach]. On hand to demonstrate the technique was John himself.

See fig. 1 for the basic cardboard strip technique. The crew used 1"-wide strips of corrugated cardboard, cut in only a minute or two on the MODEL RAILROADER staff's favorite all-purpose modeling tool, the maintenance department's bandsaw.

Using a heavy-duty stapler, they fastened the vertical strips to the plywood backdrop and the benchwork. Then they weaved in the horizontal strips and secured them with a clasping-type stapler.

Andy Sperandeo had used a hot-glue gun extensively on his Washita & Santa

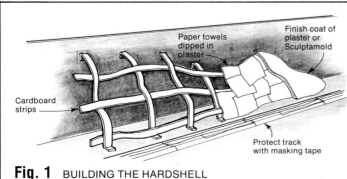

Fig. 1 BUILDING THE HARDSHELL

Cardboard strips

Paper towels dipped in plaster

Finish coat of plaster or Sculptamold

Protect track with masking tape

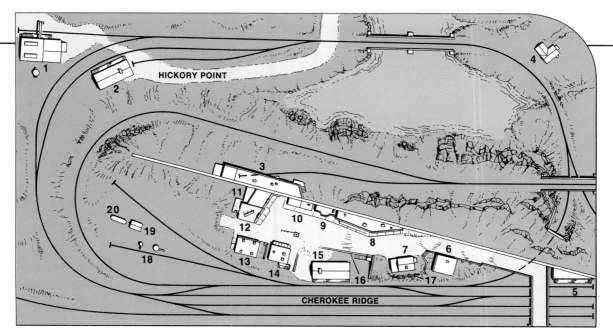

HICKORY POINT

CHEROKEE RIDGE

1   2   3   4   5

20   19   18   11   12   13   14   15   16   17   10   9   8   7   6

1 Factory annex. Kibri 9786

2 Rural station. AHM 15301

3 Furniture factory (see fig. 6)

4 Lake cottage (see fig. 6)

5 Kramdin Storage (see fig. 6)

6 Bill's Glass Shop. Magnuson Models 803 (foundation deepened with sheet styrene)

7 Rooming house. Model Power 426 (upper story and roof shortened to make upper porch; porch railings from Atlas 776 picket fence kit)

8 Corner bank. Heijan 903 (uses, left to right, front, side, and corner walls; remodeled front is from Tyco 7772B drugstore kit)

9 Herald Star Newspaper. AHM 15806 (clock tower omitted. foundation deepened, outside second-story entrance added)

10 Gemini Building. Magnuson Models 802 (third story from second Gemini kit; sice walls shortened; modernized front from sheet styrene)

11 Front from Luigi's Restaurant AHM 15810 (middle third of front is removed)

12 Nick's Pickles. Model Power 471 (front wall angled, foundation deepened)

13 Kelly's Bar, Design Preservation Models

14 Restaurant (front made from strip and sheet styrene; sides and rear from Magnuson Models 802 Gemini Building)

15 Rural station. AHM 15301 (June '85 MR, p. 62)

16 Stone wall (plastic sheet)

17 Retaining wall. Stained ⅛"-square balsa

18 Sand and fuel facilities. Stewart 103

19 Yard office. Pikestuff 5

20 Diesel oil station. Kibri 9430

Cherokee Ridge was built on a piece of ceiling tile and set in place as a single piece.

Fe and has been proclaiming its merits ever since. Somewhat skeptically we followed his advice and found this tool has a multitude of uses in layout construction. We used it to anchor cardboard strips in places that were awkward to get to with the stapler.

I believe the modeler who invests in one of these guns will soon find himself using it for all kinds of jobs. For one thing, it's perfect for attaching cleats to the tops of benchwork risers, a tedious job usually requiring three screws. Andy even used one to glue a power pack to the underside of his Washita & Santa Fe.

Once the cardboard webbing was in place Allen and John finished the scenery shell by dipping paper towels in plaster and laying them in place. John insists that Hydrocal (a plaster made by U. S. Gypsum) is best for hardshell, as it dries much harder and stronger than ordinary plaster of Paris. It would appear John's right. We have a place or two in the hardshell where you could poke your finger through without much effort. Hydrocal is hard to find, but it's worth searching for.

ROCK CASTING

Gordon Odegard and I had secretly worried that Malcolm and John might make our eastern mountains look like the Colorado Rockies — both are noted for the spectacular western scenery they've created. We need not have been concerned. These fellows can build beautiful scenery any way you want it, any time, any place. They never cease to amaze.

John provided most of the rubber molds. He had several big beauties with horizontal strata that worked out very nicely on the hill behind the pond.

Making the rocks is a matter of mixing plaster to about the consistency of thick pea soup, then pouring it into the molds, as shown in fig. 2. Furlow and Olson prefer Hydrocal because it takes detail very well and will pick up every little nook and cranny in the mold.

John had cast some of the rocks the

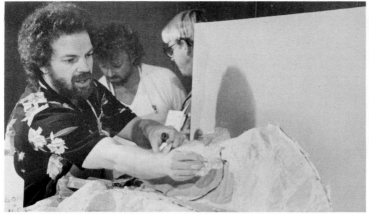
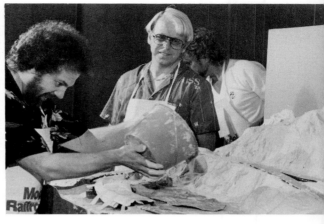

A. L. Schmidt

Fig. 2. Before making a rock casting on the layout, Malcolm Furlow decides where he wants it to go, then marks the spot on the hardshell by tracing around the mold with a marking pen. **Above.** Mike Sigmon looks on as Malcolm pours molding plaster in a rubber mold. Once the plaster

night before, to be installed during the session. Basically it was just a matter of spraying the hardshell and the casting with water, then spreading on some plaster to serve as an adhesive. (The spraying helps prevent the dry plaster from sucking the water out of the wet plaster.)

The rocks on the hillside above the branch line were all cast in place, a technique that gives a little more flexibility in shaping the rocks (the molds bend readily to follow the hardshell's contours.) To cast rocks in place, pour plaster into the mold and keep a close eye on it.

After a few minutes the plaster will thicken and crinkle when you flex the mold slightly — at least it should. The plaster of Paris our crew was using just laid there for 30 minutes before it did anything. All came out well in the end, though. The only lasting damage, I'm sure, is that Olson and Furlow will never let us hear the end of it.

Once the plaster is placed against the hardshell, it needs to be held with the hand for about 5 minutes. You can feel the mold become warm as the plaster "kicks." Then you can pull your hand

away and get on with your life. After 20 minutes the rubber mold can be peeled away without damaging the rock detail.

Dick Christianson finished up the scenery base, using Sculptamold to fill in holes and gaps.

COLORING ROCKS AND TERRAIN

Fred Hamilton, our ad sales manager, led the session on coloring the rocks and terrain, starring Dave Frary, author of *Building Realistic Model Railroad Scenery* [Kalmbach]. They were plenty nervous at the start, as those rocks made just an hour earlier still weren't really set.

Mustering his courage, Fred began by spraying the rocks with dilute India ink from a spray bottle. (A bit of liquid detergent had been added to make the water wetter.) This first wash settled into the crevices, darkening them. See fig. 3. He then sprayed on water tinted with tinting colors, using grays, browns, and tans. After the castings were dry (a matter of pretending in this case), Dave used light colors of acrylics to drybrush highlights on the castings.

To model the ground Dave first paints

the surface with a flat, tan-colored latex paint, as shown in fig. 4, then sprinkles on real dirt here and there. Next comes the foliage. Grass and plants are usually represented with ground foam (Woodland Scenics and Life-Like are popular brands), using a variety of colors and textures.

Once these materials have been sifted on, Dave sprays them carefully with a solution of acrylic matte medium (available in art supply stores) diluted with water. A ratio of about 6 parts water to 1 part matte medium works well. A little liquid dishwashing detergent added to the water helps it soak in. For lush Eastern ground cover he builds up the grass and foliage in layers, rather than trying to do it all at once.

MODELING WATER

Dave Frary, Bob Hayden, and Vera Savić demonstrated how to model water with two-part epoxy. The brand used was Ultra-Glow, although other similar products are available. Look for a product that calls for mixing together two materials in 1:1 or 2:1 ratios. Products that call for adding only a few drops of

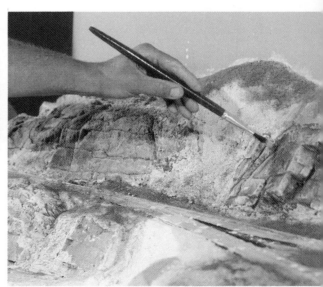

A. L. Schmidt

Fig. 3. Our rock-coloring crew first sprayed the castings with a dilute solution of black India ink. Then they sprayed on solutions of color tints.

Above. The castings were highlighted by drybrushing with light-colored acrylics. The effect can be stark at first, but softens as the paint dries.

begins setting up, it can be placed against the hill. **Above.** Malcolm sprays water on the hardshell where the casting is to go. He doesn't want

the dry hardshell pulling water from the wet casting. **Right.** Malcolm carefully peels the mold away, and voila! Beautiful stratified rock appears.

catalyst to a liquid are polyester resins. Modelers also use those to model water, but the odor released while the material is curing can literally drive you out of the house.

The first step in making the pond was preparing a flat base. The night before their demonstration Bob and Dave poured thin Hydrocal into the pond depression. The next morning they spray painted the banks and edges with Floquil's Earth. Then they sprayed the middle of the pond black, feathering the black into the earth color. See fig. 5.

Because they were doing the demonstration live, Dave hastened the paint's drying as best he could with a hot-air gun, then they mixed and poured in the epoxy. The audience was barely able to stop laughing long enough to point out a leak along the front edge of the layout.

Vera used a throw-away paintbrush to work the epoxy into the corners. Next Bob, using a propane torch per the epoxy kit's instructions, pulled the bubbles out of the water. The boat and fisherman were added last.

THE STRUCTURES

For our structures we called in Art Curren, the old pro. Art, who works for our sales department, writes all those structure kitbashing articles that are extremely popular with our readers. (He prefers to use the term "kitmingling.")

Obviously, he couldn't build all of these structures in only an hour, with or without an audience watching. He built the town of Cherokee Ridge in advance on a piece of ceiling tile that fit neatly into a recess we had provided for it. I know of no one else who could have created such a nice town in only 3 or 4 weeks.

All of the buildings have their origins in inexpensive plastic kits that Art has modified in one way or another. The key with the track plan shows the 10 structures that make up Cherokee Ridge.

Art says the fun part was "getting the buildings to look right at their various elevations." The town is 2½" higher on the right than on the left and 1½" higher at the back than at the front. These changes in elevation are subtle but add tremendously to the realism. It's rare in real life to find a group of structures built on a perfectly flat site.

To make bases for the buildings Art used ½"-thick pieces of ceiling tile and pieces of ¼"- and ⅛"-thick paneling. He says the ceiling tile worked well because it was lightweight, and also because it was a natural earth color, in case the scenic materials didn't cover everything. Ceiling tile is easy to shape with a wire brush in an electric drill. Planting trees and weeds is easy, and the dirt drilled up is the right color to just leave there.

Easy-to-bend, thin wall paneling was especially good for forming a base for

the undulating streets. Art paved the streets with premixed spackling compound to which he added lampblack for an aged asphalt look. He applied the spackle with a pallette knife. After it dried he drew on the cracks with a finetip, felt-tip pen.

Cherokee Ridge would look like a ghost town if there were no merchandise in the store windows. Art added interior detail where it counted, using odds and ends from his scrapbox as well as the interior details from the Nick's Pickles and Tyco drugstore kits. He also installed black cardstock where necessary so the viewer couldn't look right through a building.

Art used .040" styrene for the sidewalks. He carved in cracks here and there and cemented on a few .010"-thick styrene squares to represent concrete blocks heaved up by frost.

Figure 6 shows those buildings Art made which are not part of the Cherokee Ridge group.

TREES, GREENERY, AND BACKDROPS

Quick now, what makes the Eastern Seaboard in particular and the American South in general look different from the rest of the country? Red dirt, maybe, although you don't see it everywhere in the South. The main difference is the trees, trees, and more trees, as well as

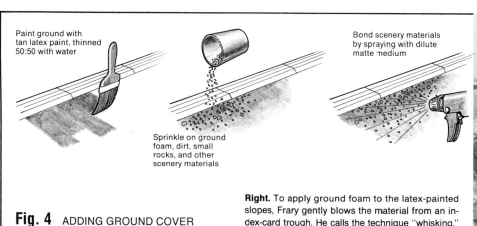

Paint ground with tan latex paint, thinned 50:50 with water

Sprinkle on ground foam, dirt, small rocks, and other scenery materials

Bond scenery materials by spraying with dilute matte medium

Right. To apply ground foam to the latex-painted slopes, Frary gently blows the material from an index-card trough. He calls the technique "whisking."

Fig. 4 ADDING GROUND COVER

A. L. Schmidt

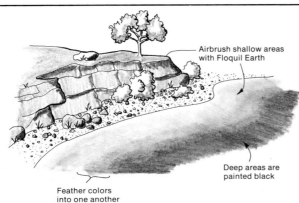

Airbrush shallow areas with Floquil Earth

Deep areas are painted black

Feather colors into one another

Fig. 5. Above. The illustration details how the pond bottom is prepared for the "water." **Right.** We used two-part epoxy to make the water. It looks like and pours like syrup. **Middle.** A small, disposable paintbrush was used to work the liquid epoxy up to the banks and into the nooks and crannies. **Far right.** It may look dangerous, but the product directions recommend playing the flame of a propane torch over the epoxy to draw out the bubbles.

A. L. Schmidt photos

plenty of other green, growing things.

Marty Oetting, our summer intern, made several dozen Woodland Scenics trees for us. We planted them all and could have used even more. As Gordy pointed out, a layout like the SC soaks up trees the way a sponge soaks up water.

To round out the greenery we also used lots and lots of lichen. Quality lichen is hard to find right now. We bought ours from Blue Ribbon Models, P. O. Box 888, Marblehead, MA 01945. Gordy added most of it to the layout, using only the fine tips. Enter the hot glue gun again. Gordy found it excellent for attaching the foliage to the hillsides. The glue sets in a few seconds, and you can keep working without having to worry about the bushes making like tumbleweeds and rolling off the hillsides.

We wanted a backdrop on each side of the scenic divider, but none of our crew professes to mastery in landscape painting. Besides, we wanted something simple that would provide a background to the scene without calling attention to itself. We want viewers looking at the modeling out in front, not at the backdrop painting.

I painted on the clouds with flat white paint from a spray can (Rustoleum, by brand name, because it was on sale, although any flat white spray paint should work fine.) For the hills I used tube acrylics, squeezing them out on a pallette and using a 1"-wide flat brush. I found for such a simple backdrop I could get by with just two colors, Chromium Oxide Green and Titanium White. For the more distant

hills I mixed a lot of white into the green, while the closer hills are green straight out of the tube.

FINAL TOUCHES

After the convention we trucked the SC back over to our building. We had to unload it in the rain, but that hardly mattered — the layout was still plenty wet around the edges anyway. We let it dry a week, then Gordy and I spent 3 days patching up some of the rough spots, ballasting the track, and adding more details to make it presentable for the magazine.

The backdrop buildings on the Cherokee Ridge side of the backdrop were made from Detail Associates backdrop scenes nos. 7501 City and 7502 Downtown. I used the technique described by

A. L. Schm

Fig. 6. Art Curren built this lakeside cottage from an AHM no. 15309 Texaco gas station. The screened-in porch fit neatly under the overhang for the pump island. To frame the porch Art used Evergreen styrene HO scale 2 x 2s, 4 x 4s, and 4 x 6s. For screen wire on the porch he used a nylon stocking. **Above right.** Hickory Point Furniture was made from four Life-Like no. 1337

Mt. Vernon Manufacturing Co. kits. The angled loading area adds relief a interest to the large, flat wall. **Right.** Kram Storage Co.'s name was suggested by its tight location. Art made it from rear walls left over from two AHM kits used in Cherokee Ridge. As the fac lettering shows, this building was once a Seaboard Central freight warehou

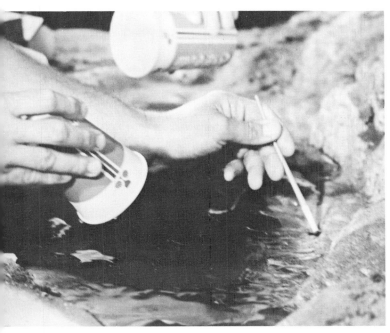

John Olson in the January 1983 MR, and also in his book, *Building an HO Model Railroad with Personality*. To wit, I cut out the paper buildings I wanted, using an X-acto knife and a straight-edge, then brushed rubber cement onto the back of the paper and the backdrop. After the cement was dry I placed the paper against the backdrop, where it stuck very well.

The rubber cement is being used as a contact cement, so you get only one shot at positioning the paper correctly. It's a good idea to use a sheet of tracing paper between the paper backdrop and the backdrop proper while positioning. Once you're happy with the alignment, you can remove the tracing paper and let the rubber cement do its thing. I used a rubber cement pick to pull away excess cement.

To ballast the track we went to the old tried-and-true bonded-ballast method. For the main line we used Highball's Limestone, and for the yard and spurs we used their Cinders.

First, we spread the ballast carefully, using a plastic drinking cup as a dispenser, then we smoothed it with a wide, flat, soft brush. A small piece of tubing is good for blowing unwanted ballast away from switch points and out of flangeways.

Then we carefully soaked the ballast with water, using a spray bottle. A few drops of liquid detergent in the water helped it soak in. Next, using an eyedropper, we dribbled on dilute acrylic matte medium (about 5 parts water to 1 part matte medium). Once the matte medium dries, the ballast looks loose and natural, but is bonded securely in place.

To me, weathering the ballasted track with an airbrush is a crucial step. HO-size crushed rock looks unnatural if left unpainted. Floquil's Earth, Reefer Gray, and Grimy Black are very good colors for weathering the track and tying it in naturally with the surrounding scenery. Be sure to clean the rail thoroughly with a Bright Boy afterwards.

We hope you enjoyed the Seaboard Central and found an idea or two here that you can use on your own layout. If you don't have a layout yet, we hope the SC will help motivate you to get started. It's fun, and the small layout you build now might one day be the heart of your basement-sized dream empire. Come to think of it, that's exactly the way John Allen got started on his legendary Gorre & Daphetid. ⌂

Jim Kelly

A pair of GP38s run light past the Hickory Point station. The thick grove of trees behind the station hides the steep branch line that ascends to the Hickory Point Furniture Co.

Building the Berkshire Division

A 4 x 8-foot HO layout featuring two seasons

BY LOU SASSI
PHOTOS BY THE AUTHOR

EVEN though we had new modelers in mind, our HO scale New Haven Berkshire Division layout goes a few steps beyond the typical flat 4 x 8-foot table.

Dick Elwell, Russ Speed, Jim Smith, and I built it with scenery and buildings we felt would appeal to many advanced modelers, yet be within the reach of beginners. We used some advanced techniques, airbrushing for one, but you could certainly build the layout without them. Besides, by the time you get that far, you won't be a beginner anymore.

We can't cover every detail of building the layout in a single article, but we think we can come pretty close. We took lots of pictures as we went along, and if you follow them through, you'll get there. Of course your layout doesn't have to turn out exactly like ours. The Model Railroad Police certainly won't come knocking on your door if you do some things your way.

If you've never built any kind of layout, we recommend you pick up a copy of *All Aboard: The Practical Guide to HO Model Railroading*, published by Kalmbach Publishing Co.

Continues on page 71

A New Haven RDC bursts from Tunnel no. 2. The trees are twigs cut from wild blueberry bushes.

TRACK PLAN

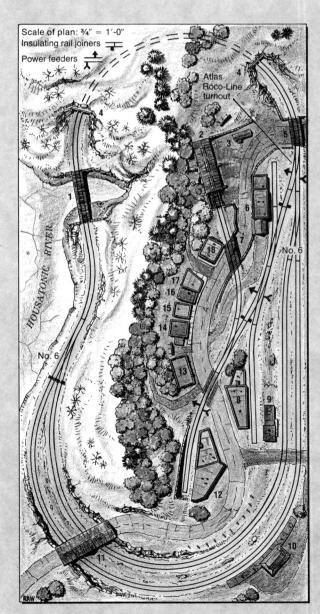

NEW YORK, NEW HAVEN & HARTFORD
BERKSHIRE DIVISION
HO scale, 4 x 8 feet
Minimum radius: 18"
Unmarked turnouts: Walthers code 83 no. 5

STRUCTURES

1. Atlas no. 885 through plate girder bridge (inverted and narrowed)
2. Mil-Scale no. 90 Jacobs Coal Co.
3. Scratchbuilt shanty
4. A.I.M. no. 110 tunnel portals
5. Atlas no. 2548 N scale bridge (inverted)
6. Litchfield Bearing, kitbashed from two Magnuson no. 523 Wischer's Washers kits
7. Atlas no. 2548 N scale bridge (inverted and staggered)
8. Design Preservation no. 103 Cutting's Scissors Co. (kitbashed)
9. Chooch yard shed (no longer made, could use AM Models no. 106)
10. Atlas no. 706 station, modified
11. Covered bridge, scratchbuilt with Campbell no. 802 metal roofing
12. National Machine, kitbashed from DPM no. 104 Moore Showroom and DPM no. 106 Laube's Linen Mill
13. John Rissman's & Sons Dry Goods, DPM no. 102 Robert's Dry Goods
14. Simmons Furniture, DPM no. 105 Skip's Chicken
15. R. M. Kellog Hardware, DPM no. 101 Kelly's Saloon
16. W. F. Whitney Drapery Store, Walthers no. 3000 Don's Shoe Store
17. Boston Seafood Restaurant, Small-town U.S.A. no. 6012, Helen's Country Kitchen
18. Atkins & Durbrow Variety Store, DPM no. 113 Carol's Corner Cafe

TRACK USED
Atlas
913 Roco-Line code 83 LH turnout, 1
921 insulating rail joiners, 1
923 rail joiners with wire leads (optional), 3
Walthers
948–803 code 83 LH turnout, no. 6, 1
948–804 code 83 RH turnout, no. 6, 1
948–815 code 83 39"-long flex track, 15
948–841 rail joiners (pkg. 50), 1
948–891 code 83 LH turnout, no. 5, 2
948–892 code 83 RH turnout, no. 5, 1

Downtown Cornwall Bridge, has that timeless small-town America look. Using little buildings helps make a small layout look much larger. The lobster is extra good at Boston Seafood Restaurant.

An elevated facility like Jacobs Coal adds lots of interest to a small layout, particularly if all the track is level. Most highway vehicles on the layout were bought from American Prototype Models (Box 2305, Stamford, CT 06906).

BENCHWORK AND CORK ROADBED

Elevating the plywood roadbed allows for a highway and a pond to be constructed below track level.

Our crew planned ahead. The ears on this roadbed section are for mounting signals by Integrated Signal Systems.

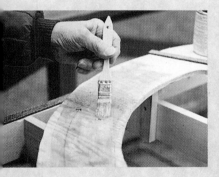

The plywood and cork roadbed were coated with contact cement, then joined after the cement dried, per directions on the can.

With contact cement, adjustments are impossible, but laying the cork accurately against the track center line is easy.

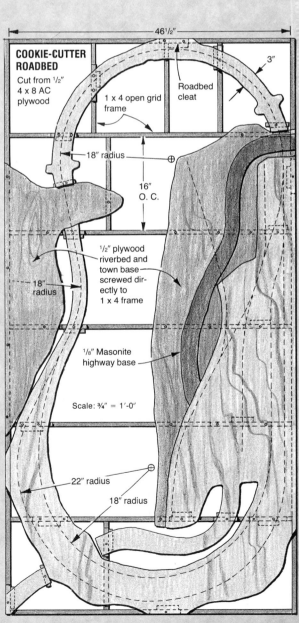

COOKIE-CUTTER ROADBED
Cut from ½"
4 x 8 AC
plywood

1 x 4 open grid frame

Roadbed cleat

3"

18" radius

16" O. C.

½" plywood riverbed and town base screwed directly to 1 x 4 frame

18" radius

⅛" Masonite highway base

Scale: ¾" = 1'-0"

22" radius

18" radius

46½"

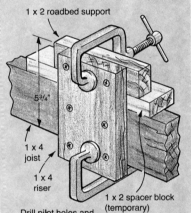

1 x 2 roadbed support

5¾"

1 x 4 joist

1 x 4 riser

1 x 2 spacer block (temporary)

Drill pilot holes and mount with drywall screws

TRACK RISERS

BENCHWORK MATERIAL

Framing
- ½" AC plywood, 4 x 8 sheet, 1
- 1 x 4, 8 feet long, 8
- 1 x 2, 8 feet long, 1
- 1¼" drywall screws, 1 box
- 4 x 8 sheet, tempered hardboard, (Masonite), 1

Legs
- 2 x 2 (legs), 8 feet long, 2
- 1 x 2 (braces), 8 feet long, 4

Cork roadbed
- 36"-long sections, 14
- water-based contact cement, 1 pint

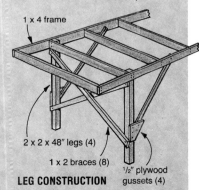

1 x 4 frame

2 x 2 x 48" legs (4)

1 x 2 braces (8)

½" plywood gussets (4)

LEG CONSTRUCTION

Traffic on Rt. 7 will be tied up while the New Haven switches National Machine Co. in the background. Those shiny John Deere "Johnny Poppers" and implements were built from Woodland Scenics kits.

Nothing says New England quite like a covered bridge. We hope the autos are obeying that 10-mph speed limit, or traffic could get tense shortly. Those two railfans could have parked more carefully.

EXTRUDED FOAM SCENERY

The scenery was built using pieces of 2″ foam insulation joined with Liquid Nails. Sold at building supply stores, the foam's color varies among manufacturers.

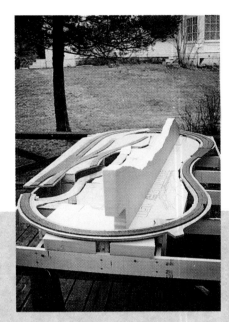

THE LAYOUT'S CONCEPT

Our railroad is set in the mid-1950s and represents a section of the New Haven's Norwalk, Conn., to Pittsfield, Mass., Berkshire branch. The branch was real, but our track plan is fiction. We did try to give it an authentic feel, though, by using real town, industry, and place names. Our village, for example, is called Cornwall Bridge and boasts a covered bridge just as its real-life namesake in Connecticut does. The pond is a backwater of the Housatonic River.

To add more interest and to make the railroad look larger, we incorporated a view block, the mountain down the middle. The track is level, but to get the look of railroading in hilly country we put lots of elevation changes in the scenery. The highway, for example, rises from below track level at one end of the village to above track level at the covered bridge.

We've included one other feature not often attempted on a layout of this size — a seasonal change from one side of the view block to the other. It's autumn in the village, but winter at Tunnel no. 2, thanks to a combination of Hydrocal plaster and "cold, dry" snow from Vintage Reproductions.

SOME PARTICULARS

The railroad is wired as one block. The track plan shows where you'll need to install insulating joiners and

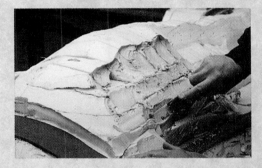

After the foam was built up wedding-cake style, it was carved with serrated knives and Surform planes.

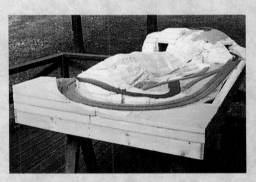

Here's the layout carved to shape. The Masonite base for Connecticut Rt. 7 has been glued in place.

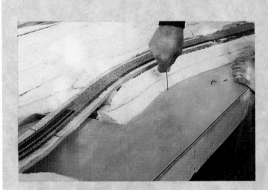

The ice is Lexan sanded lightly on each side and laid over a sheet of black construction paper.

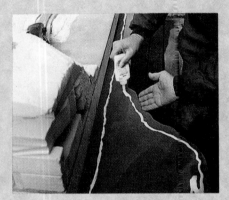

Top and above: Side panels were cut from Masonite, then glued and screwed to the railroad. Industrial-grade carpet was glued to the panels for a distinctive (and attractive) look. **Below:** This access hatch can be used in the event that cars pile up inside the tunnel.

TRACKLAYING AND PAINTING

Our builders used Atlas code 83 flexible track on the main line and Shinohara code 70 on the sidings. Needlenose pliers were used to drive the spikes.

The group weathered the track with Floquil Driftwood stain and Rail Brown paint applied with an airbrush.

Fine-grade emery paper wrapped around a sanding block was used to clean paint off the rail.

To bond ballast our crew used dilute white glue applied with a syringe they bought at a drugstore.

Graffiti on a bridge, an old-time lamppost, a sidewalk and curbing — such details combined with careful weathering add up to realism.

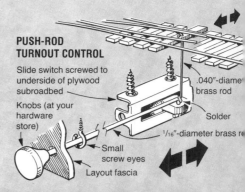

PUSH-ROD TURNOUT CONTROL

Slide switch screwed to underside of plywood subroadbed

Knobs (at your hardware store)

.040"-diameter brass rod

Solder

1/16"-diameter brass rod

Small screw eyes

Layout fascia

SCENERY TECHNIQUES

For ground our crew laid on a secret mix ⅛″ thick. The recipe is 1 cup Sculptamold, 1 cup Celluclay, and ⅓ cup white glue. Thin with water to a cake-batter consistency.

add feeder wires as you lay the track. The spur tracks won't be powered unless the turnouts are set for them, so we're able to keep our two locomotives on the layout at the same time as long as we remember that one must always be in a spur that's "turned off."

Our locomotives are by Atlas: a factory-painted RS-3 and a custom-painted RS-11. We weathered both and then added a crew and steam generator stack to the former. The cars are a mix of "shake the box" kits (Athearn for example) and more advanced Tichy and Innovative Model Works kits. To ensure good performance we equipped all the cars with Kadee trucks and couplers.

IN CONCLUSION

This story is short because we want the photos and drawings to do the talking. Believe us, the traditional 4 x 8 layout can be a lot of fun. If you decide to go all out on the scenery and details, it can keep you busy for several months, even a year or two.

Best of all, if you're short on space, you can store the railroad in the corner of a large walk-in closet. You can take it with you when you move. If you ever do get started on that big dream layout you'll have a head start, not only with models, but with skills and techniques. So rise up from those armchairs — the time to build that first layout is right now! ⱷ

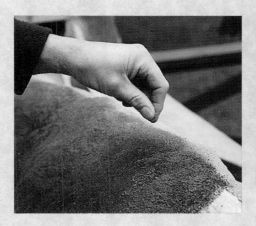

Above: The finished ground cover is dirt, gravel, ground foam, static grass, and poly fiber, along with just about anything else that "looks right." **Above right:** A road surface made out of illustration board was laminated to the Masonite base. Then the crew worked it into the scenery.

Right: Rock castings were made by pouring soupy plaster in rubber molds. Once the plaster began to set, the molds could be positioned on the layout. **Below:** Jars were used to hold the molds in place. **Lower right:** Rocks around tunnel portals were cast first, then carved to accept the portal. A little touch-up plaster blended it in.

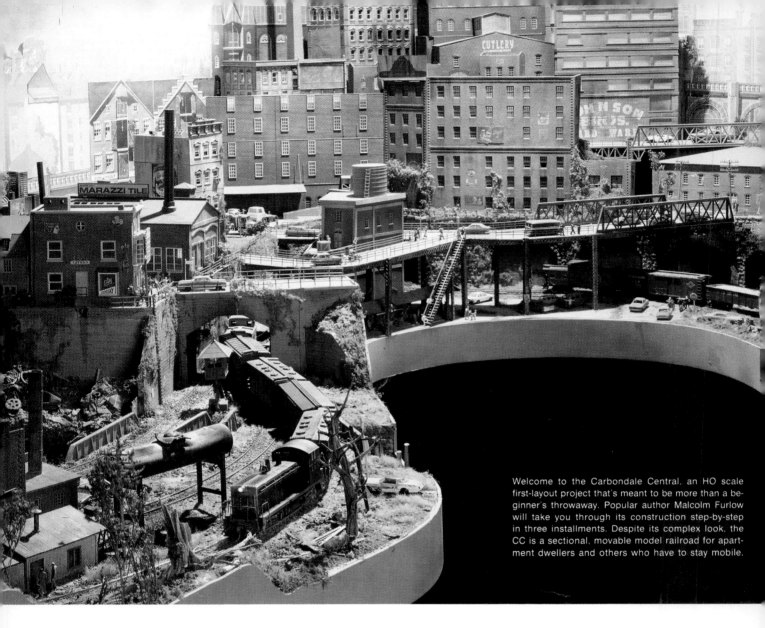

Welcome to the Carbondale Central, an HO scale first-layout project that's meant to be more than a beginner's throwaway. Popular author Malcolm Furlow will take you through its construction step-by-step in three installments. Despite its complex look, the CC is a sectional, movable model railroad for apartment dwellers and others who have to stay mobile.

Building the Carbondale Central: 1

Get started with lightweight, movable benchwork and HO sectional track

BY MALCOLM FURLOW
PHOTOS BY THE AUTHOR

THE CARBONDALE CENTRAL is an HO layout that I hope disguises itself as something a bit more than the beginner's project that it really is. It's compact and sectional so you can take it with you if you move. While it's meant as a first railroad, it's also meant to be one you'll keep rather than outgrow.

Much like John Allen's original tabletop Gorre & Daphetid (pronounced "gory and defeated"), the Carbondale Central aims to look good enough to be the start of a larger system. As you gain confidence and experience you'll be able to add to or modify the original layout, but you won't have to abandon or apologize for it.

Don't let the busy look of my CC photographs throw you. The track plan in fig. 1 is simple, and with sectional track it's simple to build. The city of Carbondale is built with plastic kits right from the hobbyshop shelf, and I'll show you easy ways to make bigger, more interesting buildings from these kits.

I'll also show you how to make the city look larger than it is by using "leading lines," mainly the roads that seem to penetrate the background and extend past the edges of the layout. By appearing to travel beyond the layout's small boundaries they lead our eyes further into the scene.

Most of the city is built on an upper-level platform above the track at the back of the layout. This adds realism by hiding the track plan's round-and-round loop, and forms a scenic backdrop for the railroad itself. It's supposed to look as if the CC, after following a water-level route like most early railroads, has had the growing city mushroom over and around its right-of-way.

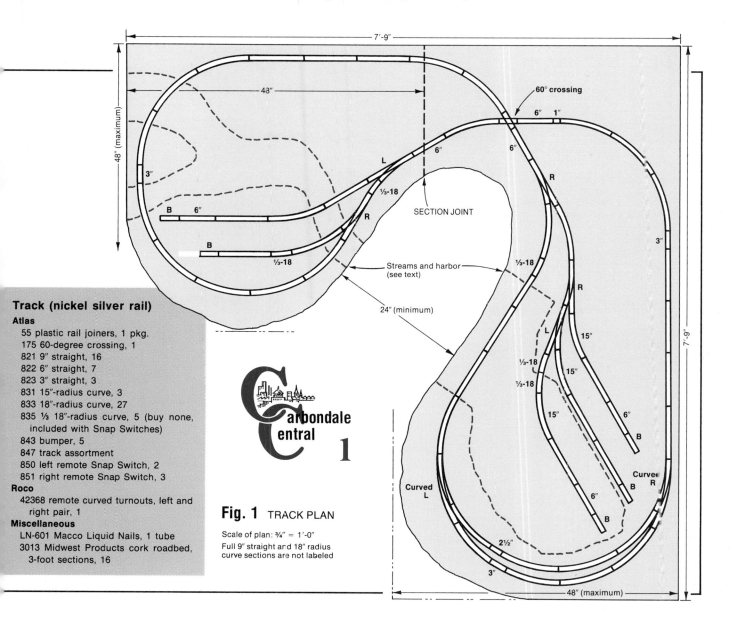

Track (nickel silver rail)

Atlas

55 plastic rail joiners, 1 pkg.
175 60-degree crossing, 1
821 9″ straight, 16
822 6″ straight, 7
823 3″ straight, 3
831 15″-radius curve, 3
833 18″-radius curve, 27
835 ⅓ 18″-radius curve, 5 (buy none, included with Snap Switches)
843 bumper, 5
847 track assortment
850 left remote Snap Switch, 2
851 right remote Snap Switch, 3

Roco

42368 remote curved turnouts, left and right pair, 1

Miscellaneous

LN-601 Macco Liquid Nails, 1 tube
3013 Midwest Products cork roadbed, 3-foot sections, 16

Carbondale Central 1

Fig. 1 TRACK PLAN

Scale of plan: ¾″ = 1′-0″
Full 9″ straight and 18″ radius
curve sections are not labeled

Just raising the city to a higher level accentuates the cityscape by adding to its height. Like rugged mountain scenery, this helps make a small layout seem larger, and creates a crowded urban atmosphere where sharp curves and small switch engines look right.

If Carbondale Central looks good to you but you want something else in the track plan, change the plan! You could expand the layout to include a more substantial yard or a longer main line. Even without expansion, track could be added to the upper level for more industrial switching. You'd need a steeply graded ramp up from the lower level, but in an urban setting that wouldn't be out of place. I've kept the track plan simple to avoid complicated construction, but you see where this thing could end up!

The Carbondale Central uses some techniques and materials that oldtimers may not be familiar with, but if you're just starting out you may as well learn something new. Mainly I'm talking about the extensive use of plastic foams for structural elements as well as scenic forms. This railroad was meant to be light in weight for portability, and it is. Two

people can set it up easily, and in a pinch I've done it all by myself.

I hope some of you younger modelers will give this little railroad a try. I had a lot of fun working with Harl Asaff, the 10-year old son of my business partner, Jimmy Assaf. Harl's wide-eyed enthusiasm tells me there are a lot of young people looking for this kind of creative project. Same thing with a young 14-year-old girl by the name of Hannah, who completely surprised me with her capabilities.

WALL UNITS

One special feature of the Carbondale Central is the framework shown in fig. 2 that supports it as a shelf layout without damaging or disfiguring your walls. That's at least as important as portability if you figure that you might have to move. The trick is that the wall units, designed by Jim Kelly and Gordon Odegard of MODEL RAILROADER, will be wedged in between the floor and ceiling, and the two legs of the ell help support each other too. Because of the wall units, the actual space needed for the 7′-9″ x 7′-9″ layout is 7′-11¼″ x 7′-11¼″.

Figure 3 shows how to put the wall units together. The carpentry is simple. Just make sure the uprights are square on the backdrop panels and the units join to make a good square corner. Don't be shy about ignoring the measurements for the inner bracket arms and just cutting these parts to fit.

I used a power circular saw to cut the lumber, and it's a good idea to wear safety goggles and a dust mask while doing this kind of work. You can use a plain 7/64″ bit to drill pilot holes for both the sheet-metal and drywall screws. The idea of the two types is to put the drywall screws where you won't want to take them out — their flat heads will turn in flush — and the sheet-metal screws where you need a removable fastener.

The wall units are designed to come apart for moving. The units separate from each other with removal of the hinge pins and one screw, the uprights can be unscrewed from the backdrop panels, and the brackets break down with the removal of three bolts each. I'm pointing this out so you'll know better than to glue a joint that you'll want to take apart some time down the road.

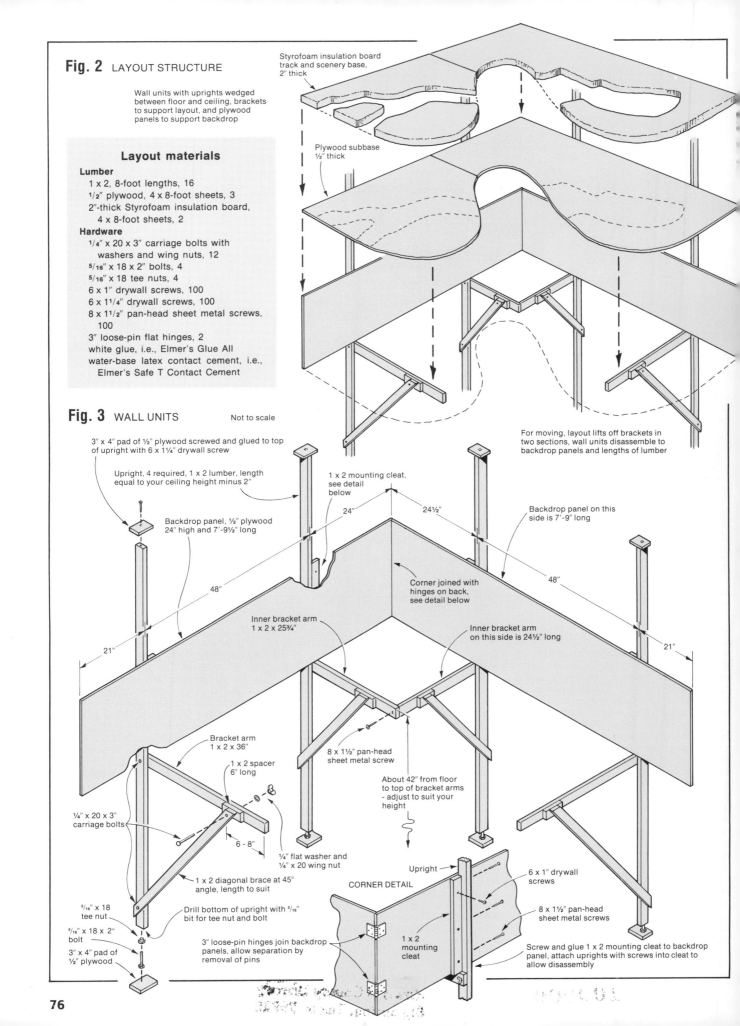

Fig. 2 LAYOUT STRUCTURE

Styrofoam insulation board track and scenery base, 2" thick

Wall units with uprights wedged between floor and ceiling, brackets to support layout, and plywood panels to support backdrop

Plywood subbase ½" thick

Layout materials

Lumber
1 x 2, 8-foot lengths, 16
½" plywood, 4 x 8-foot sheets, 3
2"-thick Styrofoam insulation board, 4 x 8-foot sheets, 2

Hardware
¼" x 20 x 3" carriage bolts with washers and wing nuts, 12
5/16" x 18 x 2" bolts, 4
5/16" x 18 tee nuts, 4
6 x 1" drywall screws, 100
6 x 1¼" drywall screws, 100
8 x 1½" pan-head sheet metal screws, 100
3" loose-pin flat hinges, 2
white glue, i.e., Elmer's Glue All
water-base latex contact cement, i.e., Elmer's Safe T Contact Cement

Fig. 3 WALL UNITS   Not to scale

For moving, layout lifts off brackets in two sections, wall units disassemble to backdrop panels and lengths of lumber

3" x 4" pad of ½" plywood screwed and glued to top of upright with 6 x 1¼" drywall screw

Upright, 4 required, 1 x 2 lumber, length equal to your ceiling height minus 2"

1 x 2 mounting cleat, see detail below

24"

24½"

Backdrop panel on this side is 7'-9" long

Backdrop panel, ½" plywood 24" high and 7'-9½" long

48"

Corner joined with hinges on back, see detail below

Inner bracket arm 1 x 2 x 25¾"

Inner bracket arm on this side is 24½" long

48"

21"

21"

Bracket arm 1 x 2 x 36"

1 x 2 spacer 6" long

8 x 1½" pan-head sheet metal screw

About 42" from floor to top of bracket arms - adjust to suit your height

¼" x 20 x 3" carriage bolts

6 - 8"

¼" flat washer and ¼" x 20 wing nut

1 x 2 diagonal brace at 45° angle, length to suit

Upright

6 x 1" drywall screws

8 x 1½" pan-head sheet metal screws

5/16" x 18 tee nut

5/16" x 18 x 2" bolt

3" x 4" pad of ½" plywood

Drill bottom of upright with 5/16" bit for tee nut and bolt

3" loose-pin hinges join backdrop panels, allow separation by removal of pins

CORNER DETAIL

1 x 2 mounting cleat

Screw and glue 1 x 2 mounting cleat to backdrop panel, attach uprights with screws into cleat to allow disassembly

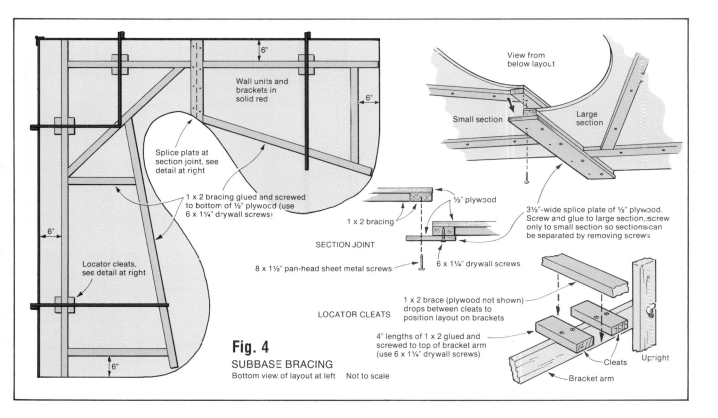

Fig. 4
SUBBASE BRACING
Bottom view of layout at left   Not to scale

Labels within figure:

6"

Wall units and brackets in solid red

Splice plate at section joint, see detail at right

1 x 2 bracing glued and screwed to bottom of ½" plywood (use 6 x 1¼" drywall screws)

Locator cleats, see detail at right

6"

6"

6"

View from below layout

Small section

Large section

½" plywood

1 x 2 bracing

SECTION JOINT

8 x 1½" pan-head sheet metal screws

6 x 1¼" drywall screws

3½"-wide splice plate of ½" plywood. Screw and glue to large section, screw only to small section so sections can be separated by removing screws

LOCATOR CLEATS

1 x 2 brace (plywood not shown) drops between cleats to position layout on brackets

4" lengths of 1 x 2 glued and screwed to top of bracket arm (use 6 x 1¼" drywall screws)

Cleats

Upright

Bracket arm

Right now, though, you're more interested in getting them set up. With the bolts in the bottoms of the uprights turned all the way in, join the two backdrop panels by installing the pins in the hinges. Move the joined units into the corner of your room and put the screw into the inner bracket arms to help hold things square. Place the plywood pads between the bolts in the uprights and the floor, and use a wrench to turn the bolts out — a little at a time all the way around — until the uprights are wedged tightly in place.

If you move the Carbondale Central into a room with a different ceiling height, it should be a simple matter to shorten or shim the uprights to fit. Even if the difference is so great that you have to make four new uprights, that's no big deal.

LAYOUT AND TRACK

The best way to mark out the material for the layout's "tabletop" sections is to assemble the sectional track on the foam insulation board to see just where it will fit. Look back at fig. 1 and you'll find that except for the two back sides and the location of the section joint, you don't have to be too picky about the overall dimensions. You do want to leave yourself a comfortable aisleway in the middle, but you also want to leave as much room as possible for scenery and structures in front of the track.

Use a felt marker to draw the outer edges of the layout sections on the foam, but don't worry about the harbors and streams yet, or the exact location of the track. Get the track safely out of the way and cut the foam to shape, then use the foam pieces as templates to mark the plywood. We cut the foam with a hand keyhole saw and used a power saber

saw on the plywood — remember your goggles and dust mask.

The mask is *really* important when cutting foam. The small particles can enter your lungs and cause irritation, and give you a sore throat too, but a dust mask will protect you.

Once you've cut the plywood, flip the pieces over and install the bracing and splice plate shown in fig. 4. Then set the two sections on the brackets, put some glue on the bottoms of the locator cleats, and slip them in place between the plywood and the brackets. Make sure you're gluing these to the bracket arms only and not to the plywood or the bracing. When the glue has set you can remove the layout sections and reinforce the cleats with screws into the bracket arms.

Now put the foam sections on top of the plywood and lay out the track again. You can do this work with the layout on the brackets, but we set it up on sawhorses instead. It's a bit easier to be able to get at the layout from all sides. When you have the track in place you can draw along each side of the ties with a marker as shown in fig. 5.

I have to admit that we cheated a bit by using a little flextrack here and there. That allows some smoother curves and saves a few rail joints, but it isn't at all necessary. MR's Andy Sperandeo set up the Carbondale Central track plan with the sectional track shown in fig. 1 and made sure that it all fits without any cutting or bending.

This is also a good time to mark the foam for cutting out the harbor and streams. You want to draw and cut near where the bottom of the banks will be, so you'll have foam to cut back into a realistic slope later on. The banks should curve and flow naturally, except where there will be bridge abutments and

retaining walls. If in doubt leave some extra foam in place. You can always cut it out, though putting some back is no sweat either.

Remove the track one more time and cut the water areas out of the foam. We won't get around to installing bridges until part two, so if you'd like you can leave narrow strips of foam under the tracks that will be on bridges. It will be easy to cut these out later. On the other hand, don't worry about the spur that will run out onto that wharf in the harbor. We know where it's going and we can just leave it until next time.

The next step is to coat the plywood and the bottoms of the foam sections with an even layer of a water-based latex contact cement. Elmer's Saf-T is a good brand that won't attack the foam (ordinary solvent-based contact cements will eat holes in it). Don't put any cement under the foam "bridges" and they'll be easier to remove.

Let the cement dry for about 20 minutes, then check to see that the plywood hasn't soaked up too much of it. There should be an even layer of cement, and you may need to do a little touchup here and there. When everything is ready, position the foam carefully over the plywood. Don't let the two cemented surfaces touch until the location is just right, and then press them together firmly. You'll have a layout with a solid foundation but a surface that's easy to shape for scenery.

But it's not much of a layout without track, and that's next. We used cork roadbed to simulate a ballast embankment everywhere except the two spurs at the left end of the layout. They can go right on the foam, with the transition in height being made across the bridges, and even this slight difference in elevation will add some interest.

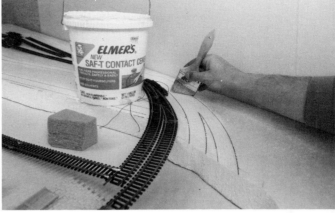

Fig. 5. Locating track. With sectional track it's easy to lay out your track plan just where it will go as a guide for marking your materials. Use a felt marker to draw along both sides of the plastic ties as shown here, then get the track out of the way while you cut and glue the Styrofoam.

Fig. 6. Cementing roadbed. You can't nail cork to Styrofoam, so simply glue it in place with latex contact cement. Brush a coat of cement on the foam following your track outlines, and brush another coat on the bottoms of the roadbed strips. When the cement dries just press the cork in place.

Follow the track outlines you drew on the foam to apply contact cement to the layout as in fig. 6, and put a layer of cement on the bottom of the roadbed strips too. Let the cement set for 20 minutes, then press the cork in place. Use a sharp hobby knife to trim the cork for the switches and crossing as you go.

The conventional way to fasten sectional track is to use small nails through the holes in the ties, but nails won't hold in Styrofoam. We found that it was quick and easy to glue the track to the cork with Macco Liquid Nails, a panel adhesive you can find in most hardware stores. Using a caulking gun and a scrap piece of cork as a spreader, spread the Liquid Nails thinly on top of a couple track sections' length of cork, press the sections in place and adjust their alignment, then move on.

When you come to a "turnout" or track switch, make sure not to get any adhesive into its moving parts. Hold it in place and mark the cork where the throwbar and points — the rails that move back and forth — will lie. Don't apply any Liquid Nails to that area. What you put on either side will be more than enough to hold the turnout securely.

You can join all the track sections with metal rail joiners and run the layout with just two wires to the rails from a power pack. That's very simple, but you'll only be able to have one engine on the track. If you want to wire your layout as we did, look ahead to fig. 7 and put plastic rail joiners in place of metal at the locations shown there.

Be sure to make smooth, tight joints between the track sections, without gaps or kinks. You can roll a car along as you lay track to test things out, or run an engine over each new stretch of track by hooking a power pack to the rails with clip leads.

SCENERY ALREADY?

Now, I tend to do things a little bit backwards, because I seem to need a bit of scenery to keep things visually interesting. That's often gotten me ahead of myself and into a few tight corners, only to find that things could have been eas-

ier had I followed a more traditional route. Still it's fun to break from the norm and make sure layout building never even scrapes the edge of boredom.

So try some scenery. Even if all the track hasn't been laid and you haven't done any wiring yet, go ahead and experiment. I've built a lot of scenery, and if you think it takes a lot of talent, you're wrong. If you think it takes some creativity, you're right. All we're talking about is a bit of foam, paint, dirt, glue, grass, weeds, and so on.

If you bought this issue of MODEL

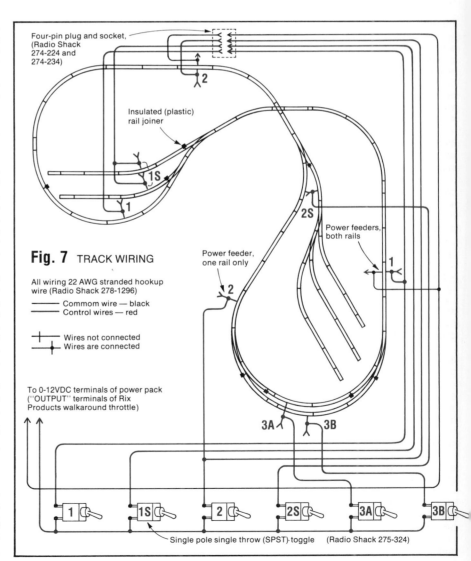

Fig. 7 TRACK WIRING

Four-pin plug and socket, (Radio Shack 274-224 and 274-234)

Insulated (plastic) rail joiner

All wiring 22 AWG stranded hookup wire (Radio Shack 278-1296)

— Commom wire — black
— Control wires — red

Wires not connected
Wires are connected

Power feeder, one rail only

Power feeders, both rails

To 0-12VDC terminals of power pack ("OUTPUT" terminals of Rix Products walkaround throttle)

Single pole single throw (SPST) toggle (Radio Shack 275-324)

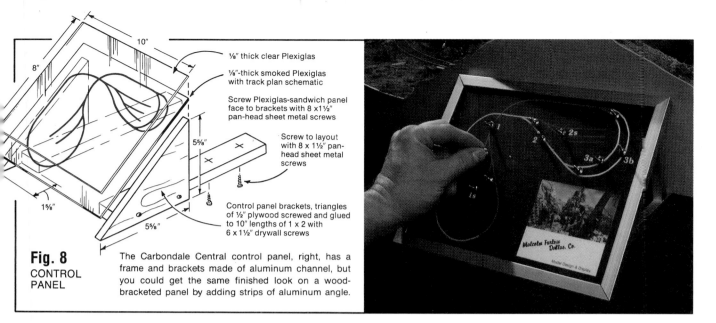

Fig. 8 CONTROL PANEL

⅛" thick clear Plexiglas

⅛"-thick smoked Plexiglas with track plan schematic

Screw Plexiglas-sandwich panel face to brackets with 8 x1½" pan-head sheet metal screws

Screw to layout with 8 x 1½" pan-head sheet metal screws

Control panel brackets, triangles of ½" plywood screwed and glued to 10" lengths of 1 x 2 with 6 x 1½" drywall screws

10"

8"

5⅝"

1⅝"

5⅝"

The Carbondale Central control panel, right, has a frame and brackets made of aluminum channel, but you could get the same finished look on a wood-bracketed panel by adding strips of aluminum angle.

RAILROADER from a hobby shop, they probably have Dave Frary's book, *How to Build Realistic Model Railroad Scenery,* or Bill McClanahan's *Scenery for Model Railroads.* Or you can get them directly from MR's publisher, Kalmbach. Read up on scenery while you're building your layout and getting the trains running, but don't hesitate to try making some scenery too.

Once you can construct a scene with all of the right elements, you'll be hooked, my friend. Trains on bare plywood or foam are one thing, but trains in a realistic setting are another. You'll be proud of what you've created, and your friends will be amazed! Scenery is what advertisers call the WOW factor.

One reason some model railroaders shy away from scenery is the "it takes an artist" excuse, but there's nothing to this "art" that you can't learn.

Another common excuse is what I call the "engineer's perspective." Modelers with this point of view build benchwork like fine cabinetry, lay flawless track, and have locomotives and cars that perform perfectly. Once they've done all this "prescenery" work, they may think, "Why make the track dirty?" Or, "Why age and weather those engines and cars? I mean, all of this stuff *is* new, so why make it look used?" And, "If I build mountains and hills, I might get plaster and paint all over the track and maybe the thing won't ever operate properly again."

Listen friends, it's not operating properly now if it's on a flat sheet of foam or plywood and we want it to look like a railroad through a little stretch of Mother Nature. Imagination is one thing, but why not help it along?

A good way to get started is to take a bare piece of plywood about a foot square and paint the thing with Pactra Dark Earth from a spray can. Sift on some good ol' dirt, maybe decomposed granite if you can locate some, or beach sand, or any dirt that has a bit of texture to it and isn't just mud.

Put some water and few drops of detergent into a spray bottle, like a plant sprayer, and wet the dirt. Now mix up some Elmer's white glue and water —

The Carbondale Central is basically a simple model railroad, but Malcolm will show you how to give it a busy, big-city look by crowding detailed urban scenery up to, over, and around the tracks.

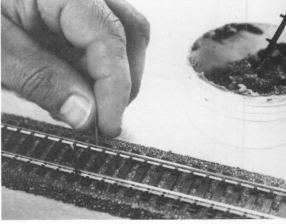

Scenic detail is Malcolm's trademark, and in MR's Carbondale Central series he'll show you fast, simple, and effective ways to get this look on your own model railroad.

Fig. 9. Soldering feeders. Bring the feeder wires up through holes next to the rails as in the upper photo. Strip the insulation and "tin" the wires by heating them with your soldering iron and flowing solder into the bare strands. Bend each wire to lie tightly against the base of the rail as in the lower photo, apply a little rosin flux (the paste in the can), then use the iron to quickly heat both rail and wire while you apply a little more solder.

⅔ glue and ⅓ water is about right. Dribble the glue/water mixture over the wet dirt, being careful not to flood everything to the point of rearrangement.

Next add a little Woodland Scenics ground foam. Try the green "blended turf" variety to start with. Just use your fingers to dust this on to the dirt here and there to look like grass. Let a little dirt show through. It's sort of like watercolor painting, and you don't want to cover up all the "whites"!

While this mixture is still damp, add some Woodland Scenics coarse turf, first a dark green and then a lighter shade for contrast. Spray on a bit more water and add a little more glue/water mixture.

Now for some finer details. Cut some hemp rope or macrame yarn into short lengths for weeds. Dip one end of a little bundle of rope fibers into undiluted Elmer's glue — squeeze some into a tin lid for easy access — and plant the weeds on your "scene." Place them in groups, not one here and one over there. Add some scale-size junk: a few broken boards, a rusty can or barrel, or some old machine parts. Get a Woodland Scenics tree kit and add it to the scene too.

That's it! Get that square of plywood looking good, and everything else will be a piece of cake. Practice making scenery while you work on wiring, and you'll be ready to jump right in on the layout next month. But first let's get trains running.

WIRING

We wired the Carbondale Central with six insulated sections or "blocks." Each block is controlled by a single-pole, single-throw (SPST) toggle switch which simply turns the block on or off. This little railroad doesn't really have room to run more than one train at a time, but with this kind of wiring you can have a couple of locomotives on the layout and park one while you run the other.

Figure 7 shows the wiring in schematic form. It might look a little complicated, but it really isn't if you take it one wire at a time. The black wire is for the "common" rail, the rail that doesn't have any plastic joiners in it and so is common to each block.

On a small railroad like the Carbondale Central you could get by with just one feeder connection to the common rail. However, we're building a sectional layout and you should have one common feeder for each section, with plugs and sockets as shown in fig. 7 to carry the wiring across the section joint.

The red wires go to the feeders for the controlled block rails, one for each except blocks 1, 1S, and 2. Blocks 1 and 2 extend across the joint, so they have two controlled feeders each. The two spurs at the left end are controlled together as block 1S, but you could separate them by adding another toggle and wire.

So you'll have some place to run the wires to and be able to test things out as you go, the next step is to build the control panel. Ours is shown in fig. 8. It has a schematic plan of the layout with the toggles located right on the blocks and turnouts they control.

After you've cut the Plexiglas to size, put the schematic and lettering on the piece of smoked plastic so they'll be sandwiched in between where they can't be scratched or marred. Use Chart-Pak crepe tape for the schematic (it can bend for curves) and dry (rub-on) transfers for the lettering. You can find the tape and transfers in art supply stores, and if you like you can use a different color of tape for each block.

When the graphics are done, clamp the two pieces of plastic together and drill holes for the toggles with a ¼" drill bit. Our panel has a fancy frame made of aluminum channel, but wooden brackets as in fig. 8 will work just fine. Make the brackets, screw the panel face to them, and mount the whole thing on the layout. While we put the panel at the end of the right section of the layout, yours could go wherever you'd like.

Now you can install the block toggles and start running wires to the track. If you'd like to be able to separate the panel from the layout, use more of the Radio Shack plugs and sockets near the control panel. Try to route your wires under the layout in a neat, organized manner so you can troubleshoot or make changes easily later on. We drilled holes through the 1 x 2 braces so we could keep the wiring flat against the underside of the layout.

Hook up the common wires first, then install the block wires one at a time, and check each block by running an engine in it before you go on. I like to color code my wiring, and black for common and red for control is a good scheme, just like fig. 7.

To make a feeder connection to the track, drill a 1/16" hole next to the outside of the rail — you'll need an extralong bit, but hardware stores have them. Run the wire up through the layout and solder it in place as shown in fig. 9.

A good 40-watt soldering iron is adequate for most track wiring. Anything hotter could soften your plastic ties and possibly cause a gauge problem. Make sure the rail is clean and your iron is hot before you start, so you can make a good solder joint quickly. Just get in and get out, as they say at NASA.

While you're soldering feeders, it's a good idea to also solder the metal rail joiners between track sections. Sometimes dirt or oxidation can find its way into joiners and cause a dead section of track. Soldering the joiners will eliminate the problem, though you want to be sure NOT to solder the joiners on the two track sections across the layout joint. You do want to be able to take the layout apart, remember, and you'll have good, solid feeders on both sides of each loose section.

Once you get the track wiring done you can move on to the switch machine wiring shown in fig. 10 (or maybe you'll want to try some more practice scenery and come back to this later). Again, the complicated schematic isn't so bad if you take it one switch machine at a time. Each one has three wires to connect, one green common wire and red and black wires for throwing the turnout to the curved or straight route.

The "momentary" toggle switches are spring-loaded to return to a center off position. It just takes a quick shot of current to energize a coil and throw the turnout, then you release the toggle and let it spring back to avoid burning out a switch machine.

You could run the Carbondale Central with any power pack, but if you like to watch trains from realistic angles, a Rix walkaround throttle is a good choice. [This throttle is made by Rix Products, 5221 Hogue Rd., Evansville, IN 47712, phone (812) 422-6810, and is also available from Wm. K. Walthers. — Ed.]

You mount the Rix circuit module, transformer, and fuse under the layout close to the control panel as shown in fig. 11. The speed and direction controls are in a handheld box on the end of a 12-foot cable. Instead of being stuck at the control panel, you can get your eyes down near track level next to a bridge or building nearby and watch 'em roll.

What's that? You say your version of the Carbondale Central doesn't have any bridges or buildings? Well, join me next month and we'll start doing something about that. So long for now. ☼

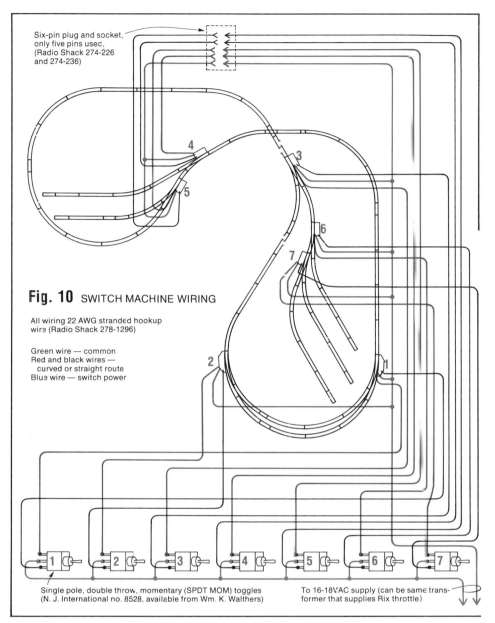

Fig. 10 SWITCH MACHINE WIRING

All wiring 22 AWG stranded hookup wire (Radio Shack 278-1296)

Green wire — common
Red and black wires —
   curved or straight route
Blue wire — switch power

Single pole, double throw, momentary (SPDT MOM) toggles (N. J. International no. 8528, available from Wm. K. Walthers)

To 16-18VAC supply (can be same transformer that supplies Rix throttle)

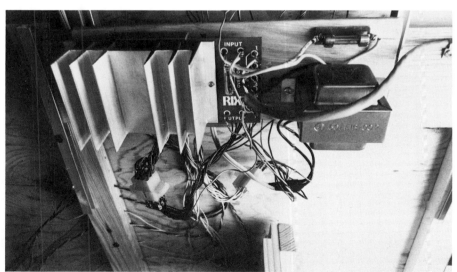

Fig. 11. Walkaround throttle. Malcolm uses a Rix no. 8 handheld transistor throttle to run the Carbondale Central. The throttle's circuit module is mounted on a removable board under the layout near the control panel, along with the power transformer (Rix no. 12) and a fuse for protection per the manufacturer's instructions. The handheld control unit is on the end of the 12-foot cable leading off to the right.

Building the Carbondale Central: 2

Add scenery and bridges, and get ready for the cityscape

BY MALCOLM FURLOW
PHOTOS BY THE AUTHOR

I HOPE you've been doing your homework on that little practice scene we talked about last time, because now it's time to get semi-serious about building a realistic environment on the Carbondale Central. Instead of a square of plywood, we'll be working with plastic foam. Foam scenery helps keep a movable model railroad light, and it can't crack or shatter like plaster scenery.

In fact you've already started to rough in the CC's scenery by cutting the harbor and river out of the blue Styrofoam insulation board last time. The leftovers and scraps of that blue foam will provide most of what you'll need to build riverbanks, hillsides and embankments, and whatever other kinds of landscape you want to have on your railroad.

You'll probably need a little more, though, and there are other types of plastic foam you can use. We got some blocks of expanded polyurethane foam at a florist's — you can also find it in craft stores. It can be cemented in place with latex contact cement or Liquid Nails, then cut and carved to shape.

Both these foams can be cut with a fine-toothed hobby saw, like a razor saw, and carved with a serrated kitchen knife. The urethane block foam can be shaped with a stiff wire brush too. Just be sure to wear a dust mask when working with this stuff, particularly the urethane blocks, as cutting or carving them makes an extremely fine dust.

You can see something of how our scenery is shaped in the photos of the finished Carbondale Central, but I hope you won't try to copy the original layout too closely. You'll do better to start with just the general idea and use your own creative energy. Don't try to make scenery for the whole layout at once, either. Work on a little area at a time to develop your skills and try different ideas.

This second installment will start you on the way to making your version of the Carbondale Central look like this. Malcolm Furlow will show how to add scenic textures and details, track ballast, bridges and abutments, and an upper level for the city scene.

Fig. 1. SCENERY TEXTURE. This is the basic technique for modeling ordinary ground surfaces. In the top photo, dirt — here decomposed granite with a variety of larger chips — is sprinkled over Styrofoam and polyurethane block foam terrain. The next photo shows how to moisten the dirt with a gentle spray of "wet" water, water with a few drops of detergent added. Use a gentle spray so it won't blow or float the dirt out of place, but keep spraying until the dirt is soaked. In the photo below, a mixture of about ⅓ water and ⅔ white glue is dripped onto the wet dirt. This soaks in and is invisible when dry. In the bottom photo ground foam is sprinkled on. Use "blended turf" foam for grass and coarser grinds for small plants. Secure the ground foam by repeating the spray and glue steps; you can continue adding layers in this way without waiting for earlier applications to dry.

Fig. 2. TRACK BALLAST. To ballast track use the technique shown in fig. 1, but with ballast from the hobby shop or clean builders' sand instead of dirt. Pour ballast over the track and roadbed as in the photograph at right, and use a brush to spread and shape it as at the far right photograph. Then spray the ballast with wet water and dribble on dilute white glue.

Often it's the kinds of things that we'd rather not see in the real world which are just what we need to lend realism and interest to a model railroad scene, such as the junk cars, trash, and other debris Malcolm has included in this view. This photo also gives you a good look at varied ground texture, caspia trees, rope-fiber weeds, and a weathered Atlas telephone pole. The HO scale figures of people and animals add life too.

TEXTURE AND DETAIL

When you have an area of foam worked to a shape you like, go ahead and paint and detail it the way you did that practice scene. We used Pactra Light Earth or Dark Earth paint from spray cans, but we made sure to hold the cans about 3 feet from the foam and sprayed in several light passes. You can't apply this kind of paint too heavily or it will attack the foam and dissolve it.

Another way would be to brush on an earth-colored acrylic latex paint. That won't affect the foam, and you won't even have to wait for it to dry before going on to the next step.

The next step, of course, is to add texture with sifted dirt, sand, and "blended turf" ground foam, then add detailing with coarser foam, rope-fiber weeds, foliage, and junk. I described that last month, and you'll see it demonstrated step by step in fig. 1. The secret to getting an interesting, natural look is to use lots of different materials for variety in size and color. I don't even mind when some of the dust from shaping green urethane block foam settles on scenery that's already in place. It just adds another sort of grass effect.

We made our trees from a plant called sugar bush, and with Woodland Scenics stretchable foam foliage applied over various kinds of twigs. Small bushes and short trees were made from caspia fern from a florist's shop. The Woodland Scenics foliage material can also be used for vines, and used in this way it's very handy for covering up spots you don't want seen, like bare spots of foam or open joints in retaining walls and buildings. We used a lot of this stuff for vines!

Ballasting track is just a variation on the basic scenery technique. For a more realistic look first spray your track with Pactra Hot Rod Primer, a dark, flat gray. You can also use Dark Earth or even Light Earth spray paints for more of a weathered, low-maintenance look. After the paint dries, clean the tops of the rails and the turnout points with a rubber abrasive track cleaner like a Bright Boy. Then add the ballast and dress it with a brush as in fig. 2, and secure it with the same water/glue/water process that we've used for other scenic

Above left. Carbondale harbor is a perfect setting for the Rivarossi "Dockside" 0-4-0T steaming onto the wharf spur. Note the piling wall next to the modified Campbell wharf, the Woodland Scenics foliage used for vines, and the sky backdrop.
Left. Here the Carbondale Central's Athearn diesel switcher starts across the International Hobby Corp. rolling-lift drawbridge that spans the harbor entrance. You can see the rusty weathering and drybrushed highlights on the bridge, and the trees and vegetation springing up almost everywhere.

3. GIRDER BRIDGES. The photographs above show how to make through [gir]der bridges, bridges with track between the girders. First cut away the Styro-[foa]m under the track, then mark the bridge deck dimensions on ⅛"-thick foam-[cor]e sheet as in the left-hand photo. With the deck cut out and wedged in place, [cut] and trim Chooch Enterprises molded urethane bridge abutments and wing walls as in the middle photo. Paint and install the deck, abutments, and wing walls, then add Atlas bridge girders on each side as in the right-hand photo. You can splice or section the girders to make them longer or shorter as needed, and you should paint them before installation. The drawings below show how to model deck girder bridges — track over the girders — using the same materials.

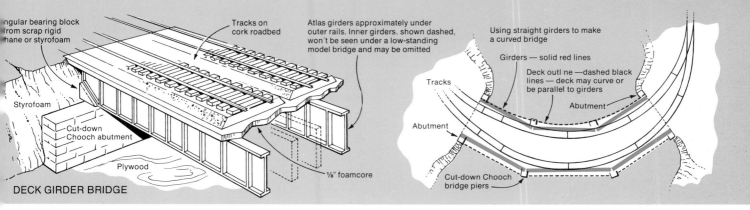

[An]gular bearing block [f]rom scrap rigid [uret]hane or styrofoam

Tracks on cork roadbed

Atlas girders approximately under outer rails. Inner girders, shown dashed, won't be seen under a low-standing model bridge and may be omitted

Styrofoam

Cut-down Chooch abutment

Plywood

⅛" foamcore

DECK GIRDER BRIDGE

Using straight girders to make a curved bridge

Girders — solid red lines

Deck outline —dashed black lines — deck may curve or be parallel to girders

Tracks

Abutment

Abutment

Cut-down Chooch bridge piers

---

textures. That's all ballast is, as far as we're concerned.

Around the turnout points you'll want to ease up and apply ballast sparingly, but whatever you do you're bound to end up with the points stuck solidly once the glue dries. Don't worry, though; just work the points back and forth with your fingers until they move freely. You'll also need to check for chunks of ballast blocking the flangeways at the frogs and guard rails. Finally, clean the rails and points again before trying to run trains over freshly ballasted track.

BRIDGES

As you work your way around the layout and come to the bridge locations, stop and install the bridges so you can work scenery up to and around their abutments or piers. We made through-girder bridges to cross the river on the left end of the Carbondale Central, as in the fig. 3 photos.

The bridge abutments and wing walls are urethane moldings by Chooch Enterprises that are easy to cut and sand to fit. We used Pactra Gull Gray spray paint as the base color for the abutments, then aged them with a wash, a very dilute mixture, of India ink and alcohol sprayed from a plant atomizer. We'll use a lot more of this basic aging spray.

Later we drybrushed the edges of the stones with white artists' acrylic paint to give the abutments more three-dimensional definition. Drybrushing is another important basic technique: you dip the tip of the brush in paint, wipe most of the paint off onto a paper towel or piece of scrap, then lightly draw it over a surface to add highlights or other subtle touches.

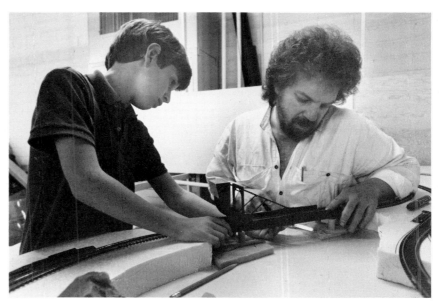

Fig. 4. DRAWBRIDGE. The Carbondale Central drawbridge is a rolling-lift type from an IHC kit. It's used with just the pier sections from the base, cut apart as shown in the photo above. At the right, Harl Asaff helps hold the bridge in place while Malcolm shapes one of the urethane foam shims used under the pier moldings to bring the bridge deck up to track level.

For the bridge deck we used foamcore, an ⅛"-thick sheet of plastic foam with smooth paper laminated to both sides. It's used for signs and displays, among other things, and you get it at art supply stores. Cut it to size as shown and paint it black before gluing it in place.

The bridge girders are Atlas flatcar girder loads — I guess these loads have been delivered! The girders can be sectioned or spliced to make shorter or longer bridges. Use a fine-toothed razor saw and cut the girders next to one of the vertical braces. Lightly sand the cut ends smooth, then cement the girders back together with liquid plastic cement for a nearly invisible joint. Be sure to paint the girders before installing them, because it'll be harder to paint them later. The girders should rest on the flat top of the abutment so the bridge looks well-supported and able to carry a heavy load.

The bridge at the far right end of the layout, the one with two tracks across the end of the harbor, we built as a deck bridge, but using the same materials — Chooch abutments, Atlas girders, and foamcore. As the drawings in fig. 3 show, the deck rests on top of the girders in this kind of bridge, and the girders go under the track. We treated all our girder bridges as "ballasted deck" types, because with ballast over the foamcore we can ignore the lack of deck detail.

We needed a drawbridge to let boats and barges into our harbor, so we modified an IHC kit as shown in fig. 4. We used the bridge sections themselves with the track laying right on top of the detailed open decks and no roadbed or ballast. We also used the foundation piers which we cut from the base sections, but we discarded the base sections themselves along with the crank mechanism. Our drawbridge is not operational, but that helps keep the trackwork and wiring simple.

UPPER LEVEL

The upper level "downtown" area of the city of Carbondale will need platforms

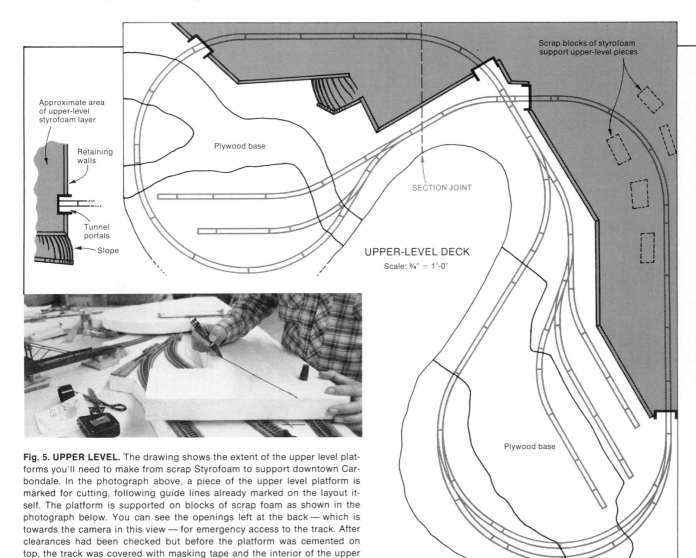

Fig. 5. UPPER LEVEL. The drawing shows the extent of the upper level platforms you'll need to make from scrap Styrofoam to support downtown Carbondale. In the photograph above, a piece of the upper level platform is marked for cutting, following guide lines already marked on the layout itself. The platform is supported on blocks of scrap foam as shown in the photograph below. You can see the openings left at the back — which is towards the camera in this view — for emergency access to the track. After clearances had been checked but before the platform was cemented on top, the track was covered with masking tape and the interior of the upper level sprayed flat black. The photograph below and to the right shows the completed upper level platform installed on the right end of the layout.

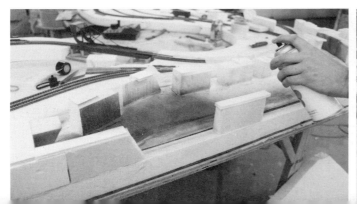

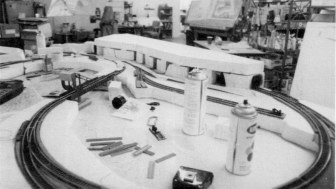

Bill of materials

Backdrop
Upson Easy-Curve, ⅛" thick, 2 4 x 8-foot sheets

Bridges
Atlas no. 790 flatcar girder loads
Chooch Enterprises no. 7016 cut stone wing walls
Chooch Enterprises no. 7027 single-track stone bridge abutments
Chooch Enterprises no. 7028 double-track stone bridge abutments
Chooch Enterprises no. 7040 cut stone bridge piers
International Hobby Corp. no. 840 rolling-lift drawbridge kit
⅛"-thick foamcore sheet

Foam
Urethane block foam (as needed)

Paint
Flat white latex
Flat earth-colored latex (optional, see text)
India ink, with alcohol for thinning
Pactra no. 10 Flat Black spray (or Krylon no. 317-0032)
Pactra no. 160 Hot Rod Primer spray
Pactra no. 2125 Gull Gray spray
Pactra no. 2145 Light Earth spray
Pactra no. 2149 Dark Earth spray
Pactra no. 20139 Sky Blue Formula U urethane spray dope
White artists' acrylic

Retaining walls and tunnel portals
Chooch Enterprises no. 7014 single-track cut stone tunnel portals, 3
Chooch Enterprises no. 7015 double-track cut stone tunnel portals
Chooch Enterprises no. 7022 single-track concrete tunnel portal, 1
Chooch Enterprises no. 7030 double-track concrete bridge abutments
Evergreen Scale Models no. 102 .010" x .040" styrene strip
Holgate & Reynolds no. 1014 red brick sheet

Wharf and pilings
Campbell no. 307 wharf kit
⅛"-dia. birch dowels
⅛"-thick wood sheet (bass or balsa)
1/32"-thick wood sheet (bass or balsa)

Scenery
Ballast (clean sand or commercial scale ballast such as Highball Products no. 220)
Caspia fern
Dirt (from your own "excavations" or use packaged dirt from the Rock Quarry and other suppliers)
Hemp rope or macrame yarn (for weeds)
Sugar bush
Twigs (for tree trunks with branches)
White glue (Elmer's Glue-All)
Woodland Scenics no. 49 green blended turf, along with an assortment of other colors and sizes of ground foam "turf"
Woodland Scenics foliage material, assorted colors

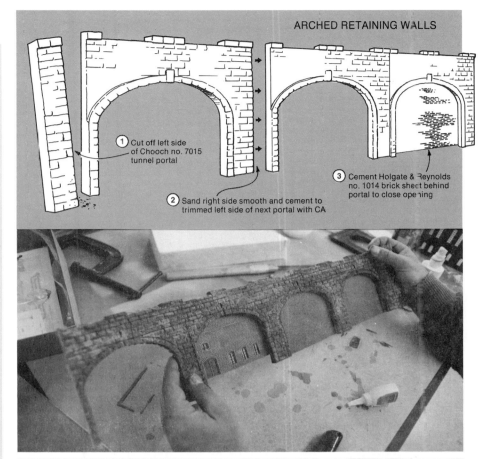

ARCHED RETAINING WALLS

① Cut off left side of Chooch no. 7015 tunnel portal

② Sand right side smooth and cement to trimmed left side of next portal with CA

③ Cement Holgate & Reynolds no. 1014 brick sheet behind portal to close opening

Fig. 6. ARCHED RETAINING WALLS. The retaining walls which line the left end of the upper level were made by splicing Chooch cut-stone tunnel portals and urethane moldings, as shown in the drawing above. The photographs show the retaining wall sections as assembled and installed. Most of the archways — originally portals — are closed off with sheets of Holgate & Reynolds plastic brick. Such spaces can be used for warehousing, modeled here by the closing of one archway with a wall left over from a Heljan brewery kit. Also notice the archway left open to be used as a road tunnel.

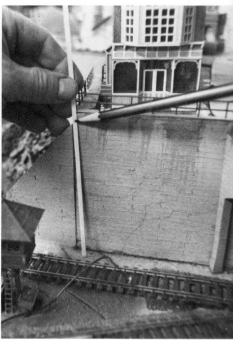

Fig. 7. CONCRETE RETAINING WALLS. Above. The left end of the Carbondale Central with its upper level in place but with scenery and bridges still to come. The retaining wall sections are Chooch double-track concrete bridge abutments; notice how these were also used to make an elevated street with railroad underpass. (Also, Malcolm has roughed in the highway viaduct using a strip of 1/8" foamcore and a pair of pliers driven into the Styrofoam!) Above right. Joints in the concrete walls were hidden with .010" x .040" Evergreen Scale Models styrene strip used as pilasters and coping.

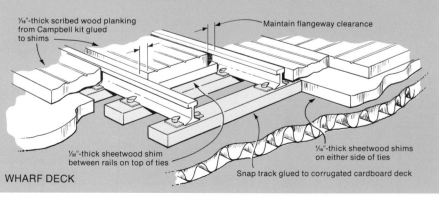

Fig. 8. WHARF. The Carbondale Central's wharf is made with bents (pier assemblies) from a Campbell wharf kit, but with a corrugated cardboard deck to simplify its construction. After the wharf spur track was laid, the deck planking was added as shown in the drawing.

1/16"-thick scribed wood planking from Campbell kit glued to shims

Maintain flangeway clearance

1/32"-thick sheetwood shim between rails on top of ties

1/16"-thick sheetwood shims on either side of ties

Snap track glued to corrugated cardboard deck

WHARF DECK

to support it over the rear tracks on both sections of the layout. Make these as shown in fig. 5 from leftover blue Styrofoam, with scrap foam risers cut about 2¾" high — you can see how we had to shim our risers a little bit with strips of foamcore.

Before you glue this stuff down, you need to make sure the risers and platforms clear engines and cars on the track. Just running a train through will do the job, but if you want to be scientific about it, you can buy a National Model Railroad Association HO standards gauge. These are sold in most hobby shops or by the NMRA itself (4121 Cromwell Rd., Chattanooga, TN 37421) for $2.50.

Figure 6 shows how we faced the upper-level platform on the right end of the layout with retaining walls. The combination of Chooch's tunnel portals used as archways with some plain stone walls keeps the retaining wall from being monotonous. These were painted, aged with India ink and alcohol spray, and highlighted with drybrushing like the bridge abutments.

Just to the right of the section joint we stopped using stone and went to concrete retaining walls made from Chooch concrete bridge abutments. This was another attempt to break up any sameness, and I wanted to make the left end of the city look a little newer. See fig. 7.

WHARF AND PILINGS

The Carbondale Central's wharf, fig. 8, started out as a Campbell Scale Models wharf kit. This wood kit is easy to assemble with white glue and comes with very good directions. It's also flexible enough to let you fit it into your layout, adjusting its dimensions to fit instead of following the instructions verbatim. We simplified the kit by using corrugated cardboard cut to size on top of the bents. Before gluing the wharf in place, spray the plywood harbor bottom where it will sit with flat black paint. Spray the foam bank with Pactra Dark Earth, again remembering to hold the can about 3 feet from the foam. When the paint is dry, you can glue the wharf in place with a little white glue.

Now lay the spur track out onto the wharf using cyanoacrylate cement — CA, or super glue. With the track in place, use sheet wood from the hobby shop and the scribed wood from the Campbell kit to make the planked deck as shown in the fig. 8 drawing. Extra stripwood from the kit can be used to hide the edge of the cardboard.

There are a lot of places around the Carbondale harbor where there isn't room for a sloping bank, like next to the wharf or beside the drawbridge abutments. We took care of these areas by making easy piling walls as shown in fig. 9. You can lay out a long stretch of piles on a strip of tape and cut off sections to glue in place as you need them.

We also put in groups of two or three pilings in various spots out away from the bank, where they'd be used as bumpers to protect piling walls, bridge piers, and the like. You can drill shallow ⅛"-diameter holes in the plywood and glue these in place.

BACKDROPS

Now is a good time to get started on the backdrops, because they'll help you appreciate the work you've done so far. We added a facing of Upson Easy-Curve to our backdrop panels. Easy-Curve is available from lumber and building material suppliers, and has a smooth, evenly textured surface — if you paint right over the plywood panels the wood grain will show through.

Remove the layout sections from their brackets and install the two flat sections of Easy-Curve as in fig. 10. This is the kind of work that Liquid Nails is made for, and it will do a good job. We didn't run the Easy-Curve all the way into the corner so we could bend another piece and snap it in place to make the curved corner. Easy-Curve lives up to its name and bends easily, and the corner piece will be removable for moving the layout.

Paint the Easy-Curve with a flat white latex paint as a base coat. A simple way to make a cloudy sky backdrop is shown in fig. 11. We used Sky Blue Pactra Formula U polyurethane model airplane dope from a spray can. Spray on irregular, rounded areas of the Sky Blue, but let lots of the white remain. All we wanted was a hazy, distraction-free background for the detailed model railroad in the foreground, so we didn't get hung up on trying to produce "accurate" cloud shapes.

Well, that's about all the new stuff I'll throw at you this month. Until next time, keep working on your "finished" scenery until you're really happy with it. If you haven't got that naturally varied look yet, add some other colors and sizes of ground foam, along with more weeds, bushes, and trees. The great thing about this is that you just about can't do anything wrong, so have lots of fun with your version of the Carbondale Central, and I'll see you in March. ○

Fig. 9. PILINGS. To make piling walls, cut pilings from ⅛"-diameter wood dowel, stain with India ink wash, and lay out on masking tape turned sticky side up. Use a straightedge as at upper left to make the bottom of the wall even. At lower right, a section of piling wall glued in place, with individual pilings set out from the bank. Use white artists' acrylic paint mixed with sand to simulate barnacle growth.

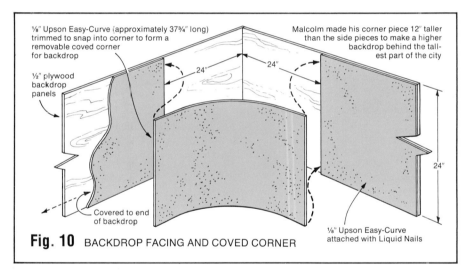

Fig. 10 BACKDROP FACING AND COVED CORNER

⅛" Upson Easy-Curve (approximately 37¾" long) trimmed to snap into corner to form a removable coved corner for backdrop

½" plywood backdrop panels

Malcolm made his corner piece 12" taller than the side pieces to make a higher backdrop behind the tallest part of the city

24" 24" 24"

Covered to end of backdrop

⅛" Upson Easy-Curve attached with Liquid Nails

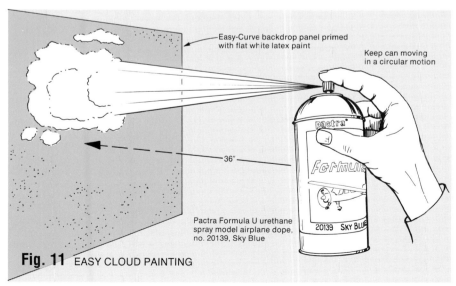

Fig. 11 EASY CLOUD PAINTING

Easy-Curve backdrop panel primed with flat white latex paint

Keep can moving in a circular motion

36"

Pactra Formula U urethane spray model airplane dope, no. 20139, Sky Blue

Malcolm Furlow concludes his Carbondale Central series this time, explaining how to add unifying road bridges, realistic water, tall city buildings, and more to the HO scale model railroad. It's a beginner's layout that doesn't look it when it reaches this stage.

Building the Carbondale Central: 3

Urban scenery completes this HO layout project

BY MALCOLM FURLOW
PHOTOS BY THE AUTHOR

HERE WE GO into the homestretch on the HO scale Carbondale Central RR. Some of what we did the first two installments may have seemed a little bit like work, but it's just about all fun from here on out. Enjoy yourself, and don't feel that you have to do everything we did right away. Buildings and bridges can take some time, and some of the kits aren't exactly cheap, so make it easy on yourself. We'll show you what you'll need to know to "finish" the

layout, but feel free to continue at a pace that feels comfortable to you.

Also, you've probably noticed by now that we didn't build our CC exactly in order as laid out in these articles. Some things do *have* to be done in order. A good example of this is that you need to finish up the bridge and highway piers, and texture and detail the stream and harbor bottoms, before you pour the polyester resin water. On the other hand, it's helpful to have a few of the city buildings at least mocked up when locating and building the road bridges.

Like I said back in part one, I've sometimes gotten myself in trouble by jumping

back and forth in what seems to be the usual sequence of model railroad construction, but I'll guarantee you that I don't get bored. So, while I'm about to start in on road bridges, don't be shy about jumping ahead to get going on a building kit or to add some printed backdrop sections. The "right" sequence for building a layout is, as far as you can, doing what you'd like to do when you'd like to do it!

ROAD AND HIGHWAY BRIDGES

The elevated roadways and viaducts give the Carbondale Central a lot of its scenic continuity. They unify the separate

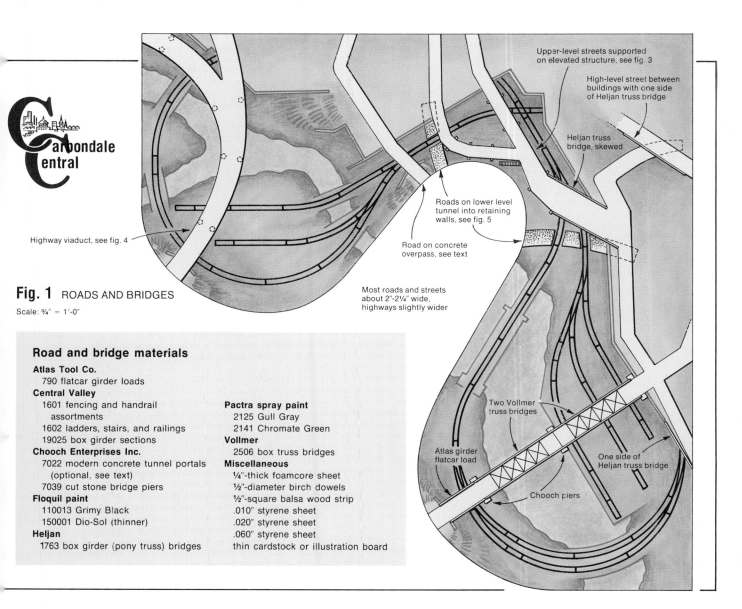

Carbondale **C**entral

Upper-level streets supported on elevated structure, see fig. 3

High-level street between buildings with one side of Heljan truss bridge

Heljan truss bridge, skewed

Roads on lower level tunnel into retaining walls, see fig. 5

Road on concrete overpass, see text

Highway viaduct, see fig. 4

Most roads and streets about 2"-2¼" wide, highways slightly wider

Two Vollmer truss bridges

Atlas girder flatcar load

One side of Heljan truss bridge

Chooch piers

Fig. 1 ROADS AND BRIDGES

Scale: ¾" = 1'-0"

Road and bridge materials

Atlas Tool Co.
790 flatcar girder loads
Central Valley
1601 fencing and handrail assortments
1602 ladders, stairs, and railings
19025 box girder sections
Chooch Enterprises Inc.
7022 modern concrete tunnel portals (optional, see text)
7039 cut stone bridge piers
Floquil paint
110013 Grimy Black
150001 Dio-Sol (thinner)
Heljan
1763 box girder (pony truss) bridges

Pactra spray paint
2125 Gull Gray
2141 Chromate Green
Vollmer
2506 box truss bridges
Miscellaneous
¼"-thick foamcore sheet
½"-diameter birch dowels
½"-square balsa wood strip
.010" styrene sheet
.020" styrene sheet
.060" styrene sheet
thin cardstock or illustration board

upper and lower levels, and link the two sections together in a believable scene that feels like it's all one piece.

Figure 1 shows where we put the roads and road bridges on our version of the CC. Your roads and bridges don't have to go exactly where ours do, but remember a couple of things I told you about them when we were just starting

out. If you use the roads and bridges as leading lines, you can make the layout itself seem larger by guiding a viewer's eye into the scene from one point of interest to another. And you can make the overall scene appear larger than the layout by having the roads seem to continue through the backdrop and beyond the layout's edge.

Mostly you can get these effects by laying out your roads and streets on diagonal lines and avoiding square corners, and by having them pass between and behind buildings as they go "through" the backdrop. Mocking things up right on the layout will help you see what to do, and if you haven't built the buildings you want yet just use kit boxes and paint cans as

Fig. 2. ROAD SURFACE DETAIL. Scribe joint lines and cracks into the foamcore or cardstock road surfaces as in the left-hand photo, then paint them Gull Gray before installation on layout. After installation, flow India ink wash into the cracks as in the right-hand photo to make them stand out.

Fig. 3. ELEVATED STREETS. Closeups show the elevated streets (foamcore) supported on Central Valley box girders and detailed with Central Valley stairs and railings. Also note the skewed Heljan truss bridge over the wharf lead and the low-level street tunneling through the retaining wall.

substitutes for the finished structures.

The roads and overpasses are not hard to build at all. A list of materials for them is included in fig. 1, and you'll already have some of what you need. For the road surfaces themselves we simply cut ¼"-thick foamcore and painted it Gull Gray. We carved in expansion joints, cracks — go easy, just a few here and there — and other details as shown in fig. 2, then aged the roads with India ink and alcohol wash. The wash accentuates the texture and helps make the detailing more visible.

On the viaduct across the harbor, the foamcore roadway runs through a couple of Vollmer truss bridges and a through girder approach span made with those good old Atlas girder flatcar loads. These bridges are supported by Chooch cut sandstone bridge piers trimmed flat on top and cut to height as necessary. The pier between the two truss bridges stands in the harbor bottom next to the wharf.

The elevated streets in the central "downtown" area are foamcore roadways supported with Central Valley box girders, both under the edges and as vertical piers. See fig. 3. The street crosses the approaches to the harbor spurs on a Heljan pony truss bridge.

The railings and stairways on the elevated streets (and elsewhere) are all from two kinds of Central Valley assortment packs — fencing and handrails, and ladders, stairs, and railings — and

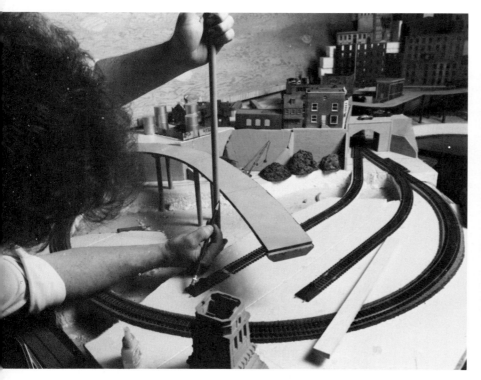

Fig. 4. HIGHWAY VIADUCT, above. Malcolm cut the foamcore highway to shape and marked the dowel piers for cutting right on the layout. At the near end see how he's arranged a joint at a future pier location, so the transverse beam can back up the splice.
Fig. 5. LOWER LEVEL TUNNEL, right. Removable foamcore roadway helps hide the section joint on the lower level. The road tunnels through the retaining wall and under the upper level.

were sprayed Pactra Chromate Green before installation. We made sidewalks here and along other streets for our city's HO scale citizens, using strips cut from .010"- and .020"-thick sheets of styrene.

The concrete overpass just to the left of the section joint is made out of foamcore roadway and Chooch concrete retaining walls, as we showed you last time. If cutting the "tunnel" openings in these walls seems like too much of a hassle, you could simply make the overpass from a couple of concrete tunnel portals, like Chooch no. 7022.

The elevated highway at the left end of the layout is supported on "concrete" piers modeled by painting ½" dowels Gull Gray. Over "land" we simply set the dowel piers into the foam terrain. Over "water" you could simply glue the piers to the plywood stream bottom, but we made stone footings for them with leftover scraps cut from the Chooch stone abutments, which adds a little interest. As you can see in fig. 4, figuring out exactly where to put them is a trial-and-error, cut-and-fit job.

Each set of piers is spanned by a big lateral concrete beam cut from a strip of ½" square balsa, and the foamcore roadway was cemented on top of these beams with cyanoacrylate (CA). We cut our roadway in a long continuous strip, but marked expansion joints above the lateral beams so it looks like it was built in sections like a real highway viaduct. The side walls are ½"-wide strips cut from .060" styrene sheet and cemented to the roadway with CA.

When it was complete we sprayed the entire highway bridge with Gull Gray, and afterwards redrew the expansion joints and added just a few cracks. Then we aged and weathered it with — what else? — India ink wash.

Figure 5 shows how I used a piece of foamcore roadway to hide the separation point of the two sections and model a tunnel running under the city on the upper level. The streets and parking lots on the upper level itself are scribed cardstock painted Gull Gray. You can really go to town weathering and aging the parking lots. Use plenty of India ink wash, and add a few spots of Floquil Grimy Black, diluted to a wash with Dio-Sol thinner, here and there to represent oil stains.

WATER

For water in our streams and harbor we poured in a two-part, transparent

The simple but effective highway viaduct at the left end of the layout leads your eye into the distance and helps make the scene seem larger than it really is.

polyester casting resin. This is a product that craft and hobby stores sell for projects like making plastic "stained glass" and small clear castings. When this resin dries hard it still looks wet, and it can produce a wavy or rippled effect that's great for model water. We used Chemco Casting Resin (made by Chemco, San Leandro, CA 94577). If you can't find that brand, Chapter 8 of Dave Frary's Kalmbach book, *How to Build Realistic Model Railroad Scenery*, lists others that will work as well.

Before pouring any resin, though, you need to make sure that you've put in all the footings, piers, and pilings which will stand in the water, that you've painted the banks and bottoms of the streams and the harbor, and that you've got texture and detail on all the banks.

To paint the plywood stream and harbor bottoms, spray Dark Earth or even Flat Black out in the middle, deep-water areas, and Light Earth for the shallows along the banks. Just let the various colors feather into each other. After the clear resin is in place you'll see an effect of greater depth in the dark areas, even though the bottom is flat.

Also, make sure that the foam banks are completely painted, or protected by walls and abutments. This is important because the resin water will attack and eat away any exposed foam. Make sure you have them well sealed with paint, though, and your banks will be okay.

To detail the banks you can add cast metal junk and broken tree limbs (small twigs) where they'll be partly or completely covered by water. They'll show up just fine through the clear resin. It's best to use 5-minute epoxy to cement these details in place, by the way, as another thing that polyester casting resin softens is white glue.

Be sure to add some drainage pipes too, as shown in fig. 6. Use soda straws painted gray for the pipes and narrow strips of Scotch tape to represent water. Flow a little CA onto the tape and hit it with a liberal spray of a cement accelerator like Zip Kicker. This makes a good three-dimensional illusion of flowing water, and it works best if done before you pour the resin.

When all the paint and glue is dry, dam up the outlets at the edges of the layout with masking tape, and check to see that there aren't any holes in the bottom where resin can leak out. This stuff finds the tiniest openings, so watch out!

We mixed the Chemco resin according to the manufacturer's directions, except that we used double the recommended amount of catalyst. The extra catalyst produces extra heat as the resin hardens,

It takes only a thin layer of polyester casting resin to make model water that looks both wet and deep. The white water in the speedboat's wake and around the tugboat was made by picking at the resin surface while it set, then drybrushing with white acrylic once the resin was hard. In the black-and-white photo, notice the drain pipe in the retaining wall at the right as well as the pipeline span modeled with a soda straw, pieces of Central Valley girders, and wire.

Fig. 6. DRAIN PIPE. To model drains from retaining walls, cement painted soda straws in place, with Scotch tape to represent flowing water. Dribble CA down the tape, then spray liberally with CA accelerator.

Fig. 7. WATER. Before pouring the clear casting resin water, all bank details must be complete and the bottom painted as shown in the left-hand photo above — avoid letting the resin come in contact with unprotected Styrofoam. Outlets at the edges of the layout must be dammed with masking tape as in the right-hand photo. Then the resin can be mixed and poured as in the photo below, to a maximum depth of about ⅛". Boats can be placed in the resin as in the bottom photo when it starts to harden (you should protect plastic boat models from the resin by painting their hulls beforehand).

and so creates a slight wave effect instead of a glassy smooth surface. The faster hardening also helps keep the resin from eating too much of any exposed foam that it might find.

Mix enough resin to cover the harbor and stream areas with a thin coat in one pouring. With the painted bottoms a layer of resin about an ⅛" thick is all you'll need for a good effect of depth, and if it's too thick it won't cure properly. Another consideration for proper curing is the weather. You'll need to open the windows and use a fan to get rid of the resin's dangerous and unpleasant fumes, and you'll want at least 70 degrees of temperature and low humidity. Pour the resin in slowly and work it out to the edges with a stirring stick; it will flow back to level itself out. See fig. 7.

When the resin starts to harden you can set small boats into it. We assembled the big Lindberg no. 7221 diesel tugboat kit ahead of time, sawed its bottom off about at the water line, and set it into the hardening resin too. Use a pointed scriber or stick to poke and whip up the resin to make wakes for the boats and rough water under those drain pipes. After the resin hardens completely, in about 24 hours, drybrush this "white water" with a little titanium white artists' acrylic color.

BUILDINGS

Our city of Carbondale was built entirely from plastic building kits. We did build a few of the buildings straight from the kit more or less as the manufacturer intended, and if you're new to this kind of modeling you can start that way to get the feel of it. To change their appearance, try painting them with Krylon and Pactra paints from spray cans, aging them with India ink and alcohol, and adding weathering and highlights with drybrushing. Figure 8 shows some basic techniques for working with plastic kits; to learn more get the Kalmbach book, *All Aboard, the Practical Guide to HO Model Railroading,* and read pages 78-83.

When we did change or "kitbash" the buildings, it was mainly to add height and make a more imposing downtown skyline. Figure 9 shows the basic ideas.

The easiest way to gain height is to just put buildings on blocks of Styrofoam, as we did at the back of the scene. Once the foam risers were hidden by more buildings around the edges, this made the buildings in back look taller than they really are. Where any spots of blue foam edge showed through we just cut a piece of brick sheet to fit, or found an unused wall section from a plastic kit, and glued it in place.

Also, these buildings to the back and around the foam risers were mostly built just as facades and not full structures — they have front and side walls where they can be seen but no backs. The kit walls that you don't use that way can be turned around and added to the facade, or can be used to make different buildings altogether. Pretty tricky, huh?

To come up with some buildings that really are taller than the original kits, and that have a different look too, we

Fig. 8. TIPS FOR PLASTIC BUILDING KITS. Cut pieces from sprues as in the above left photo — breaking them off may damage them. Sand any rough spots with an emery board as in the above right photo to make tight joints. In the first two photos to the right, Harl and Malcolm spray paint a wall before assembly so windows can show up in a contrasting color, then drybrush a brick wall with white acrylic. For neat corners, hold walls together as in the far right photo and flow liquid styrene cement into the joint from inside.

took another step and stacked two or more of the same kits, trimming or modifying the walls as necessary. This might seem like a more "advanced" kind of modeling, but it really isn't hard once you get into it. It's mainly a matter of letting yourself respect your own creative energy.

When you come up with your first building that's uniquely your own, your imagination starts working and you want to do more. After you've started thinking in terms of kitbashing (Art Curren, a master at this kind of thing, likes to call it "kitmingling"), a plastic kit will stop looking like a set of parts for a particular structure. Just because there are instructions and a picture on the box lid doesn't mean that you *have* to build the thing the way the manufacturer intended. You'll open a box and

see walls, windows, and other pieces of raw material you can use creatively.

In fig. 10 there's a drawing with short explanations of the main buildings in downtown Carbondale, plus a list of all the building kits we used. I hope you'll use these only as guidelines and go beyond them. If you like a kit that's not on our list, use it by all means. If you don't like the way any of our buildings came out, then do it your way!

BACKDROP BUILDINGS

You probably didn't notice it at first, but lots of the buildings in our city really aren't there at all. They're printed background buildings –– colored pictures — cut out and glued to the backdrop as shown in fig. 11. The ones we used are by MZZ; they're printed in Switzerland and imported by Wm. K. Walthers.

There's a big range of MZZ backgrounds, so you can have plenty of variety and avoid the repetition of some printed backdrops, and because they come as individual buildings or clusters of buildings, you can arrange them the way you want for the best effect with your three-dimensional buildings in the foreground. The MZZ line also has a lot of accessory elements like retaining walls and trees that are good for blending a scene, and there are even some big ships which make good backgrounds for the harbor.

Printed backgrounds are even easier to modify than plastic kits, and fig. 11 shows how we did a little sketching and painting on them here and there to blend in with our foreground scenery. This is a good way to extend a road off into the distance, for example, in those

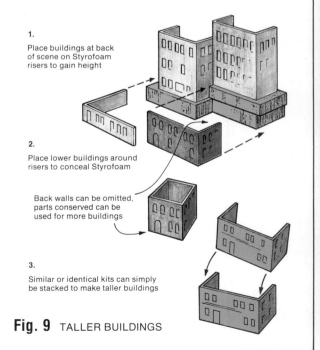

1. Place buildings at back of scene on Styrofoam risers to gain height

2. Place lower buildings around risers to conceal Styrofoam

Back walls can be omitted, parts conserved can be used for more buildings

3. Similar or identical kits can simply be stacked to make taller buildings

Rear view of layout showing Styrofoam risers with backless buildings on top.

Fig. 9 TALLER BUILDINGS

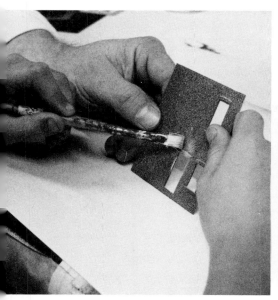

Raising buildings on foam blocks and stacking them one atop the other made an imposing downtown scene from ordinary plastic kits. The printed backdrop buildings, top center, add depth to this cityscape.

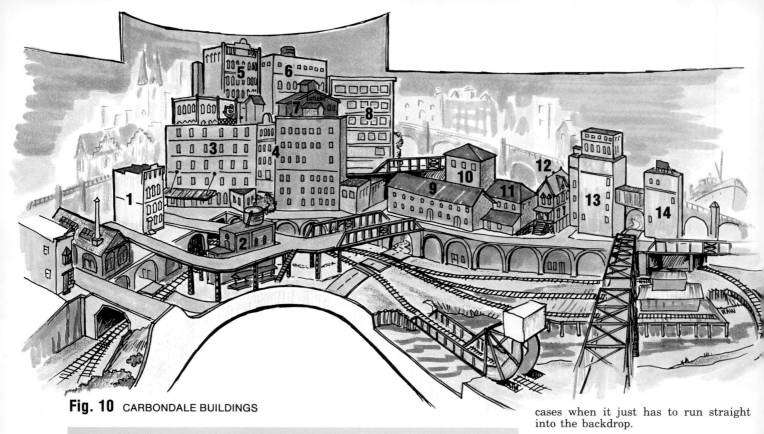

Fig. 10 CARBONDALE BUILDINGS

Downtown buildings

1. Model Power Nick's Pickles
Built per instructions.

2. A totally kitbashed structure!
Built to fit an odd-shaped space using parts left over from several kits. If you'd rather have one kit to start with, a Model Power Burlington Mills kit should work.

3. Heljan Edison's Lab
A one-wall facade made by stacking the walls of one kit, with a brick lower story made from unused portions of the Heljan slaughterhouse kit.

4. Model Power Burlington Mills
Two kits side-by-side and stacked to make a wider, taller structure. No back or left end walls — the remaining narrow walls were used to make the facade of another building, set back and to the left. Roofs are cardstock painted black.

5. Model Power IRS
Built per instructions but without back wall, raised on foam risers.

6. Heljan slaughterhouse
Two of the same kits stacked, with back walls left off.

7. Heljan 1910-era brewery bottling plant
Part of one kit on foam risers.

8. Model Power Mercedes agency
Walls from two kits stacked, with back walls used for lower stories in front.

9, 10, and 11. Heljan 1910-era brewery bottling plant
Parts of same kit used for no. 7.

12. IHC Victorian home
Built per instructions.

13 and 14. Heljan 1910-era brewery malt house
Two kits stacked to make the building at left, with back walls used to make the building at right, and other parts of the same kits used for the connecting bridge.

Building kits

Atlas Tool Co.
701 elevated gate tower
702 trackside shanty
705 telephone shanty and pole
775 telephone poles

Chooch Enterprises Inc.
9005 concrete loading dock
9015 oil storage tank facility
9024 steel water tank
9047 wood loading ramp
9049 J. E. Works gravel yard
9130 oil and water tanks
9115 Dixie's Diner

Heljan
679 1910-era brewery bottling plant*
681 slaughterhouse with cattle pens*
807 1910-era brewery malt house*
901 Two Brothers restaurant
915 Edison's Menlo Park lab*
9037 Superior Bakery

International Hobby Corp. (IHC)
1005 Victorian house
1007 colonial home
3506 sand and fuel depot
4109 signal tower
10016 Rita's antiques

Model Power
405 assayer's office*
414 Billy's Auto Body
420 urban renewal project
429 Mercedes car agency*
452 Western Union office building*
455 Burlington Mills*
465 Heinz pickle factory
470 IRS on fire
471 Nick's Pickles

Pola
813 brick pickle factory

* One or more kits modified or "kitbashed."

cases when it just has to run straight into the backdrop.

FASCIA AND DETAILS

When you're done with your scenery, bridges, and buildings, they'll still be surrounded by an edge of raw Styrofoam and plywood. Any layout gives a much better effect when it has a neatly finished profile board or fascia around its edges, just as the right frame sets off a painting. Figure 12 shows how we made the Carbondale Central's profile board from Easy-Curve.

It's the little things that can really make your city scene come alive. You can go to town adding things like street signs, water hydrants, posters, and other details, not to mention scale vehicles and figures. This is something, too, that you can work on when you're not in the mood to tackle a big project, or you're not sure what to do next. Visit a hobby shop or page through a Walthers catalog and you'll find hundreds of items you can use. For inspiration, walk down any street with your eyes open.

The youngsters who helped me build the Carbondale Central, Harl and Hannah, surprised me by quickly developing a knack for detailing scenes, and they learned mostly by experimenting, without a lot of teaching. Maybe that's because movies like *Star Wars* and *Blade-Runner* have exposed young people to the world of illusions created with miniatures. They understood the need for visual richness, and their perceptions of what they could achieve weren't limited by any ideas that they were just beginners working on a beginner's project.

I'd like to think the Carbondale Central shows you novice modelers of all ages that you already have or can quickly learn the skills you need to build a model railroad you'll be proud of. I hope it will help attract more people, especially young people, to this hobby of unlimited creative diversity. ✿

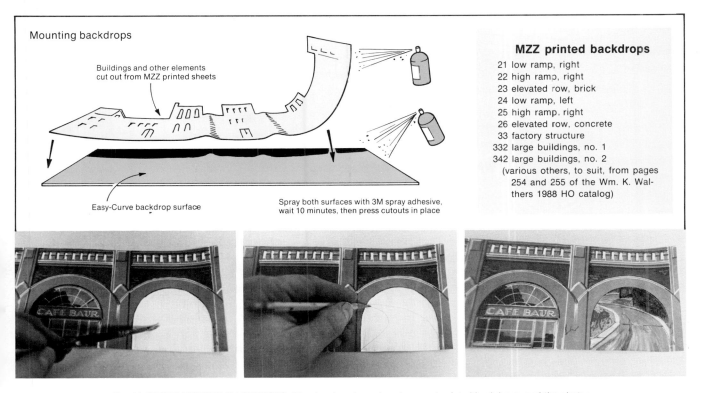

Mounting backdrops

Buildings and other elements
cut out from MZZ printed sheets

Easy-Curve backdrop surface

Spray both surfaces with 3M spray adhesive,
wait 10 minutes, then press cutouts in place

MZZ printed backdrops

21 low ramp, right
22 high ramp, right
23 elevated row, brick
24 low ramp, left
25 high ramp, right
26 elevated row, concrete
33 factory structure
332 large buildings, no. 1
342 large buildings, no. 2
(various others, to suit, from pages
254 and 255 of the Wm. K. Walthers 1988 HO catalog)

Fig. 11. USING PRINTED BACKDROPS. The drawing shows how to mount printed backdrops, and the photos show one way to modify them. At left, the archway is painted out with white artists' acrylic. Center, the extension of a foreground road is sketched in. Right, the road painted in, along with distant buildings and scenery.

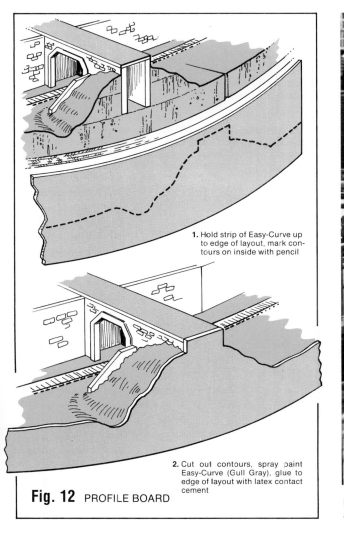

1. Hold strip of Easy-Curve up to edge of layout, mark contours on inside with pencil

2. Cut out contours, spray paint Easy-Curve (Gull Gray), glue to edge of layout with latex contact cement

Fig. 12 PROFILE BOARD

It's the little things that add life to this scene on an elevated street — people, cars and trucks, signs and stoplights and hydrants, and the birds perched on the railing.

![Santa Fe logo]

THE
WASHITA & SANTA FE
RY.
PART 1

Track planning for the Washita & Santa Fe

Modeling AT&SF lines in Oklahoma in HO scale

BY ANDY SPERANDEO

MODEL RAILROADER is modeling the Santa Fe in HO scale, with our new project railroad, the Washita & Santa Fe. (That's pronounced WAH-sha-taw, by the way, after the Washita River in Oklahoma.) It's a pretty ambitious project, but it's intended to be the sort of model railroad you'd build as your second or third layout, after you've been in the hobby for a while. I'll explain why, as well as how I do things on the W&SF, so if you're a relative newcomer this series will help you get a jump on some of the old heads.

Many of the choices involved in the W&SF series are based on our last reader survey, in an attempt to serve the interests of as many of you as possible. The Washita & Santa Fe is an HO railroad, for example, because most of you do your modeling in HO scale. While it will end up a middling large layout, we'll start it off in a space that more of you can manage, less than a one-car garage or only part of a basement.

Also, the W&SF will represent its prototype as it was in 1960, about in the middle of the late-1930s-to-present time frame that covers the great majority of your interests. And the prototype will be the Atchison, Topeka & Santa Fe Ry., because it's one of the more popular lines with you, and because you're interested in seeing more coverage of western railroads in MR. The fact that I happen to be a long-time Santa Fe fan is irrelevant, and I almost mean that seriously.

None of these choices is meant to exclude those of you whose interests are different, and the W&SF series will present techniques and ideas useful in any scale, for large or small layouts, and for any era or prototype. I hope my fellow Santa Fe modelers will enjoy the W&SF, but I'll feel most rewarded if it helps others of you to model your own favorite prototypes.

THE "WHO" & SANTA FE?

Naturally, when I say we're modeling the Santa Fe I don't mean we're trying to represent all of a system that stretches from Chicago to California and from Denver to the Gulf Coast. I've picked only a small piece of the AT&SF and compressed that piece a good deal. The idea is to make the model railroad look like a part of the whole railroad, just as you'd see only a part of such a large railroad if you went out to do a day or two of railfanning.

The part I picked is a bit of the Santa Fe's Kansas City-Texas main line in southern Oklahoma, a 35-mile stretch between the stations of Pauls Valley and Gene Autry. Pauls Valley itself is one reason for that choice. It's a small farming and oil-drilling community with several industries served by the railroad, and in 1960 it was still the junction for two branches: the Lindsay District running west to its namesake town, and the Pauls Valley District running northeast towards Shawnee and Cushing. Pauls Valley thus rated a switcher of its own, which also served as the power for the daily-except-Sunday mixed train to Lindsay.

South of Pauls Valley the main line passes through the towns of Wynnewood, Davis, and Dougherty, which I'm omitting from the model, and crosses the Arbuckle Mountains on a water grade along the Washita River. The Arbuckles aren't much in the way of mountains compared to the Rockies or the Sierra Nevada, but they're quite prominent in terms of Oklahoma terrain, and the Big Canyon of the Washita is a scenic feature that lends itself to compression on a model railroad.

The Washita River is also giving its name to the project, since Washita & Santa

Fe makes a snappier name for a model railroad than the official designation for this part of the Santa Fe: the First District of the Northern Division, Gulf Lines. The W&SF name follows the precedent of the Gulf, Colorado & Santa Fe or the Panhandle & Santa Fe, once both subsidiaries of the AT&SF.

Gene Autry is at the south end of the portion of Santa Fe main line modeled on the W&SF, and yes folks, there is a small community in Oklahoma named for the famed singing cowboy. It's really just a passing siding with a single team and elevator spur, but I couldn't resist including a

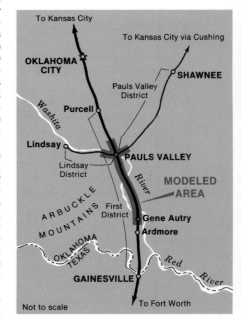

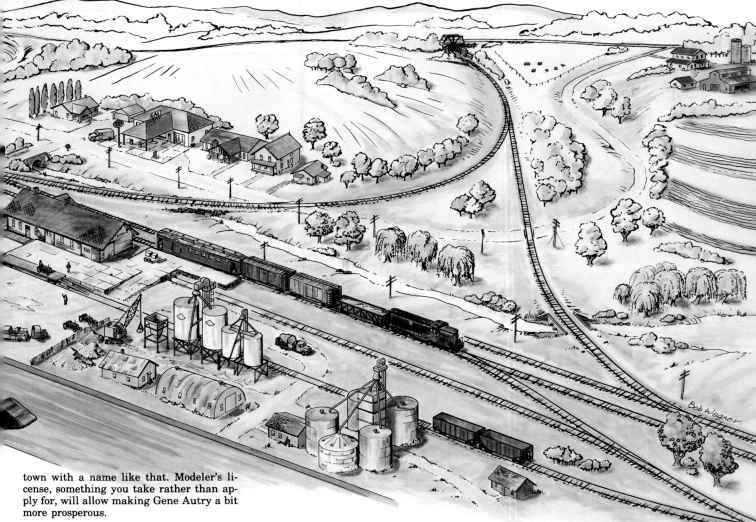

town with a name like that. Modeler's license, something you take rather than apply for, will allow making Gene Autry a bit more prosperous.

IT'S STILL THE AT&SF

This is admittedly a rather obscure section of the Santa Fe, but it still has a lot to offer in terms of the features that make the AT&SF such a popular prototype. Those railroady frame depots, for example, like the one at Pauls Valley that will form the centerpiece of that scene on the model. Or red-nosed diesels pulling stainless steel streamliners, since this is the route of the Chicago-Houston *Texas Chief*.

Like the streamliner, other interesting Santa Fe equipment will be at home on the W&SF. In 1960 high-horsepower hood diesels were taking over the transcontinental runs, so blue-and-yellow F units were joining the zebra-striped GP7s on the line to Texas. Many of the Santa Fe's original freight diesels, the 100 class FTs, ran off their last miles on the Gulf Lines at this time. For branchline flavor, we'll also need one of the "red combines," repainted passenger cars that served both as caboose and passenger accommodation on mixed runs like the Lindsay District train.

One of the attractions of modeling a real railroad, after all, is that there's a recognizable identity that will be apparent to your friends, without your having to explain that this is the way we do things on the old West Basement & Laundry Chute.

By choosing a part of the prototype that's a bit off the beaten path, we avoid having to model the double track and high traffic density of the Santas Fe's transcontinental main line. The former takes up more space and looks shorter than single track, while the latter would be hard to duplicate even

for a busy model railroad. One *Texas Chief* will suffice for the W&SF, but in 1960 the Santa Fe was running four streamliners and a mail train each way between Chicago and California.

The main line to Texas was — and is — busy enough to give the feel of big-time railroading, but easier to represent on a fairly relaxed model line. Notice also that the W&SF won't have a big yard or terminal. This helps create the feeling of being out on the middle of the railroad and lets the stations that are included be reasonably spacious.

A LINEAR TRACK PLAN

To depict the prototype I've designed a loop-to-loop track plan measuring 13 x 24 feet. It's what master track planner John Armstrong calls a "scenically pure" plan, which means that only one scene at a time is visible along the main line. To look at it another way, a train traveling from one end of the line to the other passes through each scene only once.

The idea is that since real railroads are lines stretched across the countryside, doubling back on themselves only when forced to by mountains, a model railroad will look most realistic if laid out in a similar fashion, as a single line stretching through a number of scenes. My friend David Barrow calls this "linear track planning."

Linear track plans are especially nice for representing western prototypes, where the wide-open spaces are served by widely spaced railroads, and you don't often see more than one rail line at any one place.

Linear plans also tend to be simpler than their stacked-up, looped-back counterparts, which makes them easier to dismantle and rearrange in a different shape if you have to move. Good walkaround control arrangements are another important benefit of linear track plans, and being able to walk with your train from one end of a model railroad to the other enhances the illusion of traveling through the countryside.

THE W&SF PLAN

We'll start the tour of the Washita & Santa Fe track plan at the Purcell/Shawnee reverse loop, which is the north end of the line. Actually, it's the east end by timetable direction, since on the Santa Fe anything going toward Chicago is eastbound, but for now it's easier to keep the geography straight with map directions.

This loop is not intended to be hidden below scenery, but rather behind backdrops, so there will be stand-up access to the turnouts. Hidden loops can be a pain, but this arrangement should encourage maintenance, and later in the series I hope to be able to work out an easy, mostly automatic control scheme.

It's called the "Purcell/Shawnee" loop because it represents the two division points north of Pauls Valley: Purcell on the main line, and Shawnee on the alternate route east of Oklahoma City via the Pauls Valley District. The line divides while still behind the backdrops, so that at Pauls Valley trains can come onstage over either the First District main line or the Pauls Valley District and the Gulf Junction wye.

PAULS VALLEY

Pauls Valley is the major station on the W&SF and its center of operations. Besides the junction of the Pauls Valley District with the First District main, the plan includes the Lindsay Junction turnout just north of the depot, and the start of the Lindsay District branch line. I'm leaving the branch undeveloped for the time being, but the idea is that it could run on a narrow shelf across the aisle from Pauls Valley to reach a terminal representing Lindsay in whatever space might be available.

At Pauls Valley itself there's a short, two-track version of the prototype Gulf Junction Yard, where the local switcher can sort cars set out by through freights for delivery to local industries or the Lindsay branch, and prepare blocks of cars for the through freights to pick up. The rail-served industries here include a lumberyard, a grain elevator, a ready-mix concrete plant, and a tank car loading platform serving the Kerr-McGee oil refinery.

All of these are real businesses in Pauls Valley, except the refinery which is really in Wynnewood. Since that's one of the stations selectively compressed off the W&SF, I had to either take liberties with the refinery's location or omit an important shipper. Borrowing the idea of "suggestive omission" from JOHN ARMSTRONG ON CREATIVE LAYOUT DESIGN (Kalmbach Books), I'll let the loading rack suggest that the sprawling refinery complex is just off the layout in the aisleway area.

To round out this list of switching spots at Pauls Valley, the combination depot also serves as a freight house, and the track be-

An industry to model on the Washita & Santa Fe: this interesting grain elevator with tank-like steel silos is located just south of the Pauls Valley depot and is served by a Santa Fe siding.

Another Pauls Valley industry for the W&SF: this is the Gordon White Lumber Co. no. 2 yard, located along a siding just a little north of the Santa Fe depot.

▪ wood frame depot at Pauls Valley, ▪a., is a typical Santa Fe combination ▪senger and freight station design. A ▪del of this building, somewhat com-▪ssed but of similar rambling propor-▪s, will be the focal point of the Pauls ▪ey scene on MODEL RAILROADER's Wa-▪a & Santa Fe HO project railroad.

Modeler's license will allow relocating this Kerr-McGee oil refinery from Wynnewood to Pauls Valley, and the technique of selective omission will let the large complex be represented on the W&SF by only its tank-car loading dock.

hind it is used as a team track to transfer loads directly between trucks and railroad cars.

The backdrop behind the Pauls Valley scene is forced to the far side of the layout by the Gulf Jct. wye, but that turns out to be a scenic asset. North of the wye the town can continue on the east side of the tracks, as it does in real life, and south of the wye there's space to at least suggest some open farm land. On the other side of this backdrop the country will be getting hilly and rocky, and can make up in verti-

cal surface what it loses in horizontal area.

THE BIG CANYON OF THE WASHITA

Heading south on the W&SF we follow the valley of the Washita and get to the Arbuckle Mountains rather more quickly than on the big Santa Fe. The river bank with just a portion of the river itself is on the aisle side of the track, and the hills close in on the far side. This is exactly the situation that makes the real canyon so adaptable to modeling.

Limestone and gravel are quarried from

The Jacobson Concrete Co. of Pauls Valley, below and to the left, operates a concrete ready-mix plant, and also distributes drilling mud, used to seal oil well shafts, from its blue and orange silos.

the Arbuckles in this area, and at Crusher the W&SF serves the Dolese Sand & Gravel Co's. rock crushing plant. A lot of railroad ballast comes from this plant, and the Pauls Valley switcher working out of Gulf Jct. Yard will handle cars to and from Crusher. The Santa Fe works this traffic with a switcher stationed at the town of Dougherty, which is one of the places I've selectively compressed out of the W&SF.

Around the big curve past Crusher the hills close in, and the railroad runs on a shelf between the river and a steep rock face. It's a lovely scene and not what most people expect of Oklahoma; it will do quite nicely as the major scenic feature of the W&SF. At the end of a walk-in aisle, it will be a good place to watch and photograph the model *Texas Chief*.

When the canyon opens up at its south end, the railroad diverges from the river far enough to get a good angle for a crossing. The track goes over the Washita on a deck girder span and heads for Gene Autry. We'll let the river disappear around a sharp bend into the hills.

GENE AUTRY AND GAINESVILLE

Gene Autry has only a signboard to identify it as a timetable station today, but I'm including a small depot on the plan to help make up for the towns that aren't there, and because I like Santa Fe depots. The spur serves a feed elevator and a team track just like the real one, but I've also added a small stock-loading yard. It's there because I remember seeing a lot of Santa Fe cattle cars in this area when I rode through on the *Texas Chief* in 1966. Often features you associate with a prototype do more to make a model railroad look right than strict milepost-for-milepost accuracy.

Gene Autry is out in the boonies for sure, and Haney's Gro. & Mkt. helps to give it an old-time rural flavor. This combination general store and gas station with fieldstone walls just begs to be modeled, and would give just the right dash of Wild West flavor for the W&SF.

South of Gene Autry the railroad heads into another reverse loop and holding yard. I'm calling this Gainesville after the Texas town that is the crew-change point at the south end of the First District. Ardmore, Okla., is the next station south of Gene Autry on the real Santa Fe, but First District crews run trains between Purcell and Gainesville, so that's how the W&SF is arranged.

Notice that the turnouts for the Gainesville loop and holding tracks are located adjacent to the same openings that provide stand-up access to the north-end Purcell/Shawnee holding tracks. This hidden track is important to the railroad's operation, so it has to be where it can be maintained as easily as possible.

TRAINS: Wallace W. Abbey

The Washita & Santa Fe takes the first part of its name from its most scenic feature, the Washita River's canyon through the Arbuckle Mountains. At the top, MODEL RAILROADER's Jim Hediger caught this northbound bridging the Washita just before entering the big canyon when he and the author visited the W&SF's prototype in 1980; center, a view from the *Texas Chief* as it heads south through the canyon in 1953; and bottom, the freight shown in the top photograph rounds the curve at Crusher, at the same location along the river as in the center photo.

The largest single industry on the Washita & Santa Fe project railroad will be based on the Dolese Sand & Gravel Co.'s rock crushing plant at Crusher, on the banks of the Washita River, deep in the Arbuckle Mountains of Oklahoma.

The Santa Fe hauls a lot of gravel out of the Arbuckles, and uses Hart convertible ballast cars like this one to carry company ballast from Arbuckle quarries. HO models of these cars are easy to kitbash from Athearn's quad-hopper kits.

DESIGN STANDARDS

The Washita & Santa Fe track plan has 27″ minimum radius curves on the main line and 22″ minimum radius on secondary lines — chiefly the Gulf Jct. wye and the Lindsay District lead. All turnouts are no. 6s or larger. These standards are more than adequate for four-axle diesels and 50-foot freight cars, and the main will handle full-length passenger cars equipped with truck-mounted (talgo) couplers. Even if you wanted to build a steam-era W&SF, the largest Santa Fe steam engines commonly found on this line were 4000-class 2-8-2s and 3450-class 4-6-4s, and they'd do very well on these curves and turnouts.

Space is allowed on the plan to lead into all mainline curves with short easements of larger radii, so the trains will glide smoothly in and out of the turns. The mainline curves will also be superelevated, or banked. This isn't necessary for smooth running, but a nicely modeled train leaning into a curve is a very appealing sight.

Such sights will be easy to appreciate on the W&SF, because the benchwork will be high enough to provide trackside views

nearly at eye level. The track at Pauls Valley is about 57½″ off the floor, and Gene Autry will be only 6″ lower.

Building the layout this high has other advantages besides the viewpoint. The horizon line on the backdrop behind Pauls Valley will be only a few inches above the track, which will greatly simplify the task of painting this backdrop. In the canyon the hills can easily rise to and above eye level, so only a plain sky backdrop will be required.

It's also easier to work underneath a high layout. I've already found it quite con-

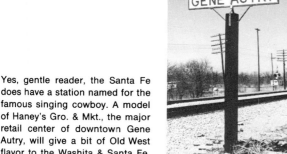

Yes, gentle reader, the Santa Fe does have a station named for the famous singing cowboy. A model of Haney's Gro. & Mkt., the major retail center of downtown Gene Autry, will give a bit of Old West flavor to the Washita & Santa Fe.

venient to roll a swivel chair under the W&SF and work in comfort. If you've ever crawled under a model railroad on your hands and knees to install and maintain wiring and turnout controls, trying to carry along soldering guns and wire cutters and other implements of destruction as you go, you'll really appreciate the change this can make in your enjoyment of the hobby.

Roll-under access will also make it easier to get into those return loop access areas behind the backdrops. There will also be a couple of access openings between Pauls Valley and the backdrop, covered by scenicked pop-up hatches. These will be needed to scenick the areas that can't be reached from the edge of the layout and to maintain the turnout at the tail of the wye.

The W&SF will be controlled with the CTC-16 command control system (MODEL RAILROADER, December 1979 through April

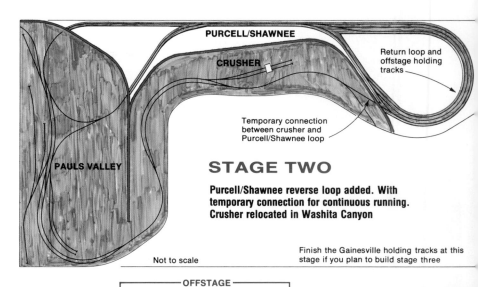

STAGE TWO

Purcell/Shawnee reverse loop added. With temporary connection for continuous running. Crusher relocated in Washita Canyon

Not to scale

Finish the Gainesville holding tracks at this stage if you plan to build stage three

STAGE ONE

Simple loop with Pauls Valley and rock crusher siding

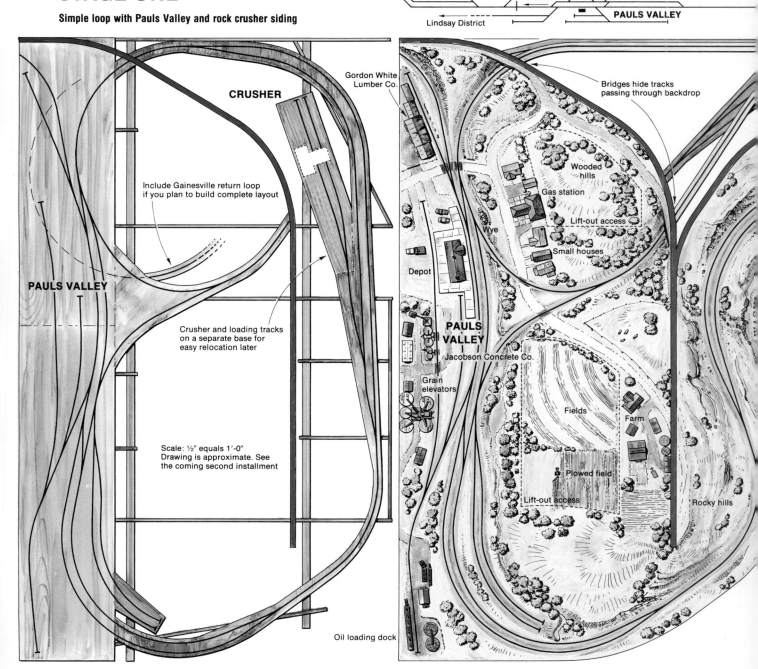

Scale: ½" equals 1'-0"
Drawing is approximate. See the coming second installment

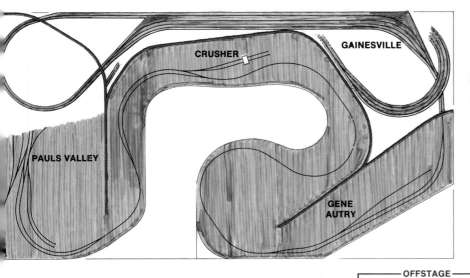

STAGE THREE

Washita Canyon completed and main line finished through Gene Autry to completed Gainesville level

GAINESVILLE

CRUSHER

PAULS VALLEY

GENE
AUTRY

COMPLETED LAYOUT

Schematic at left
Construction may vary from
these general drawings as the
Washita & Santa Fe progresses
in installments to completion

OFFSTAGE

ARBUCKLE CRUSHER

MOUNTAINS

WASHITA   RIVER

GENE AUTRY

GAINESVILLE

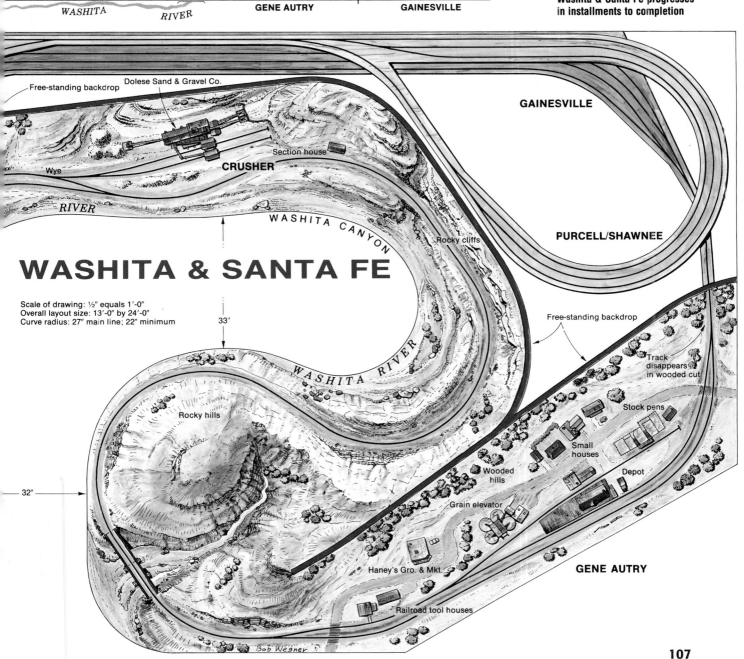

Free-standing backdrop

Dolese Sand & Gravel Co.

GAINESVILLE

Section house

Wye

CRUSHER

RIVER

WASHITA CANYON

Rocky cliffs

PURCELL/SHAWNEE

WASHITA & SANTA FE

Scale of drawing: ½" equals 1'-0"
Overall layout size: 13'-0" by 24'-0"
Curve radius: 27" main line; 22" minimum

33"

WASHITA RIVER

Free-standing backdrop

Track
disappears
in wooded cut

Stock pens

Rocky hills

Small
houses

Depot

32"

Wooded
hills

Grain elevator

Haney's Gro. & Mkt.

GENE AUTRY

Railroad tool houses

Bob Wegner

Louis A. Marre

R. S. Plummer

R. S. Plummer

This is circa-1960 power for the Northern Division, Gulf Lines. The 189 is one of Santa Fe's first freight diesels, 100-class FTs from EMC, many of which ended their careers on freight runs to and from Texas before being traded in on GP20s and 30s. The 21 is a 16-class F3, one of the Santa Fe's popular red-nosed passenger Fs. The W&SF will be a fine setting for a model of engine 21 to strut its stuff with the *Texas Chief*. The 2650-class GP7s were all-around utility locomotives, working as switchers, on branch and local freights, and even on through runs.

1980 issues), arranged for walkaround control so that engineers can stay close to their trains. The turnouts will also be set up for walkaround control, with control switches along the edge of the layout. There will be small control panels for the two reverse loops, but otherwise the W&SF won't need conventional control panels.

CONSTRUCTION IN STAGES

The Washita & Santa Fe can be built in stages, so you don't have to tackle it all at once, and so you can start in a smaller space than needed for the complete railroad. I've already begun stage one, a simple loop plan including the Pauls Valley station area in a space 7'-9" x 13'-0". This can be finished to provide a realistic scene and at least a little operation before you move on to the rest of the railroad.

The Dolese rock crusher could be included as well, with tracks and structure on their own individual base for easy relocation when you expand the layout. Notice that the first-stage plan includes the curve of the Gainesville reverse loop below Pauls Valley: the easy way to get it in place for the last stage is to put it in first.

The second-stage plan, which I'll be skipping over for our magazine project, includes part of the Washita canyon scene. It uses the Purcell/Shawnee reverse loop to complete a continuous main line more than twice as long as the first-stage loop and to provide some offstage holding tracks.

Speaking of holding tracks, the Gainesville holding yard will have to be built as the first step of the second stage, again to allow track that will be hidden to be built out in the open. Because of the amount of track in this yard it might seem just as easy to combine stages two and three, as I'll be doing, and finish the railroad on the second big leap. If you'd prefer to work in smaller steps, the second-stage plan gives you a workable choice.

The third stage completes the canyon scene and finishes the main line through Gene Autry to Gainesville. It will give you a loop-to-loop railroad with more than a scale mile of visible line on which to display and operate Santa Fe trains in scenes depicting the outstanding features of the prototype line. It will be a nice, simple-looking railroad, and its simplicity will make it easy to maintain and enjoy.

Another stage would be the addition of the Lindsay District, which I'm not giving a number because it could be done at any phase of the main layout's development. As I've said, this branch line could run along a narrow shelf on the opposite side of the aisleway in front of Pauls Valley, to reach a small stub terminal at the town of Lindsay. Because of the height of the main layout, Lindsay could be built on a shelf above a workbench. The branch might even reach into a family area in the manner of Walt Wyatt's Sweetwater RR. (September 1981 MR), and be built above a TV or stereo. We'll take a closer look at the Lindsay District and its modeling possibilities later in this series.

THE W&SF SERIES

We'll start construction on stage one of the Washita & Santa Fe in the March MR, when I'll describe how to build the L-girder benchwork and install Homasote roadbed. Construction articles detailing each phase of the railroad will appear throughout the year, and we expect to show you the finished Pauls Valley scene next December. In 1983 we'll expand and complete the railroad. From time to time we'll also be presenting related construction features, such as an article on scratchbuilding the Pauls Valley depot in styrene, and others on kitbashing Santa Fe rolling stock.

As I said at the beginning, this won't just be a series on modeling the Santa Fe in Oklahoma circa 1960. Any time you build a model railroad from the ground up, you encounter almost every aspect of model railroading along the way. The Washita & Santa Fe project is really aimed at everyone who'd like to build a model railroad, and we hope that all of you will find these articles helpful and encouraging. ✿

Here's the author installing Homasote roadbed on the Washita & Santa Fe. The next installment of the W&SF series will cover benchwork and roadbed for the railroad's first stage.

W&SF train no. 16, the *Texas Chief*, follows the Washita River on an easy grade through the lovely Arbuckle Mountains. Photo by Paul Erler.

Model railroading is many hobbies in one. Here's Andy Sperandeo enjoying the hobby of C-clamping, installing Homasote roadbed on MR's Washita & Santa Fe HO project railroad.

Benchwork and roadbed for the Washita & Santa Fe

The foundation of a model railroad

THE
WASHITA & SANTA FE
RY.
PART 2

BY ANDY SPERANDEO

THE BENCHWORK under the Washita & Santa Fe is of the L-girder design developed by Linn Westcott when he was editor of MODEL RAILROADER, with ribbon-style plywood subroadbed and Homasote roadbed. In this second part of the W&SF story I'll explain a little about how and a lot about why the benchwork is built the way it is, tell why I like to cut my own Homasote roadbed, and even show you a little about laying flexible track so you can put in the Gainesville return loop before it's covered by Pauls Valley. The bill of materials shows what you'll need to work along with me, and this month's MR Clinic covers layout construction tools.

L-GIRDER BENCHWORK

I'm using L-girder benchwork for the W&SF for a number of reasons, but one of the most important is that I'm no carpenter. The strength in an L-girder system comes from the pair of girders, which solidly support joists fastened at any angle

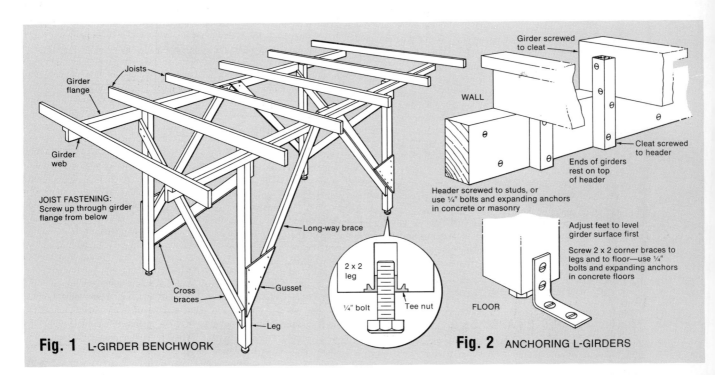

Fig. 1 L-GIRDER BENCHWORK

Fig. 2 ANCHORING L-GIRDERS

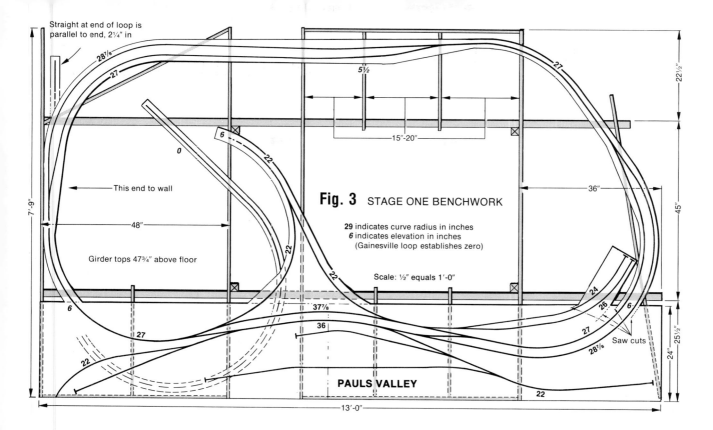

Straight at end of loop is parallel to end, 2¼" in

28⅞
27

5½

15″-20″

27

22½

6

0

This end to wall

Fig. 3 STAGE ONE BENCHWORK

22

48″

29 indicates curve radius in inches
6 indicates elevation in inches
(Gainesville loop establishes zero)

36″

45″

Girder tops 47¾″ above floor

22

Scale: ½″ equals 1′-0″

7′-9″

22

24

6

26

27

27

6

37⅞

28⅞

Saw cuts

36

27

25½″

22

24″

PAULS VALLEY

22

13′-0″

across their flanges — see fig. 1. This system doesn't require precisely squared joints between pieces of wood carefully sawn to length, so it's very fast, very flexible, and best of all, very forgiving of at least minor incompetence.

One of the design features of L-girder benchwork is that all screws and fasteners remain accessible, even after the railroad is scenicked. Linn's intention was that it would be easy to make changes on a layout built on the L-girder system, but this also makes it more practical to dismantle and move an L-girder model railroad. The Washita & Santa Fe is not designed for portability, as was MR's N scale Clinchfield RR., but if you have to move at some stage during its construction you should be able to take most of your finished work with you.

L-girder benchwork also helps make it easier to work on the W&SF. The whole 7′-9″ x 13′-0″ first stage rests on just four main legs, which, with the girders, are set well back from the edges. The whole Pauls Valley station area overhangs the girder on that side by more than 2 feet, so that there's easy access for installing and maintaining wiring and turnout controls. I've also been able to leave large open areas between the girders to allow for future access hatches behind Gulf Junction yard and on the north side of the wye, and also stand-up access to the Gainesville loop behind the backdrop.

It's not directly a benefit of the L-girder system, but the layout's height also helps to make access easy, as I pointed out in part one of this series in the January MR.

The tops of my girders are 47¼″ off the floor, which of course is also the clearance under the joists. For jobs under Pauls Valley I can sit in a castered chair, roll under the layout, and work in a comfortable sitting position with my head between the joists. To get between the girders I bend over in the chair and roll in; there's 43 1/16″ clearance under the girders, and it sure beats crawling or duckwalking.

My reasons for building the layout high, by the way, were initially all cosmetic. Trains look nice when viewed near eye level — I'm 6′-1″, and the highest track is 57¾″ off the floor. Too, with the nearly flat scenery around Pauls Valley, making the ground level high simplifies painting the backdrop by keeping the horizon low. You'll be able to appreciate these effects as

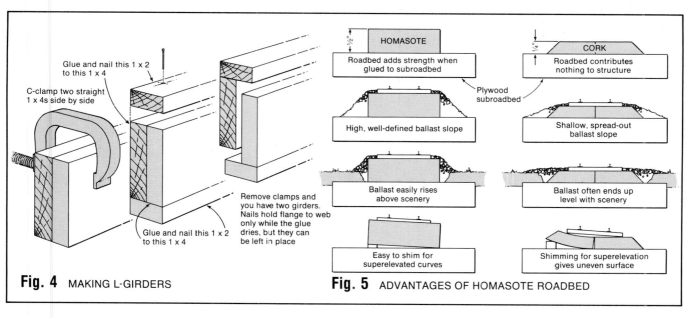

Glue and nail this 1 x 2 to this 1 x 4

C-clamp two straight 1 x 4s side by side

Glue and nail this 1 x 2 to this 1 x 4

Remove clamps and you have two girders. Nails hold flange to web only while the glue dries, but they can be left in place

HOMASOTE

Roadbed adds strength when glued to subroadbed

Plywood subroadbed

High, well-defined ballast slope

Ballast easily rises above scenery

Easy to shim for superelevated curves

CORK

Roadbed contributes nothing to structure

Shallow, spread-out ballast slope

Ballast often ends up level with scenery

Shimming for superelevation gives uneven surface

Fig. 4 MAKING L-GIRDERS   **Fig. 5** ADVANTAGES OF HOMASOTE ROADBED

layout construction progresses, but right now I can assure you that the W&SF is the easiest layout to work under that I've ever been involved with.

There are problems with high benchwork, however. The most obvious is that sometimes you need to get more of a bird's-eye view of things, especially to check the alignment of track and roadbed. I've kept a small stepladder handy, and using it to get another foot or two above the layout hasn't seemed like much of a bother to me.

A more serious problem has been that my benchwork isn't very stable resting on just the four main legs, because of the combination of the layout's height and the considerable overhangs. At first I thought of moving the girder on the Pauls Valley side closer to the edge. That, however, would put the girder right under most of the turnouts, and wouldn't help with the long overhang at the wall end, where I want to keep legs and joists out of the way for reverse loop access.

All I've done so far is attach temporary legs at the three corners where the overhang is the greatest, the 1 x 4s C-clamped to the joists that you'll see in some of the photos. Better solutions, that I'd certainly use in my own train room, would be to fasten the ends of the girders to the wall, or anchor the main legs to the floor, or both. See fig. 2. Secured in this way I don't think the layout would be tippy, and the stage two or three extension will only add stability.

CONSTRUCTION DETAILS

Scale drawings in fig. 3 show the W&SF benchwork as I've built it. Start by making the girders as shown in fig. 4, then add the legs to each girder. Next you set the girders upright and join them with temporary joists, and after that you can add the leg braces. With this basic structure complete, check to see that the girder tops define a level surface both lengthwise and across — which is why you'll want to put leveling screws in the legs — and anchor the girders or legs as discussed above. Add the permanent joists and the rest of the structure as needed to support the track boards, so you'll be sure there's a reason for every piece of lumber.

For the most part the W&SF's benchwork is pretty orthodox stuff, straight out of Linn Westcott's HOW TO BUILD MODEL RAILROAD BENCHWORK (Kalmbach Books), but I did devise an outrigger arrangement to keep the spaces between the girders clear for access. As shown in fig. 3, there are two of these on the Pauls Valley side and one on the opposite. In each, the long joists at either end support a butt-joined outrigger rail that runs parallel to the girders. The outrigger in turn supports the outer ends of short joists that reach only to the near girder, so the joists can be where they're needed for support but not in the way of future pop-up hatches.

If I seem to be overly concerned with access, it's because I know from unpleasant experience about working on model railroads that didn't have enough of it. It should be apparent that some special consideration is required with a table almost 8 feet wide and a scene at Pauls Valley that will be about 5½ feet deep.

SUBROADBED AND ROADBED

To avoid confusion with the Homasote strips that will support the track, I'm calling the plywood strips that support the Homasote "subroadbed." This is ½" interior-grade material on the W&SF, knot-free on one side only. Thicker, higher-grade, and more expensive plywood could be used, but the ½" is more than strong enough, especially with the ½" Homasote glued to it, and anyway it's supposed to end up hidden.

The roadbed itself may raise some questions; I know that some of my co-workers here at MR didn't understand what I was doing at first. It's cut from sheet Homasote, a stiff, dense paperboard, and I've made no attempt to bevel the sides. Ballast will naturally take a steeper slope when piled loose along the vertical roadbed edges than it can over beveled roadbed, so the square-cut Homasote makes it easier to model a well-maintained mainline railroad. It's also less work to cut straight rather than beveled sides, and there's no sense wasting effort on something that's supposed to be covered up anyway.

It is more work to cut Homasote roadbed than to use commercial cork roadbed, but the Homasote holds spikes much better and in general produces a more solid track structure. Figure 5 shows more of the reasons why I prefer to use Homasote.

Cutting roadbed out of the Homasote sheet can be a messy business. With ordinary toothed blades in a saber saw you'll fill the air with a lot of powdery gray sawdust, so it's best to do the work outside or at least in an area where you won't mind the dust. Breathing the stuff is uncomfortable and can't be good for you, so wear a surgical mask while sawing Homasote.

Using a knife-edged saber saw blade al-

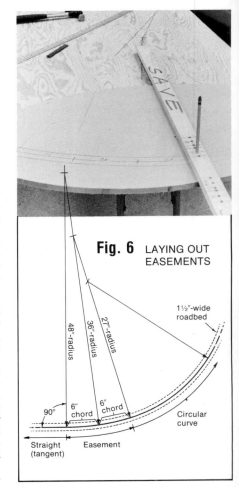

Fig. 6 LAYING OUT EASEMENTS

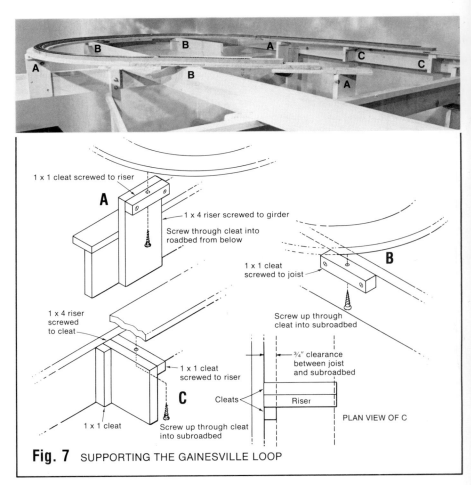

Fig. 7 SUPPORTING THE GAINESVILLE LOOP

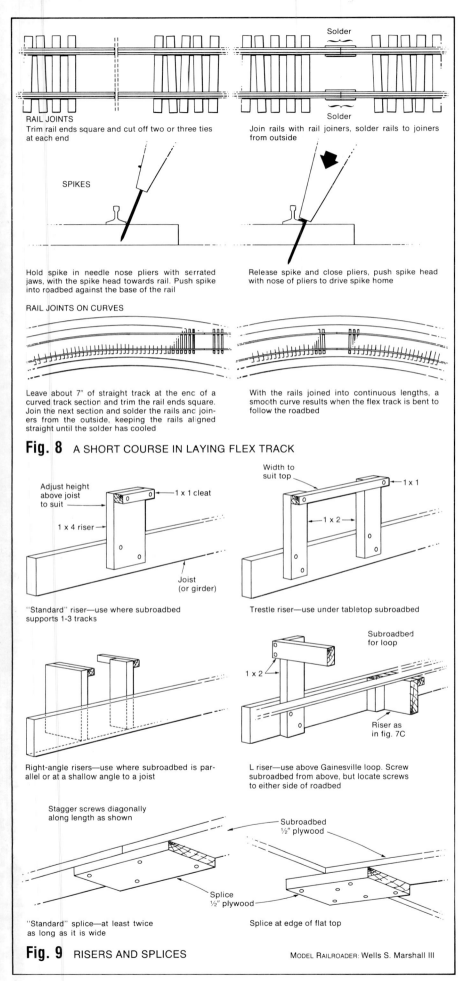

RAIL JOINTS

Trim rail ends square and cut off two or three ties at each end

Join rails with rail joiners, solder rails to joiners from outside

SPIKES

Hold spike in needle nose pliers with serrated jaws, with the spike head towards rail. Push spike into roadbed against the base of the rail

Release spike and close pliers, push spike head with nose of pliers to drive spike home

RAIL JOINTS ON CURVES

Leave about 7" of straight track at the end of a curved track section and trim the rail ends square. Join the next section and solder the rails and joiners from the outside, keeping the rails aligned straight until the solder has cooled

With the rails joined into continuous lengths, a smooth curve results when the flex track is bent to follow the roadbed

Fig. 8 A SHORT COURSE IN LAYING FLEX TRACK

Adjust height above joist to suit

1 x 1 cleat

1 x 4 riser

Joist (or girder)

"Standard" riser—use where subroadbed supports 1-3 tracks

Width to suit top

1 x 1

1 x 2

Trestle riser—use under tabletop subroadbed

Right-angle risers—use where subroadbed is parallel or at a shallow angle to a joist

Subroadbed for loop

1 x 2

Riser as in fig. 7C

L riser—use above Gainesville loop. Screw subroadbed from above, but locate screws to either side of roadbed

Stagger screws diagonally along length as shown

Subroadbed ½" plywood

Splice ½" plywood

"Standard" splice—at least twice as long as it is wide

Splice at edge of flat top

Fig. 9 RISERS AND SPLICES

MODEL RAILROADER: Wells S. Marshall III

---

most eliminates the dust and is the best alternative if you have to work alongside the railroad or somewhere else that needs to be kept clean. This also cuts a neater edge, but it is a lot slower than a regular saw blade. When helping David Barrow build his Cat Mountain & Santa Fe, I cut a lot of Homasote roadbed by hand using a utility or mat knife. This is about as fast as the knife-bladed saber saw, but takes more effort and a lot of fresh blades.

BUILD THE LOOP FIRST

The place to start is the Gainesville loop, which won't be used until the stage-three main line is complete, but which will be hard to work on as soon as Pauls Valley goes in above it. It's just as well, though, because building the loop works out to be a good introduction to subroadbed/roadbed construction, and also to tracklaying.

The loop is a single track on a 27"-radius (W&SF mainline minimum) curve with easements leading in from the straight approaches at each end. The easements are worth adding on hidden track because they contribute to smooth operation; later we'll get into superelevation or the banking of curves, but that's only for looks and not worthwhile where it won't be seen.

I first cut straight, 27"-curve, and easement roadbed sections from the Homasote, and used them as templates to lay out the plywood subroadbed. The straight roadbed is simply a strip of Homasote 1½" wide; a center line can be helpful for alignment but isn't as necessary here as it will be with curves. Use a trammel bar to lay out the curved roadbed: I made the one shown in fig. 6 from a 1 x 2 with a finishing nail for a center point and pencil-sized holes drilled at appropriate distances. For the minimum-radius mainline curve on the W&SF that means one at 27" from the center plus one each at 26¼" and 27¾".

The "SAVE" markings on the trammel in the photo show that it is my Mark II design. Mark I was not so clearly identified as a tool, and it was hacked into short bits by a colleague who mistook it for a piece of raw material.

Figure 6 also shows how to lay out the easement. It's not a true spiral but it does make a smooth transition from straight to curve, and it doesn't take up a lot of layout space. Spiral easements add more to the width needed for a turnback curve and eat up a fair bit of straightaway too, both things to be avoided on a model railroad. This kind of easement is also easier to make. The 48"-radius part of this easement will be long enough to lay out the dogleg curve on the wall side of the loop approach.

Using the roadbed sections as templates, mark out the plywood subroadbed. The subroadbed should be 3" wide for single track, and my method was to trace the roadbed outlines, use a ¾" block to make tick marks outside these outlines every few inches, and finally to connect the tick marks with freehand curves. Lay out the main curve of the loop so it will be made up of only two pieces of plywood, with enough extra circular curve on each so you can adjust the position of the joint. Use a saber saw to cut out the subroadbed.

You'll need some joists to support the subroadbed on the benchwork, so add the three long joists nearest the wall and the corner outrigger joists, all 1 x 4s, at this time. The loop subroadbed rests directly on top of the joists, and, since this is the lowest point, establishes the zero track elevation for the whole railroad.

Lay the subroadbed over the joists with the excess circular curves overlapping, so you can determine where to put the splices. See fig. 9. The joint should be away from a joist so that a plywood splice plate under the subroadbed won't cause a hump. Put splice plates on each end of the loop as well, so they'll be in position for the eventual expansion.

Position the subroadbed about ¾" away from the joist nearest the wall, to let the risers that will support the higher level subroadbed pass alongside and be fastened to the joist. Figure 7 shows the risers and cleats I used to attach the subroadbed to the joists. Note that some risers attach directly to the girders, to help keep the number of joists to a minimum.

INSTALL THE ROADBED

Now the plywood subroadbed is ready for the Homasote roadbed. I saved my original, carefully laid-out easement section to use as a template and cut new roadbed sections to install on the layout. I like to make roadbed sections as long as possible, including in this case a straight approach, an easement, and a good chunk of circular curve in one piece, to cut down on joints.

It's also a good idea to see that all joints in the roadbed and track structure are staggered; that is, that a Homasote joint doesn't fall right over a plywood joint, or a track joint over one in the Homasote. All these joints are potential trouble spots, and by staggering them you can at least avoid compounding any problems.

Use white glue to bond the roadbed to the subroadbed. The Homasote will need to be clamped every foot or so to make sure that it stays flat against the plywood while the glue sets. On narrow, single- or double-track subroadbed C-clamps do a good job, but be sure to use scrap wood to spread the pressure of the clamps. Tighten the clamps just enough to squeeze excess glue out at the sides of the roadbed, but not so much that they crush the Homasote. Let the glue dry for at least 2 or 3 hours before removing the C-clamps; overnight is a safer bet.

On wider or tabletop subroadbed, or when you run out of C-clamps, you can hold the roadbed down for gluing by driving long finishing nails through the Homasote into the plywood. Don't pound them in all the way, though. Leave about half the length of the nails exposed so you can remove them after the glue sets, and use a block of wood under your claw hammer to keep from crushing the roadbed when you pull the nails.

Sand off any unevenness at the roadbed joints and you're ready to lay track. I won't go into detail about tracklaying until the next part of the W&SF series, but if you haven't used flextrack before you'll find what you need to know right now in fig. 8. Remember to stop the track a few inches in from the ends of the roadbed, so the track and roadbed joints will be staggered.

If you use Lambert flextrack you'll find that the ties have holes to accept spikes. The Railcraft track I used doesn't have spike holes, but since this track won't be seen anyway you can simply drive the spikes next to the ties. There won't be bal-

Flat top for Pauls Valley

The south curve

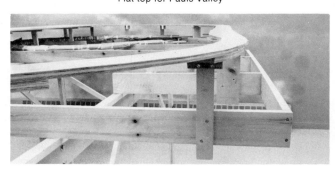
The siding at Crusher

The north curve

Fig. 10 W & SF SUBROADBED

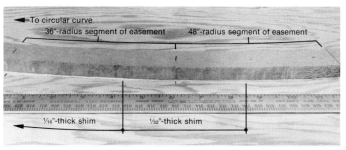
Fig. 11 SUPERELEVATING CURVES

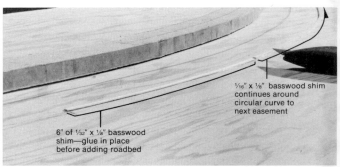

last on hidden track to help hold it in alignment, so use plenty of spikes.

When you've got the track down check it for smooth running with a full-length passenger car, and clip some power pack leads to the rails and run a locomotive. We're not coming back to use this track for a while, so make sure it works now. I found a dip over an uneven spot in the roadbed, which I corrected by shimming up the track with thin cardboard — I like to use the Lambert turnout boxes for this. When everything looked okay on the loop, I wrapped the whole thing with brown wrapping paper to keep the track clean until it's needed.

ONWARD AND UPWARD

At last we can move on to building the roadbed that will be used in the first stage of the W&SF. Start by adding the remaining long joists and the second outrigger under Pauls Valley, and then install the tabletop subroadbed along that side of the layout. This is from a single 4 x 8 sheet of ½" plywood, cut in half lengthwise, to make a flat top for Pauls Valley buildings and industrial tracks.

The flat top is supported on trestle-type risers as shown in fig. 9, with the bottom of the plywood 6" above the tops of the joists (4½" clearance above Gainesville loop track). I C-clamped the risers in place at this height, but laid the plywood top over them and checked to see that it was level before screwing the risers to the joists.

Install the plywood with screws up from below and a splice plate to join the two pieces. As a rule I try to make splice plates for single- and double-track subroadbed about twice as long as they are wide, but here I settled for one about 8" x 2'-0".

With this subroadbed in place you can refer to the track plan of fig. 3 and use roadbed sections as templates to draw in the mainline straightaways through Pauls Valley and the curves at each end. The immediate object of this is to locate the starting points for extending the subroadbed around the layout. Notice that the mainline curve at the south end is of 29" radius, to let the passing track curve maintain the 27" minimum.

You will need to cut roadbed templates for an easement leading into a 29" curve, exactly as in fig. 6 but with the larger circular curve, and for turnouts, which is why there are three of them on the bill of mate-

rials for this installment. With these you'll be able to lay out and fit the subroadbed for the rest of the first-stage continuous loop. Figure 9 shows the risers and splices I used, and fig. 10 shows the subroadbed all the way around.

There are some important points about the track plan that might not be obvious:

● I've used 2" spacing between parallel tracks on curves, but I've cut that to 1⅞" on straights. This is closer to the 13-foot spacing common on real railroads and is enough for safe clearance. It's easy to make the transition to the wider centers for curved track with the easements.

● I included the slight grade indicated by the elevations on the fig. 3 plan because in later stages the line has to start downhill south of Pauls Valley. As with leveling the flat top, clamp the risers in place and adjust them for smooth vertical curves in the subroadbed before fixing them with screws. I also put in a slight downgrade toward the end of the Gulf Junction yard.

● When laying the track around the curve at the south end of Pauls Valley, I found

there was a twist at the joint at the edge of the flat-top subroadbed. I made the "cookie-cutter" saw cuts shown on the plan to alleviate this, and I recommend that you put them in to start with.

● When you try to locate the turnouts at Pauls Valley you'll find that they won't fit around the wye and at the crossover. In the next installment I'll show you how easy it is to modify the standard turnouts so trust me for now and position them as on the track plan.

● The short curve in the main and siding across the base of the wye is large enough not to need an easement, and I also omitted them on the secondary tracks — the wye, the yard and spurs, and the Lindsay District lead.

● The short curve between the south turnout of the Pauls Valley siding and the Crusher siding turnout isn't long enough to have any circular curve: it's just two easements meeting at the middle of the curve.

● The "cosmetic curve" at Crusher came about accidentally, but it looks nice and does no harm. It's gentle enough so that no curvature is needed in the subroadbed or the roadbed; I just curved the track by eye.

SUPERELEVATED CURVES

With the subroadbed in place you can start putting in the Homasote roadbed. I think the best place to start is the north switch at Pauls Valley, so you can carefully position the tightly spaced turnouts before getting to the end curves. The curve at the south end of Pauls Valley will be the first one you come to that will be superelevated, or banked.

Figure 11 shows how to bank the curves. The Homasote is flexible enough to follow the 1/32" and 1/16" shims, but stiff enough to make smooth transitions as it twists. The 1/16" shim continues all the way around the circular curve to the easement at the other end, where you make the transition back to straight and level again.

Remember that when you superelevate the outer track on a two-track curve, you have to bank the inner one just as much to maintain clearance between the tracks. With separate roadbed for each track, as on the W&SF, you'll automatically get the correct sawtooth section across the superelevated curve. On short curves like that one that's all easement, use just the 1/32" shim, and if a curve is too short to make a smooth transition into the banking, don't use any superelevation at all.

If you haven't seen superelevated curves on a model railroad before, you're in for a treat. They add drama to a train's passage round a curve, and they add realism if you're modeling a mainline railroad. They won't cause operating problems if you're careful to make the transitions smooth and at least as long as I've shown, and if you keep the banking steady once you've made the transition. The secret is to cut the shims into inch-long sections, or to notch longer sections every inch, so they can follow the curve evenly and be right under the outer edge of the roadbed.

NEXT TIME, TRACK

That's most of what I know about benchwork, subroadbed, and roadbed. By our next installment you'll be ready to get something running, and I'll describe tracklaying, two-rail wiring, and turnout controls on the Washita & Santa Fe. ✪

A. L. Schmidt

In the next installment in MODEL RAILROADER'S Washita & Santa Fe HO project railroad series, associate editor Andy Sperandeo will cover tracklaying, two-rail wiring, and turnout controls.

With track, added in this third installment of MODEL RAILROADER'S HO scale project layout, the Washita & Santa Fe starts to become a railroad.

Laying flextrack on the Washita & Santa Fe

THE WASHITA & SANTA FE RY. PART 3

Building for smooth running

BY ANDY SPERANDEO

TRACK on the Washita & Santa Fe project railroad is plastic-tie, nickel silver flextrack with ready-to-use turnouts. This track is easy to use, it goes down quickly, and it will give years of reliable service. When painted and weathered, as I'll explain later in this series, it's a match for the best handlaid track in appearance.

I used track with Code 70 rail, which means that the rails measure .070" from base to head. In HO scale this represents prototype rail weighing 100 pounds per yard. This is actually a bit lighter than the Santa Fe was using on the Northern Division main line in 1960, but the next step up in flextrack is Code 83. This is equivalent to prototype 132-pound rail, a little too heavy for the W&SF; more impor-

tantly, no one offers ready-to-use Code 83 turnouts.

I'd rather err on the side of undersized rail, which makes a train look more massive and looks better in finished scenes. Some modelers like to use even smaller rail for sidings and industrial spurs to accentuate the difference between these secondary tracks and the main line. I may try this at other places on the W&SF, but for

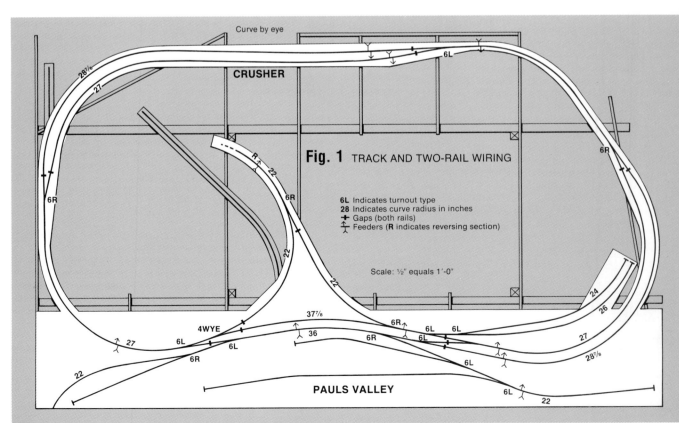

Curve by eye

CRUSHER

Fig. 1 TRACK AND TWO-RAIL WIRING

6L Indicates turnout type
28 Indicates curve radius in inches
✛ Gaps (both rails)
⟂ Feeders (**R** indicates reversing section)

Scale: ½" equals 1'-0"

4WYE

PAULS VALLEY

Fig. 2. Rail Craft flextrack has no spike holes, so you'll have to drill them yourself with a no. 70 bit. Hold a spike with pliers and start it into the roadbed, then close the jaws and push it home. Sighting down the rail is the best way to check for straightness and smooth curves as you work.

simplicity the first stage is all Code 70, and I'll use weathering and detailing to set off the side tracks at Pauls Valley.

BRANDS OF TRACK

I used flextrack made by Rail Craft Products, 2201 Atwater, St. Louis, MO 63133, with Shinohara turnouts imported by Lambert Associates, P. O. Box 4338, San Leandro, CA 94579. I probably would have used Shinohara flextrack except that it was temporarily out of stock when I was ready to start laying track.

I've been happy with the Rail Craft track, even though it doesn't have spike holes in its ties — it turns out that drilling them, as I'll show, isn't that much of a bother. Some modelers have told me that they're afraid that bending will pull the rail out of the small molded spike heads on the Rail Craft plastic tie strip. I didn't have that problem at all, and my only objection to Rail Craft track is that the line doesn't include ready-to-use turnouts.

Shinohara track has also given me very good results on other layouts, so I don't think you can go wrong whichever flextrack you choose. I do prefer Rail Craft's rail joiners and spikes — the joiners are a better design than Shinohara's, and the spikes have smaller heads that are more consistent in shape.

TRACKLAYING TOOLS

Most of the tools you need to work with flextrack are things you probably already have for model building, but I'll list them quickly in case this is new to you.

● Small needle-nose (or chain-nose) pliers, mainly for setting and pushing spikes.

● Rail nippers (flush cutting pliers). Lambert, Rail Craft, and PBL, P. O. Box 749, Chama, NM 87520, all offer nippers that I've used and been happy with.

● Needle files, for dressing and smoothing rail ends, and for adjusting turnouts. Flat and knife shapes are the most useful.

● Utility or mat knife. I prefer a heavy-duty knife for trimming plastic tie strip, which is often a very tough material.

● Soldering gun or iron, for soldering rail joints and feeders. Be sure to use resin-core solder, as rail joints are electrical connections and acid fluxes will corrode them.

● Hand motor tool, for drilling, cutting, and grinding. I use a Dremel no. 370 Moto-Tool because its built-in speed control is handy away from a workbench.

● Track gauges. A National Model Railroad Association (NMRA) standards gauge, available from Wm. K. Walthers and most hobby shops, is essential for checking turnouts and rail joints. Kadee no. 341 three-point track gauges are handy when you want to follow roadbed center lines carefully — they have pointers — and they also make good heatsinks if you're concerned about soldering to rails on plastic ties. Later I'll show you gauges you can make yourself to space parallel tracks.

TRACKLAYING TECHNIQUES

Tracklaying is essentially the repetition of a few basic techniques, so I'll describe those rather than take you around the layout rail joiner by rail joiner. You might also want to refer to fig. 8 in part two of the W&SF series, "A short course in laying flextrack" on page 71 of the March MODEL RAILROADER. The track plan here in fig. 1 shows which turnouts go where, and all the

Solder rail joints for electrical continuity and to maintain alignment. Solder joints on curves before bending to avoid kinks.

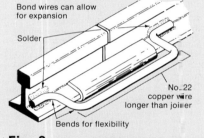

Fig. 3 SOLDERING RAIL JOINTS

track in between the turnouts is flextrack.

Figure 2 illustrates the procedure for spiking down track. Drill no. 70 holes in about every sixth tie, next to the outside base of each rail. I think this looks a bit neater than driving spikes next to the ties, and using the motor tool to drill a length of track at a time as you need it doesn't take very long. Make sure to drill the last tie left at each end of a section, as spiking these will help keep the joints aligned.

Start each spike by holding it in the jaws of the pliers, with the head towards the rail, and pushing it into the roadbed. Set the spike at a slight angle so the head will rest flat on the angled rail base. Then release the spike, close the pliers, and push the spike home with the nose of the pliers.

As you go, sight along the rail as I'm doing in the photo. This is just what the foreman of a real track gang does to check his work, and prototype or model it's the best way to get straight straightaways and smooth curves. You'll often be able to correct small irregularities just by pushing spikes to one side or another where they're already driven. Sometimes you'll have to drill a few holes and put in more spikes.

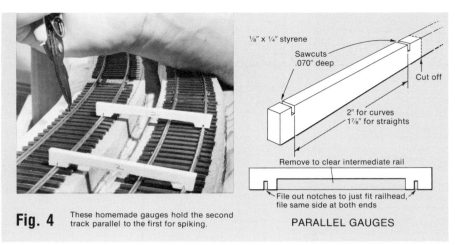

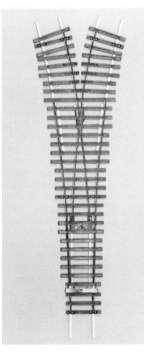

Fig. 4 These homemade gauges hold the second track parallel to the first for spiking.

⅛" × ¼" styrene

Sawcuts .070" deep

Cut off

2" for curves
1⅞" for straights

Remove to clear intermediate rail

File out notches to just fit railhead, file same side at both ends

PARALLEL GAUGES

Take special care to get mainline track straight and smoothly curved; you can relax a little on secondary tracks and spurs, but avoid kinks in curves and at joints where they can cause derailments.

Figure 3 shows how to handle rail joints: cut the ties back on each side of a joint (save the ties you cut off), trim the rails to meet squarely, join the rails with rail joiners, and solder the joiners to the outsides of the rails. Let the soldering gun tip heat up enough to melt solder, then touch the tip to the joiner and the side of the rail. Touch the solder to the rail, not to the tip, so that when the solder flows the rail will be hot enough for a good bond.

With a little practice and a clean, hot soldering tip, it's not hard to solder a joint so quickly that the plastic ties hardly get warm. In fact, if you do melt ties it's a sign

that either the work or the tip isn't clean, or that the tip isn't getting hot enough.

If you're still concerned about melting ties, place a Kadee no. 341 gauge on each side of the joint. The gauges will act as heatsinks and help protect the ties, and even if a tie does get a little too soft, the track will be held in gauge until it cools.

I soldered all my rail joints on the W&SF, and I haven't had any trouble with the track being forced out of alignment by expansion or contraction. If your railroad room is subject to extreme temperature changes, especially if it gets very hot, you may want to allow some freedom for expansion. In this case you should still solder joints on curves, but leave the joiners loose on straights, with a gap of up to ¹⁄₃₂" between rails. Unsoldered rail joiners are unreliable as conductors, so add a wire

bond as in fig. 3 for electrical continuity.

To make a smooth joint at the start of a curve, solder the joint before bending the flextrack, as I'm doing in the photo. Don't try to hold both ends of a section and pull it into a smooth curve. Start at the soldered end and bend just an inch or two at a time. Don't try to put in all the curvature you need at once; make two or three passes over a section to reach the final alignment.

Where a joint falls in a curve, leave the last 6 or 8 inches of the first track section straight. Fit the next section and solder the joint, then continue bending the flextrack to follow the roadbed.

As I said before, sight along the rail to see that the flextrack is taking a smooth curve. Also make sure not to stretch the tie strip so the ties lie diagonally between the rails. If the ties are very far from perpendicular they will narrow the gauge, besides looking just awful.

To properly space parallel tracks, use gauges like the ones shown in fig. 4. I made two pair of these, one for 2" spacing around curves, and one for 1⅞" spacing on straights (or very broad radius curves). The cutout in the center lets the gauges bridge the intermediate rail, but on superelevated curves it's still best to set the gauges on the outer, higher rails as shown.

Spike the main track in place first, then use the gauges to locate the parallel siding. You can't make the easements parallel if, as on the W&SF, you use different track center spacings for straights and curves: spot check the easements with a ruler to be sure you have smooth transitions between the narrow and wide centers.

FITTING TURNOUTS

Laying flextrack is really pretty simple.

Fig. 5. The north end of the Pauls Valley siding, right, is a good place to start fitting turnouts. Below, these underside views of the Shinohara no. 4 wye show it before, left, and after its ties are trimmed and its runners cut to fit the situation at Pauls Valley. At the lower right, notice how bending the turnout lead allows it to flow smoothly into the 22"-radius curve of the Gulf Jct. wye.

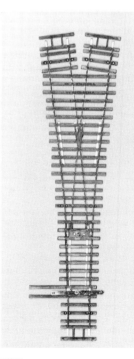

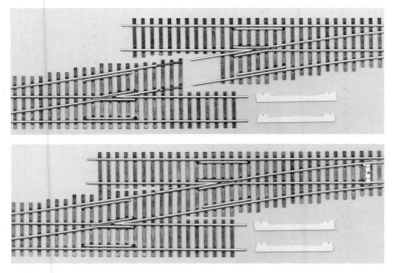

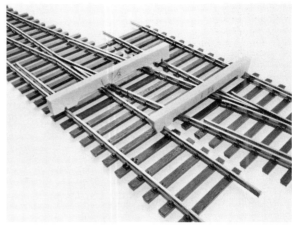

Fig. 6. Make the crossover from no. 6 turnouts: trim the ties and rails to let them overlap; check the spacing with parallel gauges.

The part of trackwork that's most likely to give an inexperienced modeler trouble is fitting the turnouts. The problems arise when you want to fit them closer together than the manufacturers allow for, or have them start curving a little sooner past the frog. The solution is just to cut the turnouts to fit the way you want them to, which isn't hard once you stop thinking of the molded tie base as a sacrosanct object.

On the Washita & Santa Fe I started laying track at the north turnout of the Pauls Valley passing siding. As you'll see in fig. 5, that meant that I started right in

squeezing turnouts together. The no. 4 wye turnout that splits into the Pauls Valley siding and the Gulf Jct. wye illustrates the necessary hacking and bending.

The before and after photos show how I trimmed ties at each end of the turnout (again, save the ties), and also how I cut out the runners between the ties under the stock rails. Cutting out the runners lets the turnout leads bend like flextrack, so I could make smooth curves into the passing track and wye. When you know which way you want the leads to bend, you only have to remove the runners on the inside of the

curve. I also trimmed the rails back farther when I put the turnout in place.

I've found that I can leave as few as two ties past the headblock — the long tie on either side of the throwbar — on the point end of a Shinohara turnout, and just one tie past the frog. All the others can be trimmed away without harming the turnout's mechanical integrity. Of course, when you have rail joints that close to the points and frog, you have to be sure the joints are smooth and in gauge to avoid derailments.

Other tight turnout locations at Pauls Valley merely require similar trimming and curving, except for the crossover in the foreground in the photo on page 116. If you just trim the ties and let the rails meet, two Shinohara turnouts make a crossover between parallel tracks on 2⁹⁄₁₆" centers. You could trim the rails too and make a conventional joint with rail joiners, but that would leave a couple of short lengths of rail in the middle of the crossover when you cut two-rail insulating gaps.

Figure 6 shows how I do it. I trim both rails and ties on both turnouts, but let the rails of one turnout overlap onto the ties of the other. The molded spike heads hold the overlapping rails in line, and the tie strip that's overlapped helps give a smooth track surface through the crossover.

I use my 1⁷⁄₈" parallel gauges to tell when I've trimmed the rails to the correct length, and then I cut the rails back a bit more to leave the insulating gaps shown in fig. 1. With the turnouts held in line by the gauges, I apply ACC to the overlapping rails and tie strip, to bond the crossover into a single unit.

FINISHING TOUCHES

In general Shinohara turnouts are very well made, but there are a few adjustments that will make them even better. Almost all of them are too wide in span, the distance between the guard rail and the heel of the frog. This can bind car and locomotive wheels, and cause a slow-moving engine to hesitate or stall.

Figure 7 shows how to check span with an NMRA gauge and how to correct it with a motor tool. The tightness is caused by plastic molded inside the rails at the heel of the frog, but Dremel no. 411 coarse sanding disks make quick work of removing this material. (Don't try to use cutting disks; the side pressure will shatter them.)

Check the span of Shinohara turnouts with an NMRA gauge. Most will need to be relieved with a sanding wheel or file.

Check span
Frog
Guard rails
Closure rail
Heel of point — **Check alignment**
Point
Headblocks
Throw bar
Stock rails — **Check fit and sharpness**

LEVELING DIPS
Fig. 7
TRACK ADJUSTMENTS
Dip in roadbed (exaggerated)
Cardboard shims, use as few or as many layers as needed, overlap layers

Fig. 8. Finish tracklaying by replacing ties at all rail joints. Regular ties can be recessed with a milling burr to give clearance below rail joiners.

There are some other potential trouble spots identified in fig. 7. Be sure that the points fit flush against the stock rails, and feather any blunt points with a file so they won't catch flanges. Also check that the point heels line up with the closure rails when the points are thrown. If they don't, file back whichever railhead sticks out where a flange might try to climb it.

Roll some cars along your track to see if they ride smoothly. If they seem to sink and sway in some spots, sight along the rail looking for vertical dips. These are easy to eliminate now by shimming as in fig. 7 — I like to cut up the Lambert turnout boxes for shims — but you want to spot and correct all dips before ballasting the track. Where cars rock or don't lean steadily on banked curves, shim just under one rail to smooth things out.

To finish up the trackwork, use the ties you've cut from flextrack and turnouts to fill in under all the rail joints. There should be enough of the recessed ties from the ends of turnouts and track sections to take care of most joints, but you'll need to cut recesses into several of the regular ties to finish up completely.

The recesses keep the ties from lifting the rail joiners and causing humps in the track. I used a Dremel no. 194 cutter in the motor tool to cut the recesses, as in fig. 8. The plastic ties are just tough enough to cut with a knife that the power tool saves a lot of time. Slip the ties under the joints; a little white glue or gap-filling ACC will keep them in place until ballasting.

GAPS AND FEEDERS

Figure 1 shows all the necessary two-rail-wiring insulating gap and power feeder locations for the W&SF. The gaps are just that, slices in both rails at each indicated location made with a carborundum cutoff disk in the motor tool — see fig. 9. Be sure to wear safety glasses while using cutoff disks, as the disks shatter easily.

I like to cut gaps close to the frogs of switches, so that trains or cars left standing on sidings won't bridge the gaps and cause short circuits. This also lets you cut the rail where the solid runners between the switch ties will help hold it in alignment; cut through the rail but try to leave the runner intact.

So far I haven't had much trouble with gaps closing due to rail creep, but it's a good idea to guard against this as it can cause especially mystifying shorts. Figure 9 shows a good way to protect gaps with strip styrene and fast-setting epoxy.

I won't go into wiring the W&SF until the next installment of this series, coming up in the September MR, but I expect that if you're building along with me you'll be impatient to get a train running on your new trackwork. You can install feeders as in fig. 9, connect them all with jumpers for each rail (skip the reversing section on the tail of the wye), and attach a power pack to the jumpers to get something running.

TURNOUT CONTROLS

One of the first things you'll notice when

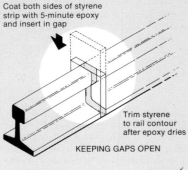

Cut gaps with an abrasive cutoff disk. Cut through the rail but not the tie-strip runner, as the runner helps keep the rails in line.

Coat both sides of styrene strip with 5-minute epoxy and insert in gap

Trim styrene to rail contour after epoxy dries

KEEPING GAPS OPEN

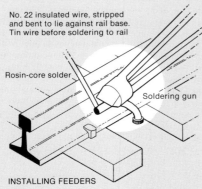

No. 22 insulated wire, stripped and bent to lie against rail base. Tin wire before soldering to rail

Rosin-core solder

Soldering gun

INSTALLING FEEDERS

Fig. 9 GAPS AND FEEDERS

Bill of materials

Track (Code 70 nickel silver):
- 32   Rail Craft FH7 3-foot sections flextrack (or 30 Lambert no. 315 1-meter sections)
- 9*   Lambert no. 303 no. 6 left turnouts
- 6*   Lambert no. 304 no. 6 right turnouts
- 1*   Lambert no. 307 no. 4 wye turnout

    Rail Craft RJ70 rail joiners
    Rail Craft SP2 spikes

* 1 less if you purchased turnouts listed in part 2

Turnout controls:
- 15   Centralab PA-1011 4-pole, 2-pos. nonshorting rotary switches
- 15   Raytheon no. 70-5-2G control knobs
- 2   GB Electronics Turnout Motors

    K&S no. 125 1/16"-o.d. brass tube
    K&S no. 126 3/32"-o.d. brass tube
    K&S no. 155 1/4"-sq. brass tube
    K&S no. 501 .032"-dia. steel wire
    K&S no. 504 .064"-dia. steel wire

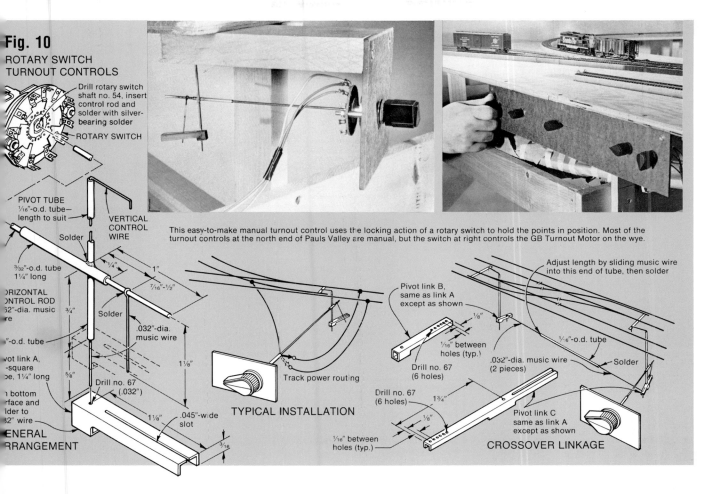

Fig. 10

ROTARY SWITCH TURNOUT CONTROLS

Drill rotary switch shaft no. 54, insert control rod and solder with silver-bearing solder

ROTARY SWITCH

PIVOT TUBE
1/16"-o.d. tube—length to suit

VERTICAL CONTROL WIRE

Solder

3/32"-o.d. tube 1 1/4" long

ORIZONTAL ONTROL ROD 32"-dia. music re

1/4"   1"

7/16"-1/2"

3/4"

Solder

.032"-dia. music wire

"-o.d. tube

ot link A, -square e, 1 1/4" long

1 1/8"

bottom face and der to 32" wire

5/8"

Drill no. 67 (.032")

ENERAL RRANGEMENT

1 1/8"   .045"-wide slot

3/16

Track power routing

TYPICAL INSTALLATION

This easy-to-make manual turnout control uses the locking action of a rotary switch to hold the points in position. Most of the turnout controls at the north end of Pauls Valley are manual, but the switch at right controls the GB Turnout Motor on the wye.

Adjust length by sliding music wire into this end of tube, then solder

Pivot link B, same as link A except as shown

1/8"

1/16" between holes (typ.)

Drill no. 67 (6 holes)

.032"-dia. music wire (2 pieces)

1/16"-o.d. tube

Solder

Drill no. 67 (6 holes)

1 3/4"

1/8"

1/16" between holes (typ.)

Pivot link C same as link A except as shown

CROSSOVER LINKAGE

you run an engine is that the Shinohara turnouts don't do a very good job of conducting current when their points aren't held in place. You'll want to install some kind of switch-throw mechanism in short order. Having spent a lot of time under layouts trying to maintain many kinds of switch machines, I have to say that I'm not overly fond of the little beasties. Still, I wanted to use something that would let me throw turnouts from the edge of the benchwork and provide switching contacts to route power around the points.

Gordon Odegard to the rescue! In the March 1981 MR, Gordy's article "Simple turnout control" showed how to use the locking action of a rotary switch to throw turnouts — see fig. 10. These controls are simple and reliable, and only take about as long to build and install as an under-table switch machine linkage. I used a rotary switch with more contacts than Gordy's, in case I get around to installing signals on the W&SF; it's also nonshorting, so there's one less modification to bother with.

When you use one of Gordy's controls for a crossover, do be sure that the control wires connect to the plastic throw bars outside the rails, as in fig. 10. I attached mine in the rivets in the metal straps between the points, which caused a dead short through the linking rod until I made insu-

lating bushings for the under-table cranks.

At Pauls Valley I mounted the rotary switches in Masonite panels screwed to 1 x 1s at the edge of the subroadbed, with each switch directly in front of the set of points it controls. The switch centers are 2 1/16" below the top of the subroadbed, which allows the horizontal control rods to clear trains on the Gainesville loop.

Later, when I install fascia or profile boards around the edges of the layout, I'll cut openings in them to let the switch panels show through. That way I'll be able to remove the fascia without disturbing the turnout controls. Away from the Pauls Valley tabletop, I screwed short lengths of 1 x 4 beneath the subroadbed to support small Masonite panels.

There are only two turnouts that can't conveniently be operated by Gordy's turnout controls: the one at the tail of the wye and the one back along the wall at the end of the Crusher siding. I've installed a GB Electronics Turnout Motor on the wye according to the manufacturer's instructions. This screw-drive device has enough auxiliary contacts to control the reversing section on the tail track, and also to be operated with the same kind of rotary switch that controls the other turnouts. I haven't installed one on the siding yet, but I'll probably use another GB Turnout Motor.

What I'm after is the decentralization of control functions. I like to operate by moving along with the train, taking advantage of the walkaround possibilities of command control. If you're tied to a control panel you can't appreciate how nice your trains look gliding over all that carefully laid track, so the Washita & Santa Fe will make it easy to enjoy the trains from up close. ☼

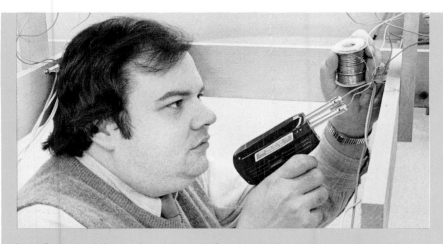

In the September MR, associate editor Andy Sperandeo will explain how to install wiring and command control in the fourth installment of the Washita & Santa Fe project railroad series.

Gordon Odegard tries out a walkaround command control throttle on the Washita & Santa Fe project railroad.

Santa Fe

Wiring the Washita & Santa Fe

Preparing for and installing command control

BY ANDY SPERANDEO

WIRING the Washita & Santa Fe is a fairly easy proposition, because the railroad uses command control. Among its other advantages, command control keeps the layout wiring simple, so there's less wiring work to do on and under the layout. Installing receivers in the locomotives is the most demanding part of the job, but that can be done in comfort and convenience at your workbench.

TWO-RAIL WIRING

Command control doesn't alter the rules of gap and feeder location in basic two-rail wiring, so that's where we start. Figure 1 shows the gaps and feeders for the first stage of the W&SF. I won't go into the details of two-rail wiring here; if you'd like to understand why the gaps and feeders are where they are, see my All Aboard article, "Two-rail wiring," in the March 1981 MODEL RAILROADER. Placed as shown, the gaps and feeders prevent short circuits with the power-routing turnouts, isolate the reversing section at the tail of the Gulf Jct. wye, and allow complete freedom in train and engine movements.

Two other factors influenced where I put the gaps and feeders. I kept the gaps closer to the turnout frogs than the "fouling point," where rolling stock on one leg of a turnout won't clear a movement on the other leg. This avoids the possibility of a short circuit across the gap through a metal car or engine wheel — if a car or engine is left clear of the fouling point, it's also clear of the gaps.

I also located feeders close to risers, so there would be a convenient place to put a small terminal strip under the roadbed at feeder locations. As fig. 2 shows, between sets of gaps you have a good deal of leeway in just where you attach the feeders, so it's not hard to do this and you'll soon see how it helps.

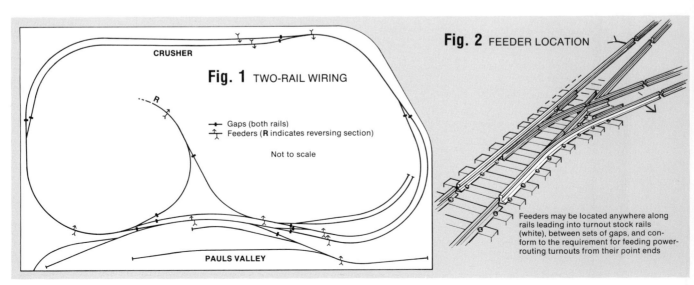

Fig. 1 TWO-RAIL WIRING

CRUSHER

R

—•— Gaps (both rails)
—↓— Feeders (R indicates reversing section)

Not to scale

PAULS VALLEY

Fig. 2 FEEDER LOCATION

Feeders may be located anywhere along rails leading into turnout stock rails (white), between sets of gaps, and conform to the requirement for feeding power-routing turnouts from their point ends

g. 3. Insulating gaps. Cut gaps over turnout tie strip, as in the photo at left, maintain rail alignment. Epoxy styrene strip fillers into the gaps, above left photo. Trim and file the fillers to match the rails, above center photo. Once you've painted the track, as in the above right photo, the fillers will disappear.

g. 4. Soldering feeders. Drill a hole for the feeder next to the outside base the rail, as at left. Bend the stripped and tinned feeder to shape as shown above left. Hold the feeder in place, above center, and heat the *rail*. Again, the feeder won't be very noticeable when you've painted the track, above right.

GAPS AND FEEDERS

In the last W&SF installment, back in the May MR, I showed how to cut and fill gaps, and how to solder feeder wires, but I'm including figs. 3 and 4 here to refresh your memory. The gaps can be cut with an abrasive disk and simply left open, but filling them with styrene as shown ensures that they won't "grow" together with rail expansion. I've left most of mine open on the W&SF, but if your railroad will be subjected to a wide range of temperatures, you'd do well to fill all your gaps.

I "tin" each feeder, or coat it with solder, before soldering it to the rail. Then I apply a little liquid rosin flux to the side of the rail and hold the feeder in place with an aluminum soldering aid. Never use an acid flux, even one labeled "noncorrosive," for soldering electrical connections.

I use a 140-watt soldering gun and apply the tip to the rail, not to the wire. When the rail is hot enough to melt solder, the solder from the tinned feeder flows onto the fluxed area of the rail, making a strong,

neat joint. Remember, there's no need to worry about melting plastic ties if the soldering tip is hot and the work, both feeder and rail, is clean.

The feeder wires themselves are no. 22 insulated wire. I used stranded wire for flexibility, and I tinned the stripped end of each feeder before bending it to shape so the solder would keep the strands from separating. This makes the feeder connections about as neat and inoffensive as they'd be with solid wire.

The simple wiring needed for command control lends itself to simple color coding. I used yellow wire for all the outside rail feeders, the ones represented by arrow tails in fig. 1, and green wire for the inside rail feeders, the ones represented by arrowheads. With this code established, all I had to remember when working under the railroad was to connect yellow wires to yellow wires, and green to green.

I used the yellow/green code also for wiring around turnout points, but added to the code as in fig. 5 by using blue wire for the frog feeders. This made it easy to tell

where each went when looking up at them from underneath.

POWER BUSSES

Good performance from command control systems demands heavier than ordinary power wiring. The no. 22 feeders are just short lengths dropped through the roadbed; underneath they connect at terminal strips to no. 14 power busses. Fig. 6 shows how I routed these around the layout and joined them to the feeders.

I used the same yellow/green code for the power busses to keep everything straight, but if you really want to make sure, you can test with a power pack as you go. Connect the pack to the power-bus screw terminals and run an engine into each new section as you connect its feeders to the busses. If the engine crosses the gaps and continues smoothly into the new section, your wiring is okay so far and you can move on to the next set of feeders.

The tail track of the wye is a special case, because it's a reversing section. I wired its feeders through the GB Turnout

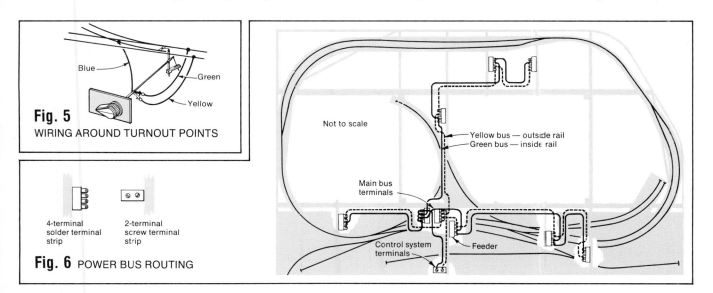

Fig. 5 WIRING AROUND TURNOUT POINTS

Blue — Green — Yellow

4-terminal solder terminal strip

2-terminal screw terminal strip

Fig. 6 POWER BUS ROUTING

Not to scale

Yellow bus — outside rail
Green bus — inside rail

Main bus terminals

Control system terminals — Feeder

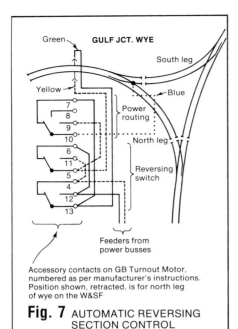

GULF JCT. WYE

Green

Yellow

South leg

Blue

Power routing

7
8
9
10
6
11
5
4
12
13

North leg

Reversing switch

Feeders from power busses

Accessory contacts on GB Turnout Motor, numbered as per manufacturer's instructions. Position shown, retracted, is for north leg of wye on the W&SF.

Fig. 7 AUTOMATIC REVERSING SECTION CONTROL

Motor's auxiliary contacts as shown in fig. 7, so that the reversing section's polarity is automatically changed whenever I throw the turnout.

I'm sure my wiring isn't neat enough to impress any master electricians, but since it isn't meant to be seen anyway, my only concerns are to keep it trouble-free and out of the way. Here's a rundown of my methods, some of them shown in figs. 6 and 8:

• I use terminal strips under every set of feeders and at the main bus connections, to keep the heavy wiring from hanging from the rails or from splices.

• Between terminals I use bits of electrical tape to gather wires into loose cables.

• I use large cup hooks to hang the wiring along the L girders and joists; these keep the wires out of the open spaces to allow easy access, and they also make it easy to make changes.

• I leave a few inches of slack at each end of a run of wire, so any wire can be moved if it later turns out to be in the way.

When you've done everything I've explained so far it'll be a good time to hook up a power pack to the screw terminals

and run a train for a while. Besides being enjoyable and a nice break from soldering wires, this will give you a chance to make sure that everything so far works. If you run into problems later on, you'll have them isolated to the extent that you'll know your track and power wiring is okay.

FASCIA AND HOUSE CURRENT

There are a couple of other things to take care of before you'll be ready to install a control system. The Washita & Santa Fe won't ever have a large central control panel, as I've explained before. Most of the controls will be mounted on the layout's fascia or profile board, so you'll need to put up at least part of the fascia at this time. Figure 9 shows how I installed the fascia along the Pauls Valley side of the W&SF.

The fascia is ⅛"-thick tempered Masonite — mine is smooth on both sides but the kind with one rough side would be just as good. I made it 14¼" deep so it extends to the same level as the bottoms of the L girders, and mounted it with screws so I could remove it if necessary without damage.

When you cut the fascia strips from 4 x 8-foot sheet Masonite, plan how you'll hang it on the layout to make the best use of the original machine-cut edges. I wanted a smooth, straight edge along the front of the Pauls Valley scene, so I used the original edge there, and I also used two original edges where the strips have to be spliced.

I saber-sawed cutouts for the turnout controls and tried to make them neat and straight, but I was disappointed with the wavy edges I ended up with. The ⅛" Northeastern basswood angle makes a nice molding, however, and gives the cutouts a finished look. Eventually I'll paint the fascia, probably with an earth tone to match the scenery, but since I'm bound to mess it up when I scenic the railroad, it's better left unpainted for now.

Finally, I screwed a six-socket power panel to the benchwork leg under Gulf Jct. wye, and wired it through a wall-type switch mounted in the fascia as in fig. 10. This gives me a convenient place to plug in power supplies and an easy way to turn the whole railroad on and off. Be sure to consult an expert if you're unfamiliar with house-current wiring.

COMMAND CONTROL

At this point you can install any com-

Bill of materials

Qty.	Item
	No. 22 green stranded wire
	No. 22 yellow stranded wire
	No. 22 blue stranded wire
	No. 14 green stranded wire
	No. 14 yellow stranded wire
9	4-terminal solder terminal strips
1	2-terminal screw terminal strip
	Large cup hooks
	Electrical tape
	No. 6 x ½ roundhead wood screws for mounting terminal strips
1	4 x 8 sheet ⅛" tempered Masonite
	No. 8 x ¾ panhead sheet metal screws for mounting fascia
	⅛" Northeastern milled basswood angle
1	Wall switch with pilot light
1	Switch box for above
1	Wall switch plate
1	6-socket power panel
1	Heavy-duty grounded extension cord, length to suit
	Digipac 316 command control system:
1	321-3 control station
1	322-2 power station
1	334 wall plug transformer
2	or more walkaround cabs
3	or more 345-18 selector plug receptacles
1	receiver and 1 matching channel selector plug per locomotive
	Floquil Polly S Grimy Black
	Floquil Polly S Dirt
	Rubbing alcohol

mand control system and connect it to the power bus screw terminals; the railroad wiring described here will work with any system. Command control lets you make the whole railroad electrically continuous, as I've done here, and control trains independently with signals sent through the rails to uniquely coded receivers installed in the locomotives. Put another way, it lets you control trains directly, rather than controlling the track as with cab control.

If you wanted to use cab control on the

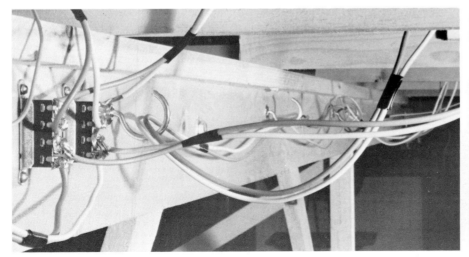
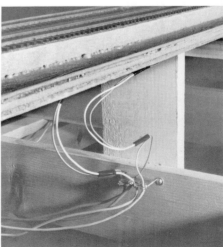

Figure 8. Wiring technique. Left: wiring under Pauls Valley, with main bus terminals at left. Right: wiring under Crusher siding, with feeder terminals.

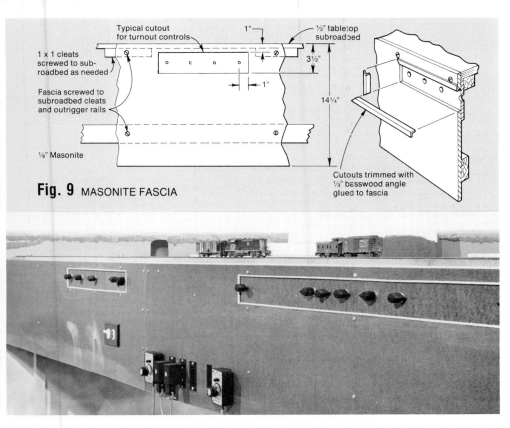

Fig. 9 MASONITE FASCIA

Typical cutout for turnout controls

1 x 1 cleats screwed to subroadbed as needed

Fascia screwed to subroadbed cleats and outrigger rails

⅛" Masonite

1"

½" tabletop subroadbed

3½"

14¼"

1"

Cutouts trimmed with ⅛" basswood angle glued to fascia

The Masonite fascia at Pauls Valley, with train controls, turnout control cutouts, and master switch.

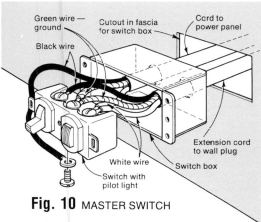

Fig. 10 MASTER SWITCH

Green wire — ground

Black wire

Cutout in fascia for switch box

Cord to power panel

Extension cord to wall plug

Switch box

White wire

Switch with pilot light

Finish the installation by adding a switch plate.

W&SF, you could consider every stretch of track between gaps in fig. 1 to be a control block and wire the blocks as John Olson did in Part 3 of the Jerome & Southwestern series in the June MODEL RAILROADER. The only thing you'd have to do differently from what I've described would be to run individual feeders to at least one rail of each block from your cab control panel, rather than wiring the feeders to busses.

You'd do well to think again about command control, however, because it's better suited to the W&SF and because it's a more enjoyable way to run trains. The Washita & Santa Fe is designed for walk-around control so that you can follow the trains around and enjoy them up close. That's not impossible with conventional methods, but it's a lot easier when you don't have to worry about keeping cabs linked to blocks with selector switches.

Also, command control is the way we've always wanted to run our trains since our first model railroads. The throttle you use to run an engine controls that engine directly, and controls no other. You can give all your attention to the train and the scene, and ignore the control system while you use it.

Finally, command control is ideal if, like me, you like realistic operation. With the locomotives under truly independent control, you can work out switching moves and passing manuvers just as on the prototype, without having to worry about keeping trains or engines electrically isolated.

I had originally planned to control the W&SF with Keith Gutierrez's CTC-16 command control system, described in MODEL RAILROADER in the December 1979 through April 1980 issues, with additional information in the December 1980 MR. That's a good system, and a good choice for the Washita & Santa Fe if you don't mind building it yourself.

When I reached this point on the railroad, however, I didn't have time to build my own CTC-16, and Russ Larson suggested that it might be better in any case to use a system that anyone could purchase. That's why the W&SF has a commercial command control system, the Digi-

Fig. 11. Digipac 316 installation. In the photo above, the power station is at upper right, the control station below it, and the transformer in the upper center. To the left in the same photo are the six-socket power panel and an MRC power pack for turnout motor power. The photo to the left shows the throttles and channel selector plugs, and the one below a no. 327-3 receiver in an Athearn GP7.

pac 316 by Mann-Made Products. (See the review in this month's Trade Topics.)

Before discussing the Digipac 316, I'd like to mention a couple of other systems that you might want to consider. Our Kalmbach employees' club railroad, the Milwaukee, Racine & Troy, has been operating for about 2 years now with the Dynatrol command control system manufactured by Power Systems Inc. We've been very happy with its performance and have the greatest confidence in it; if a train won't run on the MR&T it's the operator and not the control system that's at fault. Dynatrol was covered in my "Command control comparison" review article in the April 1980 MODEL RAILROADER.

Also, if you like sound effects, including not just diesel noise but controllable horns and bells as well, you'll find that the Onboard command control and sound system by Keller Engineering is the only system currently available that offers full sound features. Russ reviewed Onboard sound and control in Trade Topics in our December 1981 issue.

These are both systems with cab and receiver arrangements that would suit the Washita & Santa Fe. Again, any command control system could be connected to the W&SF's bus terminals; no system that I'm aware of would require any change in the layout wiring.

DIGIPAC 316

I chose the Mann-Made system because I'd seen it perform successfully on Allen McClelland's Virginian & Ohio railroad, because it's really just a ready-to-use version of the CTC-16, and because I wanted to learn about a system I hadn't used before. The Digipac 316 worked correctly the first time I hooked it up, and so far I've found no faults with it.

Digipac incorporates a memory walkaround feature, called "Plugaround," which allows you to get a train started and then unplug the handheld cab, so you can follow a train around the railroad. This feature especially makes the Digipac well suited to the W&SF's walkaround design. So far I have throttle-plug sockets only on the Pauls Valley side of the W&SF, but when I expand the layout I'll add more every few feet around the aisle.

Figure 11 shows the main features of the W&SF's Digipac installation: the power and command stations under the benchwork, the cabs and plugs on the layout fascia, and a receiver installed in an Athearn GP7. The power transformer is plugged into the power panel controlled by the main switch.

I added Velcro hook-and-loop fastener strips to the backs of the throttles and the fascia. This is a convenient way to hang

Painting the track is the first step in scenicking.

any handheld throttle without hooks or other projections that might snag clothing. These fastener strips with self-adhesive backing are available from Radio Shack, catalog no. 64-2345.

The numbers on the channel plugs are Digipac channel numbers. I plan to add engine numbers to these, so the engine number will be all I'll need to match a plug with a locomotive.

The locomotive is an Athearn GP7 with the receiver wired as per Mann-Made's instructions. This installation does take a little adjustment and modification as in the following steps:

1. Be sure that the locomotive runs well on regular DC power, and that its current drain is within the receiver's capacity — ½ amp continuous load and 1 amp slipping or starting for the Digipac receiver. You might also want to replace the wheels with North-West Short Line's no. 7140-4 nickel-plated wheels in the interest of better contact.

2. Discard the silver-colored contact strap on top of the motor and solder a length of flexible wire to the two truck contacts. You'll also need a place to connect a wire to the frame. I drilled and tapped for a 00-90 screw at one side of the rear frame bolster, but you could use the original headlight mounting bracket, which I removed, for a solder connection.

3. Remove the motor and insulate it from the frame by removing the contact fingers on the bottom brush clip and by covering the frame between the motor-mount holes with electrical tape. Before reinstalling the motor, solder a length of wire to the bottom brush clip to serve as a receiver connection — I find it best to remove the clip for soldering so as not to melt the plastic motor parts.

4. On the Digipac receiver the two blue wires are for track pickup. Solder one to one of the truck contacts, and attach the other to the frame.

5. The red and black receiver wires go to the motor. My unit runs in directions that match the cab reversing switch with the red wire attached to the top brush clip and the black to the bottom. A capacitor, not shown, can be installed across the brushes, or between the red and black wires, to reduce electrical "noise" from the motor.

6. Insulate any wire splices with electrical tape or heat-shrink tubing — I use Modeltronics no. 3010 tubing. Install the receiver in the top of the body with double-faced foam tape, and make sure that all the wiring is out of the way of flywheels and other moving parts.

PAINTING TRACK

Once you've gotten everything running the way you want it to, and are sure that all the track feeders are in place and working, its time to paint the track. Ready-to-use turnouts and flextrack are really very nice-looking, but silver rails and shiny plastic tie strip just don't have the earthy look of real railroad track. I sprayed the track on the W&SF with Floquil Polly S flat paints and cleaned off the railheads after the paint had set.

Before spraying I cut narrow strips of masking tape and used short lengths of it to protect the contact faces of all switch points and stock rails. Then I sprayed the track with an airbrush using three Polly S colors: Grimy Black on the main line; Dirt on the Pauls Valley industrial tracks; and a half-and-half mixture of Grimy Black and Dirt for the passing sidings, wye, and yard tracks.

For airbrushing use a spray mix of three parts Polly S to two parts rubbing alcohol. Be sure to spray each length of track from at least three angles, so you'll be sure to cover all the corners and overhangs.

When the paint has set, in about 15 to 20 minutes, remove the masking tape and clean off the railheads and inside corners of the running rails with an abrasive track cleaner. This gives the track an overall grungy look that's both pretty good as-is and a good base for detail weathering. ✿

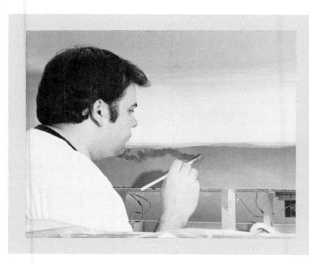

Associate editor Andy Sperandeo will show you how to put up and paint a free-standing backdrop on the Washita & Santa Fe project railroad, coming soon in the November issue of MODEL RAILROADER.

With an easy-to-paint backdrop, the Washita & Santa Fe starts to look scenic even before any scenery is in place.

A backdrop for the Washita & Santa Fe

The "layered landscape" method makes it easy

BY ANDY SPERANDEO

I DIDN'T know if I could paint a backdrop before I painted this one for the Washita & Santa Fe. But I knew the railroad needed a backdrop to define and separate its scenes, and to give them a photogenic background. I was surprised at how easy it was to do and how well it came out, and I'm sure that you can enjoy the same success with the methods I used.

You'll notice that you can't see much detail on the W&SF backdrop, and that effect is quite intentional. I wanted to suggest enough of the rolling plains of Oklahoma to give the feeling of wide-open spaces, but without making the backdrop so interesting that it would draw your attention away from the railroad. For the same reason I didn't try to paint clouds in my sky, but simply blended white into the blue to give the feeling that there is a sky above the trains you're watching.

Keeping the backdrop simple contributes a lot to its good effect, and of course I expect it to look even better when there's modeled scenery in the foreground. Its simplicity certainly made it easier to paint, as did the layout's height. Because the W&SF is up near eye level, I needed only a narrow strip of painted landscape just below the horizon. See fig. 1.

SOMETHING TO PAINT

I used ⅛" tempered Masonite to make a free-standing backdrop for the W&SF. This material is rigid enough to stand alone with support only at its bottom edge, especially when it's curved, as at the north end of the Pauls Valley scene, or when two sheets are laminated together, as at the south end of the scene.

Figure 2 shows the position of the backdrop and the arrangement of the Masonite

---

Fig. 1 BACKDROP DIMENSIONS

Top of backdrop: 81" above floor

Eye level: 67½" for Andy Sperandeo

Horizon: 62" (19" below top)

24"

Possible scenery contour

Bottom of backdrop: 57" above floor

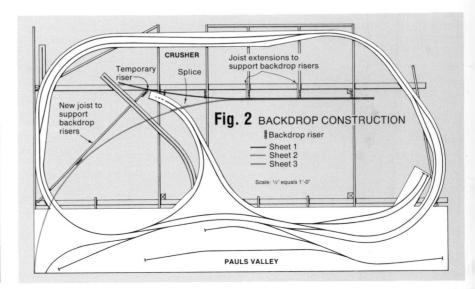

CRUSHER

Temporary riser

Splice

Joist extensions to support backdrop risers

New joist to support backdrop risers

Fig. 2 BACKDROP CONSTRUCTION

Backdrop riser
— Sheet 1
— Sheet 2
— Sheet 3

Scale: ½" equals 1'-0"

PAULS VALLEY

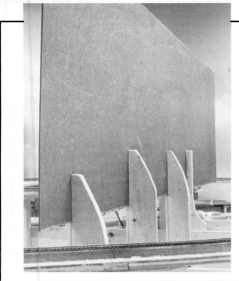

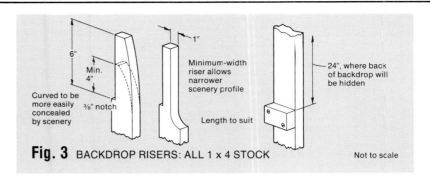

Fig. 3 BACKDROP RISERS: ALL 1 x 4 STOCK — Not to scale

6" — Min. 4" — Curved to be more easily concealed by scenery — ³⁄₈" notch

Minimum-width riser allows narrower scenery profile — 1" — Length to suit

24", where back of backdrop will be hidden

The risers for backdrop sheet 1, left, are tapered so they'll be easier to hide under scenery.

The tall risers, below left, will support sheet 2 as it curves to the north end of Pauls Valley. Below, sheet 2 installed with blocks to help hold the curve at right, and the free end of sheet 1 at left. Notice the diagonal joist supporting the center riser.

sheets. I may not have painted a backdrop before, but I've built others like this, and I have confidence in this kind of construction.

I sawed the 4 x 8-foot sheets of Masonite into 2 x 8 strips. With the bottom edge of the Masonite resting on top of the Pauls Valley subroadbed, the backdrop stands 81¼" off the floor. It could be lower if your ceiling height is less, but in general the further it extends above your eye level the better the effect.

When you're ready to put up your backdrop, it's a good idea to get one or two friends to lend their hands, as you'll have long, flexible strips of Masonite to manhandle over your track. We have lots of talented help around the MR offices, and I shanghaied Gordy Odegard and Allen Keller.

I installed the backdrop sheets in nu-merical order as indicated in fig. 2, after first attaching the backdrop risers shown in fig. 3 to the joists. I used a level to be sure that the notches where the backdrop rests are the same height as Pauls Valley and in a straight line with each other.

Next I applied white glue (Elmer's Glue All) to the vertical notches in the risers, and set sheet 1 in place with the original, machine-cut edge to the top. I reinforced the glue joints with flathead wood screws, using a counter-sink pilot drill and driving the screws flush with the Masonite, then got ready to add sheets 2 and 3.

I spliced sheets 2 and 3 before installing them, since the splice came at a point in midair. After installing the risers for sheet 2, and protecting the track with scraps of Homasote, Gordy and Allen helped me

with setting sheet 2 in place and estimating the length of sheet 3.

Next we laid sheet 2 face down on a flat table. It's true that both sides of this 2 x 8 piece were still really the same, but I started thinking in terms of the face that would show on the layout at this point, to be sure I was making the best use of the material. I wanted a machine edge along the top of sheets 2 and 3, and machine ends on both sheets at the splice.

As fig. 4 shows, I slipped a length of waxed paper under the splice end of sheet 3 and C-clamped the Masonite to the table, allowing room for about 18" of sheet 3 to also rest on the table. I cut sheet 3 to the estimated length plus about 12", carefully aligned it for a butt joint with sheet 2, and clamped it to the table. Both sheets hung

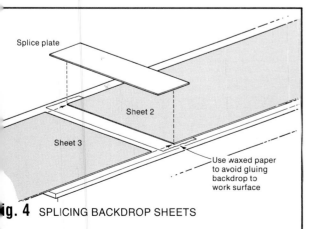

Splice plate

Sheet 2

Sheet 3

Use waxed paper to avoid gluing backdrop to work surface

Fig. 4 SPLICING BACKDROP SHEETS

Fig. 5. Clamping the backdrop. Here MR associate editor Andy Sperandeo gets an-other chance to enjoy his favorite hobby-within-the-hobby: C-clamping. Notice the short 1 x 2s clamped horizontally to hold the top edge of the laminated section.

At right are the things you need to
paint a sky backdrop: sky blue la...
paint (Sears Larkspur here), flat wh...
latex paint, paint roller and pan, a...
a wide brush. Farther right are s...
plies for painting layered landsca...
Mars Black, Chromium Oxide Gre...
and Green Gold artists' acrylic colo...
acrylic matte medium; and both...
and round brushes. Art supply sto...
and some hobby shops handle the...
ists' items; check your Yellow Pag...
under "Artists' Materials & Supplie...

Fig. 6. Painting the sky. After brushing blue paint across the top third of the backdrop, Andy brushes white up from the bottom and blends the two colors using long, horizontal strokes.

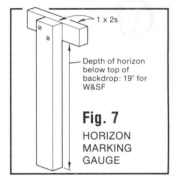

1 x 2s

Depth of horizon below top of backdrop: 19" for W&SF

Fig. 7
HORIZON MARKING GAUGE

Fig. 8. Layered landscape — beginnings. Here are the first two layers of landscape color added to the painted sky, Horizon Blue along the horizon and Distant Green below or in front.

Fig. 9. Layered landscape — finished. From the horizon down the color layers are: Horizon Blue, Distant Green, Tree Green, Tree Shadow, and Grass Gold. The brushwork isn't delicate, but it's good enough for the overall effect.

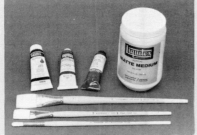

BACKDROP COLORS

Sky Blue:
    Sears Larkspur
White:
    any flat white latex paint
Horizon Blue:
    3 cups White
    1 cup Sky Blue
    6″ Mars Black
Distant Green:
    3 tablespoons Horizon Blue
    9″ Chromium Oxide Green
    ½ teaspoon matte medium
Closer Green:
    1 teaspoon Horizon Blue
    1 teaspoon matte medium
    3″ Chromium Oxide Green

Grass Yellow:
    2″ Green Gold
    2″ Chromium Oxide Green
    1 teaspoon matte medium
Tree Green:
    1 teaspoon Horizon Blue
    1 teaspoon matte medium
    2″ Chromium Oxide Green
    2″ Green Gold
Tree Shadow:
    9″ Chromium Oxide Green
    6″ Green Gold
    1″ Mars Black
    1 tablespoon matte medium

off at the ends, but I supported them with stools and sawhorses to keep the joint as flat as possible.

The splice plate is a piece of Masonite 24″ long — I made mine 6″ wide, but 8″ to 9″ would be better. After applying white glue to the splice plate, I clamped it over the splice using scrap lumber to distribute the pressure evenly. I let the assembly sit for 24 hours, so the glue would be thoroughly dry before we put any stress on the splice.

After the splice had dried, we lifted sheets 2 and 3 into place temporarily, to locate the holes where the main line and wye tracks pass through the backdrop. Then we laid these sheets down again, and I cut out openings roughly 3¼″ wide and 3¾″ high. Another dry fitting of sheets 2 and 3 let me check the openings with an NMRA standards gauge — allowing for a little extra clearance width on curves — and then we were ready for the gluing.

With Allen and Gordy standing by for quick action, I brushed full-strength white glue onto the back side of sheet 1, and the risers for sheets 2 and 3. Then we put sheets 2 and 3 in place for the last time, and clamped them tightly to sheet 1 and the risers. Figure 5 shows how I used scrap lumber and lots of C-clamps to hold everything together. Where the sheets are laminated it's important to keep the edges tight together, especially at the top and ends.

For extra reinforcement I drove panhead screws through the lamination and into the risers, keeping them low so they wouldn't show above the scenery later. I also glued short 1 x 1 blocks to both the Pauls Valley subroadbed and the back of sheet 2, as shown in fig. 3, to help hold the curve at that end.

I let the backdrop dry under clamp pressure for another 24 hours, then removed the clamps and trimmed off the extra length I'd left on sheet 1 with a saber saw. The joint between sheets 2 and 3 was very tight, but just to be sure I applied spackling compound with a putty knife and sanded it smooth when dry. It's very hard to see the splice on the painted backdrop.

I had the advantage of a good-sized room to move around in, so splicing and handling a strip of Masonite over 14 feet long wasn't too big a problem. If your space is more restricted, the way to go after getting sheet 1 in place would be to add sheet 3 alone. Add sheet 2 only after the lamination has set, making the splice in place on the layout.

This splice probably won't be as tight as one made on a flat surface, but keep it as close as you can and the spackling can take care of the rest. Also, make sheet 3 a little longer so there will be some excess to trim off at the far end of sheet 2, just to be sure that sheet 2 doesn't come out too short.

Either method will give you a stable, rigid scene divider that's largely self-supporting. Notice in fig. 2 that I put in a temporary riser to curve the free end of sheet 1 — this will be the starting point for the backdrop extension when we expand the W&SF.

PAINTING THE SKY

That long expanse of dark brown Masonite won't seem like a very attractive addition to your model railroad, so plan to paint it quickly. The first thing to do is to give it a coat or two of flat white latex to serve as a base. This goes quickly with a roller, and I painted the face of sheet 1 at the same time even though I wasn't planning to paint the sky on that side for some time. The plain white just looks a lot nicer than that dull brown.

When the white is dry, you're ready to start painting sky. The technique I used here comes from Dave Frary's book REALISTIC MODEL RAILROAD SCENERY, though my sky blue color is a little different. I used some paint that we had on hand which I thought was left over from painting the sky wall in our MODEL RAILROADER project room. It turned out not to be the same as the paint on the wall, but it is a nice, lively blue. The Sears color in the bill of materials is the closest match I could find for it.

Figure 6 shows the work in progress. After applying a heavy coat of blue to the top third of the backdrop, I brushed on more white, working up from the bottom until I reached the blue. Then I blended the still-wet paint with light, horizontal strokes of a wide brush, to get a sky that goes from nearly full white at the bottom to a strong blue at the top. Use as light a touch as you can to avoid brush streaks; the desired effect is a gradual layering.

The paint has to stay wet while you blend it, so don't try to do too wide an area at once. I found that I could handle about 4 feet at a time. Start at one end and do one such length, then overlap and blend the next area.

If the paint does start to dry too soon, moisten the brush in water and keep going. You can also brush on more blue and white paint, but try to avoid this unless it's absolutely necessary, because it makes the blending take still longer.

I'll admit that as I was blending my sky I didn't think it was going too well, but I pressed on thinking that I could always roll on some more flat white and start all over. I was a lot happier the next morning, though, because the dry paint looked a lot better. I did use a no. 16 flat brush to touch up a few too-obvious streaks by blending on small amounts of white and blue, and then I was pleased with the overall result.

I should have remembered Dave Frary's advice all along: "Don't be too fussy. As long as the top of the sky area is blue, the bottom is white, and there are no brush marks your backdrop will look great."

DISTANT HORIZONS

The backdrop behind Pauls Valley is supposed to represent gently rolling prairie country stretching off to the horizon. Again I followed Frary's book, using his technique of layering on gradually stronger colors starting at the horizon and working down. I used horizontal and nearly straight lines, however, because I didn't want any mountains or even prominent hills. When you head south from Pauls Valley and come to the Arbuckle Mountains the contrast is striking, so this backdrop gives no hint of what will be on its other side.

The formulas in the color list above are based on Dave's, but I modified them to include a technique I learned from watching LuAnn Barrow paint the backdrop for her husband David's Cat Mountain & Santa Fe Ry. I carried the sky blue down, or "forward," into the landscape colors, which gives the effect of reflected skylight and increases the appearance of distance by suggesting atmospheric haze.

The paint formulas use ordinary kitchen measurements, except for the tube acrylic colors which I've given in inches. I used a piece of thick styrene sheet for a palette and penciled 1″ divisions along one edge. After squeezing out the appropriate length of paint on the palette, I used a rubber spatula to scrape the color into one of the empty pickle and mayonnaise jars I used as mixing containers.

For a backdrop the size of the Washita & Santa Fe's you'll want to mix up at least a pint or so of Horizon Blue, since that color is used in other mixes as well as on its own. The other colors are best mixed in small amounts as you need them.

There's one more thing to do before you start painting, and that's to establish the height of the horizon and mark it on the backdrop. The easy answer to the question of how high the horizon should be is "eye level," but there are other considerations. Low-angle photos of the layout will look nicer with sky showing above the horizon, which argues for a low horizon. A low horizon also makes the backdrop easier to paint, just because you'll need less landscape. It turns out that the horizon can easily be 6″ or 8″ below your eye level without looking unnatural, so I set mine at about 61″ — my eye level is 67½″.

I made the simple marking gauge shown in fig. 7 and used it to make a series of light pencil marks on the backdrop 19″ down from the top, which works out to 61″ off the floor on the W&SF. With the horizon level established, I was ready to paint.

LAYERED LANDSCAPE

The first paint layer is, appropriately enough, Horizon Blue. Use a 3″ or even wider brush to paint a stripe of this color all the way across the backdrop, with its top edge just covering the pencil marks. Try to use straight, even strokes, but don't worry about any slight undulation or feathering along the horizon — these will actually help the effect. By the time you've worked from one end to the other and washed out the brush, the paint will be dry enough to take the second layer.

The next color is Distant Green, and again you want to sweep it on across the backdrop with a wide brush, overlapping the Horizon Blue. This layer can be a little less straight than the first, and even come up to the horizon in places, but generally its top edge should be ¼″ or so below the horizon line. Figure 8 shows the W&SF backdrop after I'd applied the first two layers.

Working forward from the distance, the next color is Closer Green. Make the top edge of this layer, too, a series of long, gentle waves. Keep it generally ¼″ below the top of the Distant Green layer, but you can let it rise to and even slightly above that edge in a few places. Continue this layer right down to the bottom of the backdrop. You could stop right here and I think you'd find your backdrop pretty effective, but the next steps are still simple and make the painted landscape a lot livelier.

The next layer isn't really a full layer at all, but a series of short brushstrokes with Tree Green to suggest lines of trees between the distant fields and along streams. You can see in the photos that there's a main tree line that runs roughly horizontal. This is composed of vertical strokes applied with the edges of the no. 10 and no.

Bill of materials

Construction:
  2 4 x 8-foot sheets ⅛″ tempered Masonite
  4 8-foot 1″ x 4″
  scrap 1 x 4 and 1″ x 2″ for clamping, including at least 7 2-foot lengths
  No. 8 x 1″ flathead wood screws
  No. 8 x 1″ panhead sheet metal screws
  Ready-to-use spackling compound, such as MH Ready Patch or Dap
Painting:
  Sears color 114 Larkspur latex paint, no. 8921X flat base
  Any flat white latex paint
  Liquitex acrylic artists' colors:
    Chromium Oxide Green no. 166
    Mars Black no. 276
    Matte medium no. 5132
  Aquatec acrylic artists' color:
    Green Gold
  9″ paint roller and pan
  3″ to 4″ brush
  No. 5 round artists' brush
  No. 10 flat artists' brush
  No. 16 flat artists' brush
  Kitchen measuring cup and spoons

16 flats; the strokes are about ½″ to ¾″ long, and they run between ¼″ and 1″ below the top of the Closer Green layer.

Don't be too concerned about making these brushstrokes look like trees. The idea is not to represent individual trees, but to give the impression of masses of trees in the distance. Stroke from the top down, beginning each stroke with just the corner of the brush, and the spread of the brush will automatically give you rounded, feathered treetops that will look very natural in terms of the overall effect. Figure 9 shows what these tree strokes should look like.

After brushing in this main line of trees, add a few diagonal lines of strokes running both back, or up, to the edge of the Closer Green layer, and forward, or down, from the main tree line. Make your strokes longer and wider as you come forward, and shorter and lighter as you go back. This

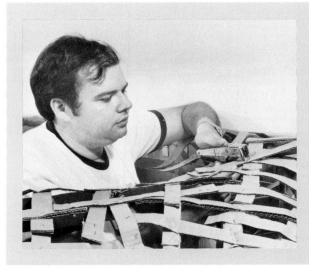

In the February 1983 issue of MODEL RAILROADER, the Washita & Santa Fe HO project railroad series returns with associate editor Andy Sperandeo showing how to build pop-up hatches and basic scenery.

isn't a true perspective painting by a long shot, but this is a perspective technique that adds depth to the layered landscape. See fig. 9 again and the photo on page 120.

Just where these diagonals are doesn't matter, but if you relate them to the rise and fall of the waves of Closer and Distant Green you'll find that they add quite an impression of terrain contours. Particularly with the lines stretching back towards the horizons, make the tree strokes follow the valleys and thin out toward the peaks.

Using painted foliage to suggest contour is another touch I learned from watching LuAnn at work on the CM&SF. My technique is very crude compared to hers, but it's good enough to be effective.

The next step is an example of serendipity, because it didn't work out at all the way I intended but I like the effect anyway. In my notes the color listed here as Grass Gold is called Closer Trees, because I mixed it with the intention of painting some lighter, brighter trees more towards the foreground. It looked like trees on the palette, but on the backdrop it was too transparent and simply gave a golden tone to the Closer Green.

Having learned my lesson about being too fussy and judging the results from just a few brush stokes, I simply continued a series of light, vertical strokes of Grass Gold all the way across in front of, or below, the main tree line, as you can see in fig. 9. When I stepped back to see if I'd made a mistake, I saw that the Grass Gold made the nearer terrain brighter and less gray than in the distance, and so added to the effect of depth. If I weren't trying to help you paint your backdrop, I'd pretend that I planned it that way all along.

Now I thought I was finished, so I invited some of my co-workers here at Kalmbach Publishing down to the MODEL RAILROADER project room to view the results. Most were as approving as I could want, but Bob Hayden offered advice. Despite the fact that only a few days before I'd been politely appreciative of his backdrop painting on the new Carrabasset & Dead River Ry., Bob told me that my trees looked too flat and thought some painted shadows would give them depth.

Actually his painting looks very good and I welcomed his advice. Besides, his idea about shadows made sense. I mixed up the Tree Shadow color starting with the same paint I'd used for the trees, and used the no. 5 round brush to add short horizontal strokes of Tree Shadow across the bottoms of the Tree Green strokes. You can see these shadow strokes in fig. 9.

As you paint in the shadows remember to keep the proportion of the brushstrokes consistent with the size of the tree strokes, to maintain the illusions of perspective and contour. Like the other effects these shadows are rough suggestions rather than detailed pictures, but they help make the Tree Green brushstrokes look a little more like trees and that's enough for this kind of painting.

Now the backdrop is finished, which means that I think it's good enough to serve its purpose of giving an illusion of distance behind the Pauls Valley scene and separating that scene from the rest of the railroad. On the other hand, I found painting the backdrop very enjoyable, and felt drawn to do more. Now that I've developed this much skill, I'll probably try to go farther on my next one. ◇

Basic scenery at Pauls Valley on MODEL RAILROADER'S Washita & Santa Fe HO project railroad: open farm land in the middle distance with low, rolling hills near the backdrop.

THE
WASHITA & SANTA FE
RY.
PART 6

Basic scenery for the Washita & Santa Fe

Terrain for the Pauls Valley scene

BY ANDY SPERANDEO

SCENERY on the Washita & Santa Fe is a basic plaster shell colored with latex paint and textured with ground foam. Its basic features are laid out in fig. 1. As I've done all along in this series* I tried a few methods and materials I hadn't used before. Some worked and some didn't, but scenery is a very forgiving kind of modeling.

If you haven't built much scenery before, keep in mind that the most important characteristic of a good scenery modeler is optimism. Nothing has to come out precisely as you planned it, and you can just keep working over any difficulty until you get something that satisfies you. The difference will most often be for the best.

The work isn't hard but it can get messy, and while in progress it's not too attractive. Keep thinking of the overall effect. The benchwork, track, and wiring were necessary foundations, but it's the scenery that gives them life and makes your layout start to look like a railroad.

ACCESS HATCHES AND FASCIA

First, however, a little more foundation work. The Pauls Valley scene is more than 6

*This series began with "Track planning for the Washita & Santa Fe" in the January 1982 MR. Other installments were "Benchwork and roadbed for the W&SF," March; "Laying flextrack on the W&SF," May; "Wiring the W&SF," September; and "A backdrop for the W&SF," November 1982.

feet deep, too far to reach to build scenery in the first place, and too far for maintenance and operational mishaps. Access hatches are among the things that I'd never done before, but in blind confidence I designed the W&SF so that it needs two of them.

I made the liftout hatch covers of extruded

Styrofoam insulation board, the same blue plastic foam that Gordon Odegard used to such good effect on MODEL RAILROADER'S N scale Clinchfield RR. There are a couple of Styrofoam liftouts on the Clinchfield, and they're light as well as rugged.

The track plan, fig. 1, shows where the

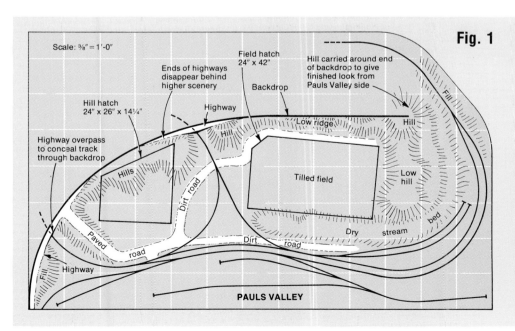

Scale: ⅜" = 1'-0"   **Fig. 1**

Ends of highways disappear behind higher scenery

Field hatch 24" x 42"

Hill carried around end of backdrop to give finished look from Pauls Valley side

Backdrop

Hill hatch 24" x 26" x 14¼"

Highway

Low ridge

Hill

Hill

Highway overpass to conceal track through backdrop

Hills

Dirt road

Tilled field

Low hill

Paved road

Dry stream bed

Highway

Dirt road

Dirt road

Fill

Fill

PAULS VALLEY

Fig. 2. HATCH CONSTRUCTION. The hill hatch frame being built around its Styrofoam liftout.

Fig. 3. HATCH INSTALLATION. The field hatch in position on the railroad, supported by risers.

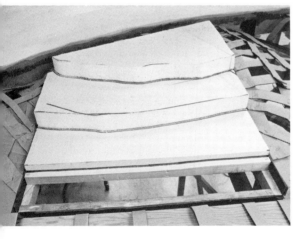

Fig. 4. HATCH CONTOURS. Foam layers for the hill, with the hatch trimmed smaller (see text).

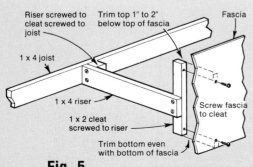

Riser screwed to cleat screwed to joist

Trim top 1" to 2" below top of fascia

Fascia

1 x 4 joist

1 x 4 riser

1 x 2 cleat screwed to riser

Screw fascia to cleat

Trim bottom even with bottom of fascia

Fig. 5
HORIZONTAL RISER FASCIA SUPPORT

hatches are located, and fig. 2 shows how I made them. Gordy's liftouts are just additional layers of the same material the rest of the Clinchfield's scenery is made from, but for the W&SF I needed hatch frames to hold the liftouts and to support the plaster scenery around them. First I cut the liftouts to size from 2"-thick foam, and then I built 1 x 2 frames around their edges.

Next I added coamings around the outside of the frames. The liftouts fit into the coamings and sit on top of the frames. Make the coamings at least as high as the full height of the liftout plus the depth of the hatch frame. That's 4" for my field liftout, but 8" for the hill liftout, to allow for layers of foam to build up the height of the hill.

I made my coamings of ⅛" Masonite screwed and glued to the frames, but I wouldn't do that again. The thin top edges of the Masonite coamings don't have enough surface for the plaster to bond to, and so don't give the scenery much support. Also the high corners of the hill hatch could spring apart until I had some very sturdy plastering around them. The next time I make hatches I'll use ½" or thicker plywood for the coamings, with lapped, glued, and screwed joints at their corners.

Remember those open spaces that the short joists left between the L-girders? The hatches go above those so you can stand up inside them. Figure 3 shows the field hatch in place, supported on cleated risers attached to the joists, girders, and even a backdrop riser.

The risers are set to hold the tops of the liftouts — the top of the bottom layer of the hill liftout — just slightly above the level of the Pauls Valley subroadbed. Keep the liftouts in the frames while you screw the frames to the cleats, so you won't accidentally skew the frames out of alignment.

With the hatches in place I visualized the scenery I wanted around them and used a felt-tip marker to draw its contours at the hatch edges onto the coamings. The field is just a little below the level of Pauls Valley on its front side and rises gradually towards the backdrop. The hill is about level with Pauls Valley for its front 8 to 12 inches, then rises gently into a rounded ridge at or a bit above horizon level.

After marking these contours I removed the hatch frames, sawed the coamings to shape with a saber saw, and remounted the hatches. I added two more layers of foam to the hill liftout as shown in fig. 4, using acrylic latex contact cement. The exact shape of these layers isn't important, but it helps to cut them to rough contour lines while allowing enough extra material to be shaped down to match the coamings.

Leave the contour shaping of the liftouts until later, but use a marker to draw the coaming contours onto the liftout edges now, while you can still reach all the way around them from below. You'll also need handles on the bottoms of the liftouts. I contact-cemented a couple of lengths of 1 x 2 under each one, leaving plenty of clearance for the hatch frames.

Figure 4 also shows how I corrected a mistake. I originally made my hill hatch a little larger than shown in fig. 1, but decided that that wouldn't leave enough room for the buildings I plan to put in front of it. So I lopped a 6"-wide strip off the front of the liftout, then sawed a length of 1 x 2 down to the coaming contour and screwed it across the frame as shown.

I used a shorter length of 1 x 2 to make the angle across one of the back corners of the field hatch. After making it a regular rectangle at first, I found that I didn't have enough room for the road I wanted to run around behind it. I'd still start out with a rectangle, though, because that's easier than framing a short angled corner.

One other preliminary is extending the fascia around the end of the layout, both to support the front edge of the scenery and to define its shape. I used 14¼"-deep strips of Masonite as I did along the Pauls Valley side, adding additional framing as necessary to support it. Mostly this was a matter of fitting "horizontal risers," fig. 5, every 18" to 24" behind the curved portion of the fascia.

With the fascia in place I saber-sawed its top edge down to a level generally below the subroadbed. I wanted the scenery below the track around the end of the layout, both to avoid obscuring the view and to give the effect of a low fill. Here again I was visualizing the scenery I planned to build, but with the next step it started to take real shape.

CARDBOARD WEBBING

A web of corrugated cardboard strips supports the plaster scenery shell on the W&SF — see fig. 6. I hadn't used this technique before, but it's one of the oldest in model railroading. It appealed to me because the material is easy to work with, and because it makes it easy to see — and therefore to adjust — the shape of the scenery before adding the plaster.

I cut single-ply corrugated box cardboard into strips about ¾" to 1" wide. Cut the strips perpendicular to the "grain" of the corrugation so they'll bend easily. The length isn't too important. A foot or so is enough because it's easy to splice strips when you need longer ones.

Figure 6 also shows tools for making the webbing: a staple gun to attach the strips to the plywood subroadbed, a plier stapler to join strips to each other where they crossed, and an electric glue gun to hot-glue cardboard to the Masonite backdrop and coamings. The glue gun was also handy in close quarters where neither stapler could reach.

Building the web is simple and fun. Just start along one edge of an open area and attach strips perpendicular to it. Then add more strips across the first batch, stapling them together where they cross.

You'll find that you can push, pull, and bend the strips to make them stand at any height you want where you join them, and this is how you shape the scenery contours. The web will be self-supporting and needn't attach to anything else except at its edges.

The fun is in seeing the contours develop as you work, which is where this method really shines. Compared to other scenery supports I've used, cardboard webbing gives a much better preview of the scenery's final shape. If something doesn't look right, just snip the strips with scissors, and either shorten them when you rejoin them or splice in additional pieces to make them longer.

The staplers and hot glue make the work go quickly, but remember to keep your fingers out of the glue until it cools. I ended up with a half dozen small blisters on my fingers when my webbing was complete.

Some other tips on cardboard webbing:

• The strips should be about 6" apart, though this isn't critical. Mine are a little closer, which doesn't hurt but takes longer.

An eye-level view of the W&SF at Gulf Junction Yard. This is how a visitor sees the railroad, and the illusion of depth and distance is apparent.

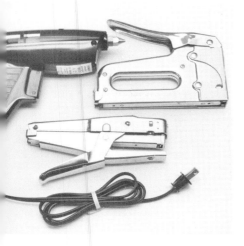

Fig. 6. WEBBING. Above, webbing fasteners: an electric glue gun, a staple gun, and a plier stapler. Below, the cardboard scenery-support web in place, with roughed-in roads and overpasses.

• Staple strips to the edges of the plywood subroadbed so they stand straight up, then bend them over. I realized from the first that stapling cardboard on top of the subroadbed reduces the relative height of the Homasote roadbed. It took me longer to realize that stapling the webbing to the bottom of the plywood causes sharp steps in the scenery rather than natural contours. No matter; it wasn't hard to fix.

• I screwed short blocks of 1 x 2 about every 9" just below the top edge of the fascia and stapled strips of cardboard along them parallel to the Masonite. I attached the webbing to these parallel strips rather than to the fascia itself. Though I hope I won't have to remove the fascia, I think this gives me a fighting chance to do so without too much damage to the scenery.

• I cut wide strips of cardboard and hot-glued them over webbing and plywood to rough-in road locations. The paved roads in the foreground are 20 scale feet wide, and the dirt roads are 16 feet. These are narrow

to save space, and I made them narrower still farther back in the scene. The highway over the tail of the wye is only 14 feet wide at most. It's easy to get away with this on a railroad that's close to eye level, where you can't look down on the narrow roads.

• I ran the highways right across the First and Pauls Valley Districts. I'll worry about bridges later, but I did put cardboard abutments on each side of the tracks so I could shape the scenery around them.

• Except at the roads, I rolled the back edge of the webbing down where it joins the backdrop, so you can't see the joint between modeled and painted scenery. Again the railroad's height helps this to work.

When you think you've finished your webbing, don't be in too big a hurry to start plastering it (unless you're working against a magazine deadline). It's so easy to change that it's worth taking a couple of days to look it over carefully, maybe running or posing some trains, to see that you've got what you want. Then it's on to the messy part.

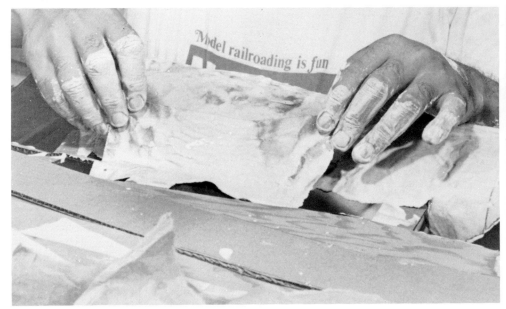

Fig. 7. SCENERY SHELL. Applying paper soaked in molding plaster to the cardboard support web.

Fig. 8. SCULPTAMOLD AND PAINTING KN

PLASTER AND SCULPTAMOLD

The Washita & Santa Fe's scenery shell is made of molding plaster applied in two or more layers with torn-up brown paper bags, with an additional application of Sculptamold in some places for finished shaping and corrections. I've done this kind of plastering with various kinds of paper towels and been successful, but this time I thought I would try using medium-weight brown paper shopping bags. That turned out to be a mistake.

I've seen others get good results with paper bags, and mine were mostly okay too, but in several places the shell came out very weak, flaking and chipping easily. The bag paper wasn't as flexible as towels and probably left too many air pockets between layers, and it didn't soak up the plaster as well as towels.

I used molding plaster to show that you don't necessarily have to use U. S. Gypsum's Hydrocal to build a hard scenery shell. Molding plaster is the name for large quantities of the same stuff called plaster of paris in small packages. It's available from several manufacturers and stocked at most cement and building material outlets, so it's easier to find than Hydrocal.

A molding plaster shell isn't as hard as one made with Hydrocal, but applied in two layers it's more than hard enough. The problems I had weren't due to the plaster. I tried fixing some of my shell's weak spots by using paper towels to apply another layer of molding plaster, and that worked perfectly.

Before going any further protect the parts of the railroad that you don't want to plaster and paint. I draped a plastic drop-cloth over the backdrop and pulled it down through the webbing. I covered the track with 1"-wide masking tape and also used tape to mask the top edge of the fascia around the end of the layout.

Meanwhile Gordon Odegard, who joined me to help with the plastering, covered most of the Pauls Valley subroadbed and the front of the fascia with brown wrapping paper. Notice that, except for the highway fill, Pauls Valley isn't plastered or textured on the west side of the main line — we'll take

care of that when we install the structures. We also spread a drop cloth on the floor and changed into old clothes. Scenery gets to be a dirty job, but somebody's got to do it!

Now gather the tools and materials for your plaster shell. You'll need:

● Molding plaster and an airtight container to store it in. I put a plastic garbage bag in a large plastic trash can and put my 100-pound sack of plaster inside the bag.

● Paper towels torn into pieces about the size of your hand. (Do as I say rather than as I did.) Any kind of towel that won't fall apart when it's wet will be fine.

● Mixing bowl — I used a couple of rubber dishpans. A rubber spatula is handy for mixing plaster and scraping out the pans.

● Measuring cups. Get two the same size and use one for water only and the other for plaster. This saves cleanup time and keeps moisture out of your plaster supply.

● Water. If there's no running water near your railroad, you'll want one bucket of clean water for mixing and one for cleanup.

Always mix plaster and water in exactly equal proportions, and pour dry plaster

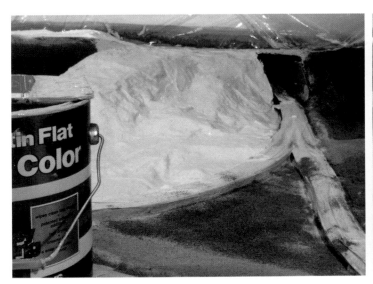

Fig. 10. COLOR AND TEXTURE. Left, **a**, paint scenery with earth-color flat latex. Right, **b**, sprinkle earth and grass texture materials over wet paint.

Fig. 9. FINISHED SHELL AND LIFTOUTS

into water to avoid lumps. The plaster mix will seem thin at first, but it thickens quickly. Don't add extra water or plaster to adjust setting time, because that spoils the chemical reaction which sets the plaster.

I found we could apply all of a batch made with two cups of plaster and two of water before it got too thick. If you want to work slower use smaller quantities but maintain the 1:1 proportion of plaster to water.

When the plaster's mixed, dip a piece of towel into the bowl, pull it back and forth to fully coat both sides, and lay it in place on the webbing. Dip and apply another piece, overlapping the first by about one-half or one-third, and continue until you get one such layer over everything you want to plaster. See fig. 7. Let this first layer set hard, then apply a second layer of plaster and towels to give adequate strength and make sure you haven't left any thin spots.

Two people working together as Gordy and I did can cover a large area very efficiently, with one applying plaster-soaked towels and the other cleaning bowls and mixing new batches — that's why we used

two mixing bowls. It doesn't matter much where you start so long as you work methodically to make sure the shell is fairly even. You can stop at any point and pick it up again, so you needn't rush to do the whole railroad all at once.

Give special attention to the eges of the shell. The plaster-soaked towels should lap well over onto the plywood subroadbed, over the top of the hatch coamings, and over the top edges of the fascia. When the plaster sets you can use a matte knife and a sanding block to trim the shell so the liftouts will fit and so you'll have a neat edge around the outside of the layout.

Almost inevitably you'll find places where the shape of your scenery isn't just what you want. I did. like those sharp steps I mentioned earlier, but I was able to fix them by troweling on Sculptamold — a product of the American Art Clay Co. sold in art-supply and some hobby stores — and building up more-pleasing contours. You could use molding plaster for this, but Sculptamold, shown in fig. 8, has some advantages.

Sculptamold is a wood-fiber and plaster

product that has a claylike consistency when mixed with water. It's neater to use than plaster because it doesn't run or dribble. It stays where you put it, and it eases cleanup chores. Although it starts to set about as fast as plaster, it stays workable longer. When set it's rock hard and rigid, and I also used it over a few weak spots.

For spreading and shaping Sculptamold get a trowel-shaped painting knife like the one shown in fig. 8. This is another artist's-supply item — mine is by Grumbacher — and its thin, slightly flexible blade makes it just right for our purposes. Leave your kitchen utensils and putty knives alone; you will be much happier using a tool that's suited to the job.

The next step is to shape the Styrofoam liftouts to match the contours of the plaster scenery. The best tools for this are Stanley Surforms, grater-like rasps that let you carve foam to shape a little at a time. For rough shaping over large areas you might want to get a rotary Surform, a drum-shaped cutter you can chuck in a ¼" variable-speed electric drill. Either way you'll make lots of foam dust, so work in a well-ventilated place and wear a dust mask. Be sure to wear safety glasses too if you use the rotary cutter in a power drill.

The coaming contours marked earlier will be a useful guide for shaping the foam, but they won't match the plaster scenery exactly. You'll have to try the liftouts in place a few times and work gradually towards the shape you want. If you go a little too far, just use Sculptamold to build the liftout up again.

You'll need some Sculptamold for sure on the hill liftout, because the foam will break up when it's shaved thin along the joints between layers. Fill the rough edges with Sculptamold to match the overall contours.

Use the Surforms to smooth out any gross tool marks on the foam surfaces, but don't worry about the general irregularity left by the cutters. Paint and texture will hide that.

Before going any farther, however, I removed all the masking from the track and fascia. Lots of plaster chips come off the masking when you do this, and I wanted to vacuum up all the loose stuff before painting. Figure 9 shows how the W&SF looked at that time, before I remasked the track and fascia in preparation for the next step.

Above, **c**, spray textured scenery with dilute matte medium bonding spray.

Fig. 11. VARIED EFFECTS. The dirt road, dry stream bed, and tilled field.

The hill at the south end of the Pauls Valley scene rises to obscure the end of the painted horizon. Eventually the addition of trees and other foliage will soften the break at the end of the backdrop.

PAINT AND TEXTURE

For the Washita & Santa Fe's basic color and texture I used Dave Frary's water-soluble scenery technique, as described in his book, HOW TO BUILD REALISTIC MODEL RAILROAD SCENERY. This has three steps:

1. Brush earth-colored flat acrylic latex paint over the plaster shell and any exposed subroadbed — fig. 10a. I used a Sears custom color called Burro Beige, a slightly reddish earth tan. You can use any earth-tone latex paint that looks good to you, but keep it light. A lot of this color will show through the texturing, and if it's too dark your scenery will be dull and lifeless.

2. Sprinkle texture materials — ground foam, dirt, sand, whatever you choose — onto the wet paint — fig. 10b. I saved some old jars and punched holes in their lids to use them as scenery material shakers.

3. Spray the texture with a bonding solution of one part acrylic matte medium and four parts water, with a few drops of detergent or Kodak Photoflo per quart of solution as a wetting agent — fig. 10c. First dampen the texture with a light mist, and then soak it thoroughly. When dry the texture will look loose but be solidly bonded to the paint.

Repeat steps 2 and 3 as many times as you wish with different materials to create varied earth and grass textures. Doing an area 18″ to 24″ square at a time is most convenient, but if some paint dries before you get to texture it, just spray it with matte medium solution and proceed.

You'll also want to keep a second sprayer filled with "wet" water — water with a few drops of wetting agent. Spraying with this helps the bonding solution soak into thick layers of texture.

The bill of materials lists the texture products I used on the W&SF. I used the Highball Earth everywhere to give the latex paint a sandy surface. For general grass and dried grass areas I used Woodland Scenics Grass and Earth blended turf, which are ground-up and dyed foam rubber, hence "ground foam."

For more specialized effects I used Highball Dirt on the dirt roads, and John's Lab Red and Brown Earth for the dry stream bed, for the results shown in fig. 11. I also sprinkled Woodland Scenics Grass fine turf along the rear heights of the scene to blend with the greens of the backdrop. I painted the paved roads with earth paint, but didn't model the paving at this stage.

You might want to use earth and dirt gathered from nature instead of the Highball and John's Lab products. This is especially worthwhile if you can gather soils from the area you're modeling. I just wanted to show you that there are good, down-and-dirty materials waiting at your hobby shop.

I removed the liftouts while texturing the other scenery, and gave them the same treatment on the bench before replacing them. I needed to stand in the hatches to reach the back of the scene, and anyway I didn't want to seal the liftouts in place with paint and matte medium.

I tried to make the color and texture on the hill liftout match the scenery around it. The joints do show when it's replaced, although, because of the railroad's height, not as much as you might think. Later on I'll camouflage them a little better.

The field liftout isn't supposed to match the scenery around it. I darkened some earth paint with burnt umber all-purpose paint tinting color, available from paint and hardware stores, using 3 teaspoons of tint to 1 cup of Burro Biege. I used this to paint the field, then textured it with Woodland Scenics Earth turf. You can see part of the field in fig. 11.

THE UNVEILING

At last it's time to pull off all the masking tape and drop cloths and really see what the railroad looks like. I found a few plaster and paint spots on the backdrop, but when you've painted your backdrop yourself you can easily touch it up.

I have to admit that when I did this I found a mistake in last November's backdrop article, part 5 of the W&SF series. The mix for Tree Green should not have any Horizon Blue, just matte medium, Chromium Oxide Green, and Green Gold.

When you get your railroad to this stage I think you'll really be happy with it. Not that this is finished or detailed scenery. I'll cover that later in the series, but this is a good base for development and finished enough to make the trains look good.

So stay optimistic while you're up to your elbows in plaster and paint and foam. It gets messy, but the payoff is worth it. ◊

The next step on the Washita & Santa Fe project railroad is finishing the Pauls Valley scene with foreground terrain, roads, ballast, foliage, and small details. This will be part 8 of the W&SF series, which Andy Sperandeo hopes to bring to you early next fall in MODEL RAILROADER.

Paul A. Erler

The canyon scene on MR's Washita & Santa Fe HO project railroad. Elements from fascia to sky help set off models like the rock crusher and the *Texas Chief.*

THE
WASHITA & SANTA FE
RY.
PART 7

Washita Canyon on the Washita & Santa Fe

Building an HO scene from the benchwork up

BY ANDY SPERANDEO

THE Washita & Santa Fe HO project railroad series concludes this month with two articles. In this one I'll show you how we built the Washita Canyon scenery on this month's cover, and in the article beginning on page 63 Gordon Odegard tells how to build the Dolese rock crusher that forms the centerpiece of our Crusher, Okla., vignette.

This won't be all you'll see of the Washita & Santa Fe. I'm planning other articles on rolling stock and details for the W&SF, but this is the last of the layout series as such. Previous installments were planning in the January 1982 issue of MODEL RAILROADER, benchwork in March 1982, flextrack in May 1982, wiring in September 1982, backdrop in November 1982, basic scenery in February 1983, and structures in June 1983, with a special feature on the Pauls Valley station.

WASHITA CANYON

The scene at Crusher is supposed to give an impression of the canyon that the Washita (say WAH-sha-taw) River cuts through the Arbuckle Mountains. This canyon gives the Atchison, Topeka & Santa Fe an easy grade through the only rugged country in south-central Oklahoma, so the railroad follows the river closely. Crusher takes its name from the rock crusher that converts some of the mountains into ballast for the railroad. Crusher is a place but not a town, and doesn't rate even a Santa Fe station sign.

The major elements of the scene, then, are the riverbank with the railroad running on top. the rocky canyon walls, and the crusher structure. Figure 1 shows how I included these on the phase 1 W&SF layout, in a space measuring about 2 x 12 feet. The crusher spurs came out a bit differently than in the original track plan in the January 1982 MR, but were built just as explained in the March and May 1982 issues.

Figure 2 is a cutaway view showing how we — Jim Kelly, Gordy Odegard, and myself — built the Crusher scenery. Much

of this duplicates earlier parts of the W&SF series, and I'll concentrate here on explaining what's new and different.

Starting with the track and backdrop in place, the first thing we added was the riverbed. This is a 1 x 4 plank supported on risers so that its top is about 4" higher than the tops of the joists. The front edge of the riverbed plank is in line with the face of the outrigger joists, so the Masonite fascia can be attached directly to the bed and the outriggers.

We kept the bottom edge of the fascia level with the bottom of the L-girders and trimmed the top edge along the river to form a lip ¼" higher than the riverbed. This lip, the bed, and the riverbank form a trough to hold the plaster layer which represents the river surface. The bank is part of the scenery shell, however, and that's what we built next.

Between the subroadbed and the backdrop we put up the shapes of the rocky canyon walls and hilltops with a cardboard web, as described in the February 1983 MR. Again, I was pleased with the

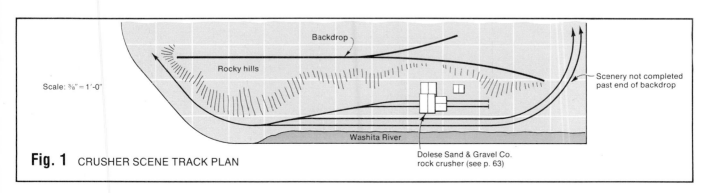

Fig. 1 CRUSHER SCENE TRACK PLAN

Backdrop

Rocky hills

Scale: ⅜" = 1'-0"

Washita River

Scenery not completed past end of backdrop

Dolese Sand & Gravel Co. rock crusher (see p. 63)

Paul A. Erler

Following Oklahoma's Washita River along the rocky cliffs of the Arbuckle Mountains, Santa Fe no. 16, the Chicago-bound *Texas Chief*, passes Crusher. Compare this view with the cutaway picture in fig. 2 to see how the scene was built.

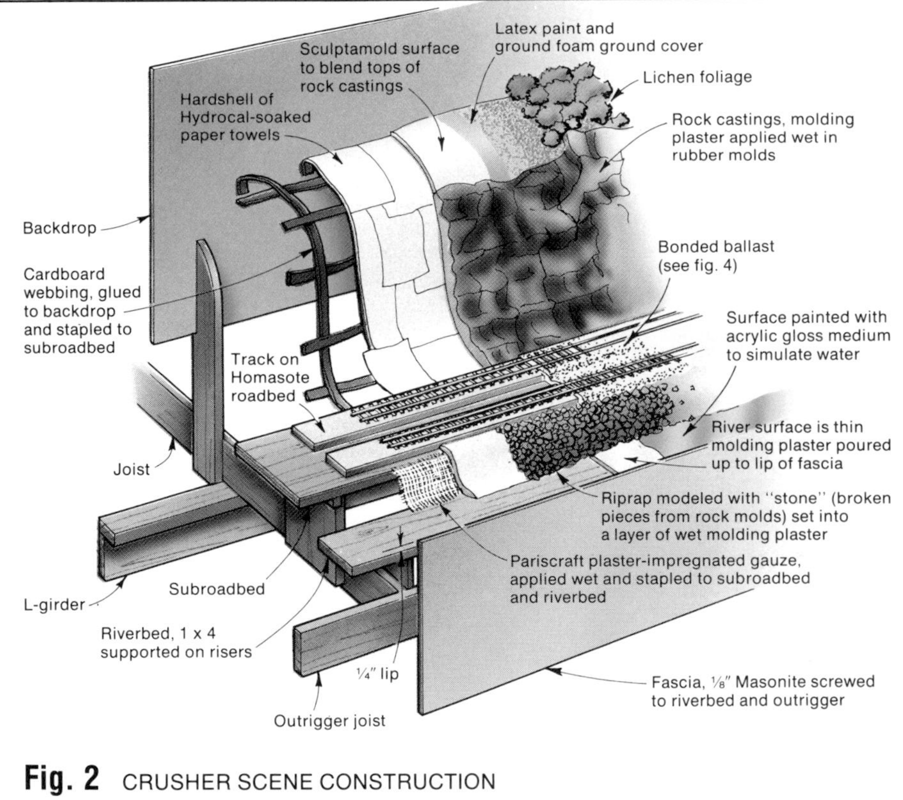

way this method let us preview and adjust the shape of the finished scenery.

We did use Hydrocal plaster and paper towels for the scenery shell this time, which worked better than the molding-plaster-and-paper-bag shell on the other side of the layout. I think the improvement is mainly due to the paper towels, which do a better job of carrying the plaster and holding it until set.

Hydrocal is a product of U. S. Gypsum, and if you have trouble finding it where you live, you can get help from the U. S. Gypsum sales representatives in most major cities. Hydrocal's chief advantage, as far as I'm concerned, is speed. You can build just as strong a shell with molding plaster, but it takes longer because you'll need to use twice as many layers of plaster-soaked towels.

The riverbank needed just a narrow swatch of scenery shell, so we used a product called Pariscraft. This is plaster-impregnated gauze strip sold in art- and craft-supply stores; you could use the medical type, as used to make casts for broken bones, but Pariscraft is cheaper. You simply cut handy lengths off the 2"-wide roll, dip them in water, and apply. We also stapled its edges down to keep it from sagging before it set.

ROCKS AND THE RIVER

The Arbuckle Mountains are the edge of a layer of sedimentary rocks, limestones and sandstones, that has curled up into an east-west ridge across southern Oklahoma. The Washita River flows from north to south, cutting our canyon through the Arbuckles.

For purposes of scenery on the W&SF, this means we need rugged hills having lots of exposed rock faces along the river with upthrust, nearly vertical striations. The railroad's riverbank right-of-way is always in danger of being washed away, so it's protected by riprap, an embankment of boulders and broken stone.

We used molding plaster in rubber molds to cast the rock faces in place on the layout. This is a three-step process:

● Place the mold open-side-up on a flat surface and spray it with "wet" water — water mixed with a few drops of liquid detergent or Kodak Photo-flow wetting agent. Mix a small batch of plaster, using equal parts of plaster and water, and fill the mold. The wet water spray will help the plaster fill all the details and crevices of the mold.

● When the plaster in the mold begins to thicken, after 2 or 3 minutes, spray wet water onto the scenery shell where you want to place the casting. A dry shell will absorb water from the casting and prevent it from setting properly. Carefully press the mold onto the shell. Since the plaster won't yet be solid,

Fig. 2 CRUSHER SCENE CONSTRUCTION

Labels in figure:

Sculptamold surface to blend tops of rock castings

Latex paint and ground foam ground cover

Lichen foliage

Hardshell of Hydrocal-soaked paper towels

Rock castings, molding plaster applied wet in rubber molds

Backdrop

Bonded ballast (see fig. 4)

Cardboard webbing, glued to backdrop and stapled to subroadbed

Surface painted with acrylic gloss medium to simulate water

Track on Homasote roadbed

River surface is thin molding plaster poured up to lip of fascia

Joist

Riprap modeled with "stone" (broken pieces from rock molds) set into a layer of wet molding plaster

L-girder

Subroadbed

Pariscraft plaster-impregnated gauze, applied wet and stapled to subroadbed and riverbed

Riverbed, 1 x 4 supported on risers

¼" lip

Fascia, ⅛" Masonite screwed to riverbed and outrigger

Outrigger joist

Fig. 3. **Rock casting.** Jim Kelly uses a putty knife to blend castings while waiting for the mold at left to set. To the right are castings already made in place on the scenery shell and the Pariscraft shell along the riverbank.

Fig. 4   BALLASTING STRAIGHT-SIDED ROADBED

To conserve commercial ballast, first pour in a partial layer of builder's sand

Flextrack on ½" Homasote roadbed

Ballast forms natural slope when poured on loose. Spray with wet water and drip on a matte medium bonding solution to fix

Let ballast overlap other scenery

the mold can bend to follow contours.

● After placing the mold you'll need to hold it against the shell for another 2 or 3 minutes, until it will stay in place when you take your hand away. Depending on the temperature of your room and the thickness of your mold, you may feel the mold get warm when the plaster starts to set. That's when you want to strip the mold away to reveal the casting, which still won't be solid enough to tear detail out of the mold.

With the casting in place you can use a palette or putty knife to break away any of the oozed plaster that doesn't look like rock and to blend the surfaces of

the new casting with any previous ones. See fig. 3. Then you're ready to wash out the mold and repeat the process. We were able to apply four molds at a time, with two of us holding two molds each while the third man cleaned up and refilled others. In a couple of hours we had cast all the rocks we needed.

We used several molds to avoid obvious repetitions of any one casting. Some were commercial molds from Color-Rite Scenery Products, which makes a line of eight molds in a variety of sizes. We also used some homemade molds borrowed from a friend. If you'd like to make some rock molds of your own, Dave Frary tells

how in his book, *How to Build Realistic Model Railroad Scenery*, from MR's publisher, Kalmbach Publishing Co.

We had a lot of broken pieces of rock castings left over, and I saved them to make the riprap. I spread small batches of molding plaster over the Pariscraft and set the rock pieces into it. Plaster is a better bonding agent for this than glue or matte medium, because it will accept the coloring we used just like the rocks themselves. Similarly, if you want to replace a large piece broken from a casting, use plaster instead of glue.

We used Sculptamold (see the February 1983 installment) to blend the edges

Fig. 5. **Cloud painting.** Andy uses a sponge on a stick to pat clouds onto the backdrop. The method is neat, and the foreground didn't need protection.

of the rock faces into the hilltop and hillside contours. Like glue, Sculptamold won't take color exactly like the plaster rocks, so use it only where you'll paint over it with earth-colored paint.

COLOR AND FOLIAGE

Jim Kelly did most of the rock coloring, and he used spray tints rather than paint or dye. All-purpose tinting colors are sold in paint and hardware stores, and for coloring rocks you mix them with water in very dilute solutions and spray them on with spray bottles. Thin solutions of tint are transparent, and they stain rather than paint the plaster rocks. They are also easier to use and more permanent than dyes.

For the basic gray tone Jim used a very thin solution of lampblack tint. He followed that with a burnt umber solution to warm up the gray and a burnt sienna tint for the reddish accents that we saw in photos of the real rocks.

When wet these tints look darker than when dry, so it took several applications to get just the color we wanted. We sprayed until things looked right, then the rocks dried overnight and looked too light, so we sprayed again and waited to see how that would come out. The easiest mistake to make in coloring rocks is getting them too dark, and this method helps avoid that by letting you gradually work up to the colors you want.

We painted the rest of the hills with earth-colored flat latex paint (Sears Burro Biege), sprinkled on Woodland Scenics blended turf ground foam (T-49 Green and T-50 Earth), and fixed this ground cover with an acrylic matte medium bonding spray. I sprinkled some Highball Products no. 520 Real Gravel and no. 510 Real Dirt over the riprap to vary its texture and color, and fixed that with the matte medium spray as well.

While we were spraying all this matte medium around, Kelly tried something I hadn't heard of before but that turned out very well. He sprayed matte medium over the rocks, and when it dried it had sealed them and given them a slightly reflective glaze. This adds highlights that help to show off the shape and detail of the castings, and gives the rocks a nice effect of depth and solidity.

We glued clumps of lichen over the tops of the hills to simulate the prototype forests. I had gathered several different brands of lichen, including Campbell, Kibri, Life-Like Scene Master, and Noch, to get a variety of colors. I also trimmed off some smaller, finer clumps to place in flat spots on the rock faces, because the cliffs along the Washita aren't bare or lifeless. My favorite adhesive for this is Walthers Goo, which is sticky enough to hold the lichen on sloping or uneven surfaces.

At this stage Gordy set his rock crusher model in place, and ballasted the track and around the bases of the buildings. I've had more questions about how we would ballast the straight-sided Homasote roadbed than on any other aspect of the W&SF, but fig. 4 shows there's really nothing to it. Gordy poured on Highball no. 330 Limestone ballast as in the photo, shaped it with a flat brush, and glued it

Fig. 6. Plaster river. The Washita River surface is thin plaster poured into the trough between the bank and the fascia lip. Wet water helped the plaster flow around the riprap, and it was self-leveling.

Fig. 7. Gloss medium water. Andy brushes a coat of acrylic gloss medium along the riverbank. The gloss medium goes on milky white but dries clear and shiny, as you can see along the layout edge.

down with the matte medium solution.

This method is excellent for well-maintained track with a high ballast shoulder, but does use up a lot of ballast quickly. If you need to be more sparing with ballast, first put a layer of sand partway up the side of the roadbed as shown on the left side in the fig. 4 drawing.

CLOUDS AND WATER

We had painted the backdrop solid blue back before we started on the hills, using Sears Larkspur flat latex. For the most part the hills rise above eye level, so I didn't need to paint a sweeping horizon, but I did want to add some clouds. I decided to try the sponge-painting method John Nehrich described in his article, "Summit scenery on the NEB&W," in the March 1984 MODEL RAILROADER, and it worked beautifully.

In fig. 5 you can see me at work on the clouds, using a piece of sponge stapled to the end of a stick to pat on some distant clouds with a mixture of sky blue and flat white latex paints. You should see John's article for more details, but the basic technique is to pat on high, large, overhead clouds with straight white; then add low, small, distant clouds with the blue-white mixture; and finally to fill in the space between with intermediate sizes and colors. A gray mixture, blue-white with a few drops of lampblack or raw umber all-purpose tint, is used to add shadows which give the clouds a three-dimensional look.

I also used a no. 5 round artist's bristle brush to paint some of the very smallest clouds, when even just the corner of the sponge seemed too large. My technique was the same with the brush as with the sponge, patting paint onto the backdrop with just the tip of the brush. Also, I got out the horizon-colored paints I'd used for the Pauls Valley backdrop and put in just a bit of landscape in the notch behind the crusher.

In less than half an hour I had painted enough clouds for the whole scene, in fact, more than enough! I took John's advice and waited until after lunch to decide, but on my first try I'd put in too many clouds and made them too regular. It was easy to fix: with the sky blue I painted out some

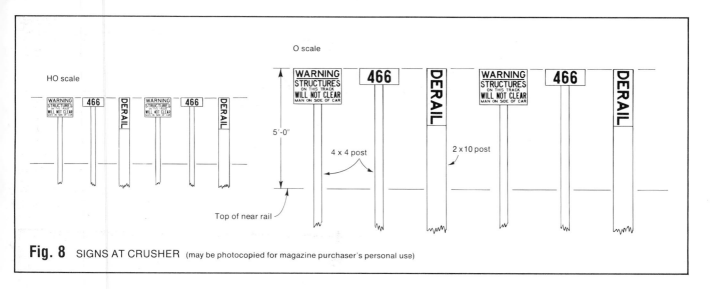

Fig. 8 SIGNS AT CRUSHER (may be photocopied for magazine purchaser's personal use)

clouds entirely and divided others into two or three, then dabbed in just a few more clouds in new positions.

Next came water for the Washita. I used plaster for the river surface, after first sealing the joint between the river bed and fascia with masking tape from underneath, and also taping a cardboard dam across the river at the end of the layout. I mixed about three parts of water to one of molding plaster, and poured it into the bed up to the lip of the fascia.

The thin plaster can flow around the riprap, especially when helped by a few squirts of wet water, and it levels itself. It won't set to full strength, but that doesn't matter because it has a solid support and will be thoroughly sealed. Figure 6 shows the unpainted plaster river surface.

To turn the white plaster into a wet-looking river, I used acrylic gloss medium as explained by Dave Frary in the January 1984 MODEL RAILROADER. Gloss medium is like the matte medium we've been using as a bonding agent, only

shiny. Using it to model water is a two-stage process: first you paint the surface with flat colors to simulate the bottom and give the effect of depth; then you brush on gloss medium for the wet look.

For a bottom color I used Polly S Earth, airbrushing it over the river surface and along the lower part of the riprap bank. To give an effect of greater depth farther out, I sprayed the surface with Polly S Grimy Black along the very edge of the layout. I also added a streak of Polly S Rust just above the waterline on the riprap. The Arbuckles aren't red-clay country themselves, but the Washita paints its banks red with colors it brings from upstream.

In fig. 7 you see how I applied the gloss medium. Straight from the jar it goes on milky white, but dries clear and shiny. Actually I brushed on several layers. The first was tinted blue, with a very small amount of ultramarine blue acrylic mixed into some gloss medium, so the river would seem to be reflecting the bright

blue sky on the backdrop. I let this lap just a little way over from the Grimy Black "depths" onto the Earth "shallows." Next came a brown-tinted layer, with Polly S Earth in the gloss, between the blue water and the bank.

I let the first gloss medium layers set about 20 minutes and then brushed on two heavy coats of straight gloss medium at about 10-minute intervals. I brushed from left to right, "downstream," so the brush streaks would help give the impression of flowing water. As a final touch, I mixed a little gloss with a dab of titanium white acrylic, and used a smaller brush to add some streaks of white water trailing downstream from projecting rocks and rough spots in the river surface.

I added a little lichen shrubbery in various colors along the bank, especially some in "autumn" reds for a clay-stained look. I also used some coarse stems of lichen for driftwood at the water's edge. We've only modeled the edge of the Washita, but it looks wet enough to let this riverbank scene make sense.

FINISHING UP

Gordy added the final details, including the signs in fig. 8, which are reproduced from *Santa Fe System Standards, Vol. One,* by courtesy of Kachina Press, 1025 Elm Street, Dallas, TX 75202-3112. The switch stands are brass models of the Santa Fe's high Star types, no. 1502 from the San Timoteo & Live Oak Ry. Co., 1130 W. Shullenbarger Dr., Flagstaff, AZ 86001. Dolese Sand & Gravel's GE 25-tonner is a brass model by Fomras of Japan (see ad on page 147 of May 1984 MR).

I painted the fascia with the latex earth color, Sears Burro Beige. I used the flat paint we had on hand, but you'd do better to get the semigloss version of the same shade. I like the effect of a light-colored fascia, but the flat paint will be hard to keep clean.

So that concludes the series. We've covered all the basic skills and types of construction you'd need to finish the layout. Much as I'd like to see the W&SF completed, we need to get on with other projects in the MR shop. Good luck to those of you who are pushing on to Gene Autry and Gainesville, Texas. ⚙

R. H. Kindig

A 1946 view of the prototype for the W&SF's Washita Canyon scene. Train no. 6, the eastbound *Ranger,* predecessor of the *Texas Chief* on the Texas-Chicago run, is shown just south of Crusher.

Index

OUTSIDE
THE
LINES, TOO

Outside the Lines, Too

An Inspired and Inventive Coloring
Book by Contemporary Artists

Curated by
Souris Hong

A Perigee Book

PERIGEE
An imprint of Penguin Random House LLC
375 Hudson Street, New York, New York 10014

OUTSIDE THE LINES, TOO

ISBN: 978-0-399-17205-2

First edition: September 2015

PRINTED IN THE UNITED STATES OF AMERICA

10   9   8   7   6   5   4   3

For Lulu

and her outstanding friends:

Aaron, Abby, Abigail, Adele, Aebfinn, Ai-Linh, Akira, Alanna, Albert, Alejandro, Alexandra, Alicia, Alyona, Amani, Amaryllis, Anabella, Anders, Andrew, Anela, Angus, Ari, Ariana, Ariana Valentine, Artemisia, Asher, Ashley, Athena, Atreya, Atticus, Audrey, August, Ava, Aya, Ayla, Ayumi, Baby Jamigan, Bailey, Banksy, Bao Bao, Bella, Billie, Bodhi, Boots, Braden, Briley, Brooks, Byron, BZ, Cairo, Caleb, Camtinh, Carla, Caroline, Cedella, Charles, Charley, Charlie, Chase, Chime, Chloe, Christian, Christopher, Claire, Clara, Clark, Clem, Cleo, Coby, Coco, Cole, Cosima, Cosmo, Cotton, Dakota, Daphne, Darby, Dash, Dashiell, Declan, Delcy, Derby, Desmond, Didion, Dosa Weir, Dottie, Eames, Eavan, Echo, Eithne, Ekoh, Elcie, Eli, Elijah, Eliot, Elise, Elizabeth, Ella, Elliott, Elodie, Emi, Emil, Emily, Emma, Emme, Emmet, Emmy, Enki, Ethan, Eva, Evan, Eve, Evelyn Flower, Ever, Everly, Ezra, Farrah, Fauna, Felix, Felixe, Fletcher, Flora, Forest, Francoise, Frankie, Freya, Gabriel, Gavin, Genevieve, George, Grace, Gracie Cash, Grace, Grady, Guy, Harmony, Harper, Hazel, Henry, Honey, Hugo, Iain, Iggy, Ilai, Io, Iris, Iroha, Isaac, Isabel, Isabella, Isabelle, Isadora, Isla, Iverson, Izzy, Jack, Jackson, Jacob, Jaden, Jaiden, Jake, James, Jax, Jaya, Jenn, Jenny, Jess, Jessica, Jessie, Jet, Jett, Jette, Joseph, Josephine, Joshua, Josie, Julia, Julian, Julianna, Juniper, Kaeli, Kahlil, Kai, Kaia, Kailani, Kaisei, Kaitlin, Kan, Kanata Ibn Umar, Kate, Keaton, Kepler, Kiran, Kosei, Kristina, Kyler, Lake, Lana, Lara, Layla, Lea, Lee, Lena, Leo, Lev, Liem, Lila, Lilas, Lillian, Lilly, Lily, Lily Gray, Liv, Llisa, Loen, Logan, Lola, Lou, Louisa, Lucas, Lucca, Lucia, Lucie, Luella, Luis, Lula, Lulu, Luna, Madeline, Mae, Mahina, Makena, Malcolm, Malin, Manal, Mariah, Marina, Marlowe, Martin, Marty, Mateo, Matt, Matteo, Matthew, Mattie, Max, Maxwell, Maya, Maybeline, Meg, Mena, Mia, Mica, Michelle, Michio, Miles, Mischa, Miuccia, Miyuki, Myra, Natassje, Nate, Nathan, Neko Marker, Nesyah, Nico, Nicolas, Nina, Noah, Noam, Nola, Ocean, Olivia, Ollie, Oscar, Owen, Paige, Patrick, Penelope, Penn, Peribeau, Petra, Phoenix, Pilar, Poesy, Poppy, Porter, Prince Pepito, Quentin, Radha, Raiden, Raul, Ravi, Ray, Reagan, Reed, Ren, Rich, Rips, RJr, Ro, Romy, Ronan, Rosa, Rowan, Rowe, Ruby, Ruslan, Ryan, Sadie, Sailor, Samantha, Sammy, Sanaya, Sato, Satya, Sayer, Scottie, Seamus, Sean, Sebastian, Shannon, Siavash, Sira, Sirocco, Skye Raine, Sloane, Sofia, Sol, Sonja, Sophia, Stella, Stormey, Sunny, Taisei, Tatjana, Tenzin, Terra, Tessa, Theo, Thomas, Tia, Tigerlily, Toby, Toki Anna, Tom, Tommy, Toussaint, Travis, Tristan, True, Truman, Twyla, Tyler, Van, Vanessa, Victoria Rose, Victoria, Violet, Vivienne, Wawo, Wilder Jack, Willa, Yaya, Yu, Yuna, Yuri, Zachary, Zachery, Zeke, Zephyr, Zinash, Zion, Ziv, Zoe, Zoe Rose, and ZZ!

INTRODUCTION

My daughter, Lulu, inspired *Outside the Lines: An Artists' Coloring Book for Giant Imaginations*.

You inspired *Outside the Lines, Too: An Inspired and Inventive Coloring Book by Contemporary Artists*!

When I first endeavored to compile line drawings by today's most creative and radical masterminds, I thought mostly of my friends, the artists, and Lulu. With this follow-up title, I thought of my friends, the artists, Lulu, and you, the audience.

Since *Outside the Lines* launched in the fall of 2013, I've received many comments about how young and old folks alike were inspired to research and learn about the artists in the book. I've been told over and over how parents engaged with excited children about art and how they discovered artists together.

Outside the Lines appealed to all ages. And while adult coloring books have taken off, the book the *Huffington Post* declared "the best thing we've ever seen" seemed to really engage fans in a conversation about contemporary art—what is appropriate artwork for children to color? How do you color a black square box? (Ask any child and they choose light-colored crayons instantly.) How is an architect's output so different or the same as a graphic illustrator's? Whatever the answer, conversations about art were had by many and that inspired me to reach out to my artist friends again.

I hope that *Outside the Lines, Too* will bring a smile to your face, engage you, and help you discover a whole new batch of artists.

Now, let's color some more!

CREATE YOUR OWN
Paper EAMES Elephant

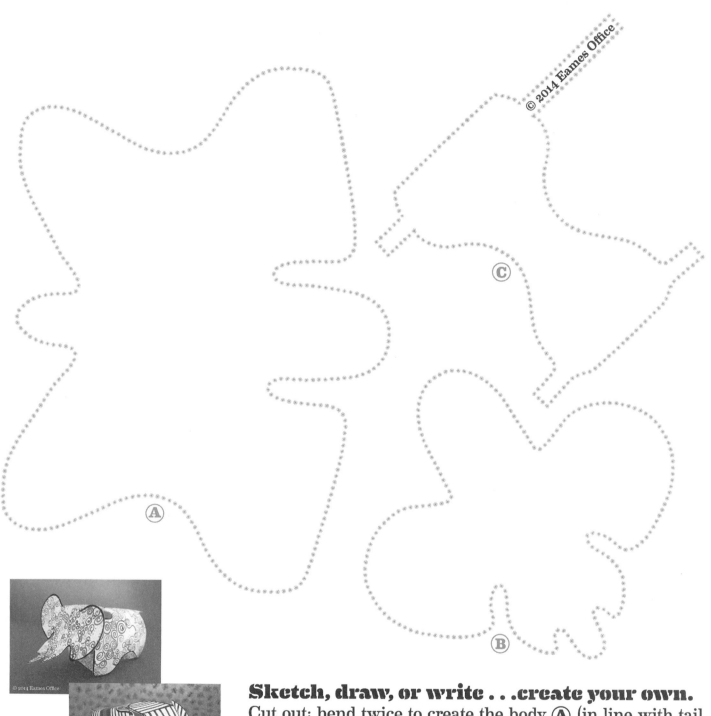

© 2014 Eames Office

Sketch, draw, or write . . .create your own.

Cut out; bend twice to create the body **Ⓐ** (in line with tail and neck); form the ears and trunk **Ⓑ** —and, finally, if desired, attach legs to "ground" **Ⓒ** so that your elephant stands just like its cousin, the Vitra Miniature *Eames Elephant*, also a design by Charles and Ray Eames from *1945*.

ARTWORK © Susie GHAHREMANi/
BOYGIRLPARTY ®

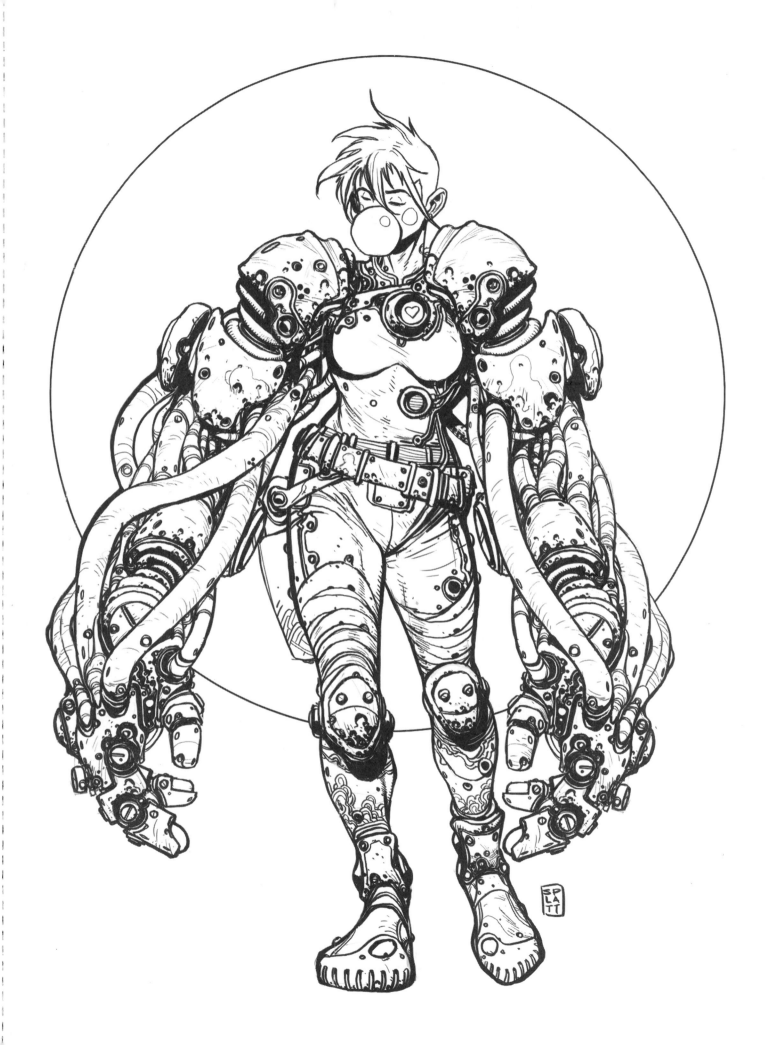

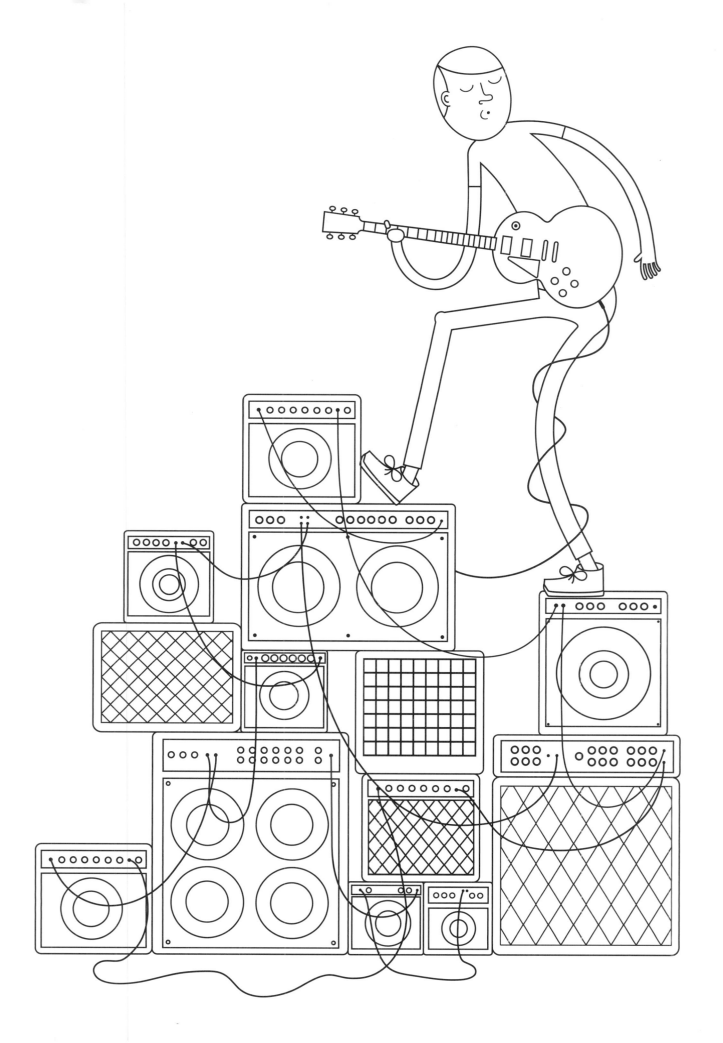

AKO

WE'LL MEET SOME DAY IN THE SO FAR AWAY.

THIS HAS BEEN A JEREMYVILLE COMMUNITY SERVICE ANNOUNCEMENT.

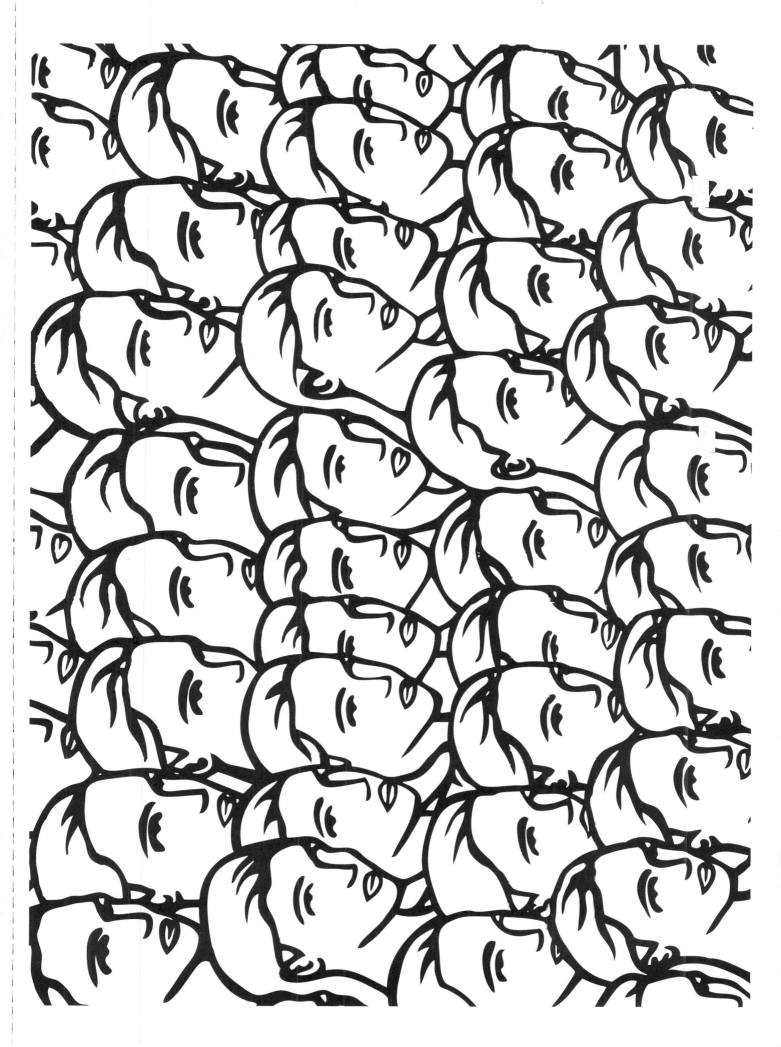

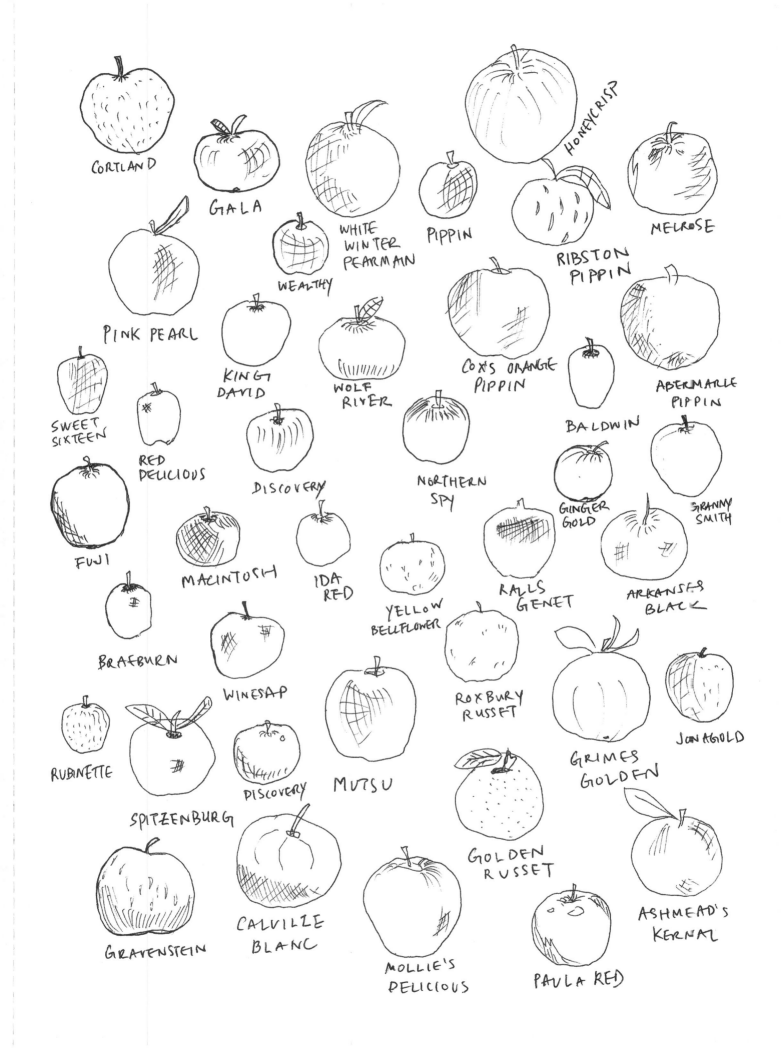

CORTLAND

GALA

WHITE WINTER PEARMAIN

WEALTHY

PIPPIN

HONEYCRISP

RIBSTON PIPPIN

MELROSE

PINK PEARL

KING DAVID

WOLF RIVER

COX'S ORANGE PIPPIN

BALDWIN

ABERMARLE PIPPIN

SWEET SIXTEEN

RED DELICIOUS

DISCOVERY

NORTHERN SPY

GINGER GOLD

GRANNY SMITH

FUJI

MACINTOSH

IDA RED

YELLOW BELLFLOWER

RALLS GENET

ARKANSAS BLACK

BRAEBURN

WINESAP

MUTSU

ROXBURY RUSSET

GRIMES GOLDEN

JONAGOLD

RUBINETTE

SPITZENBURG

DISCOVERY

GOLDEN RUSSET

ASHMEAD'S KERNAL

GRAVENSTEIN

CALVILLE BLANC

MOLLIE'S DELICIOUS

PAULA RED

Make a table, two stools, fruit bowl and tiny coloring book. Cut and fold then, color, sticker, pattern to create your own worlds. Fill up your tiny book. Use scraps of colored paper to make fruit.
Fill your bowl. Photocopy the page or use it directly. *Solid lines are for cutting. Dotted lines are for folding.*

book

table

stools

bowl

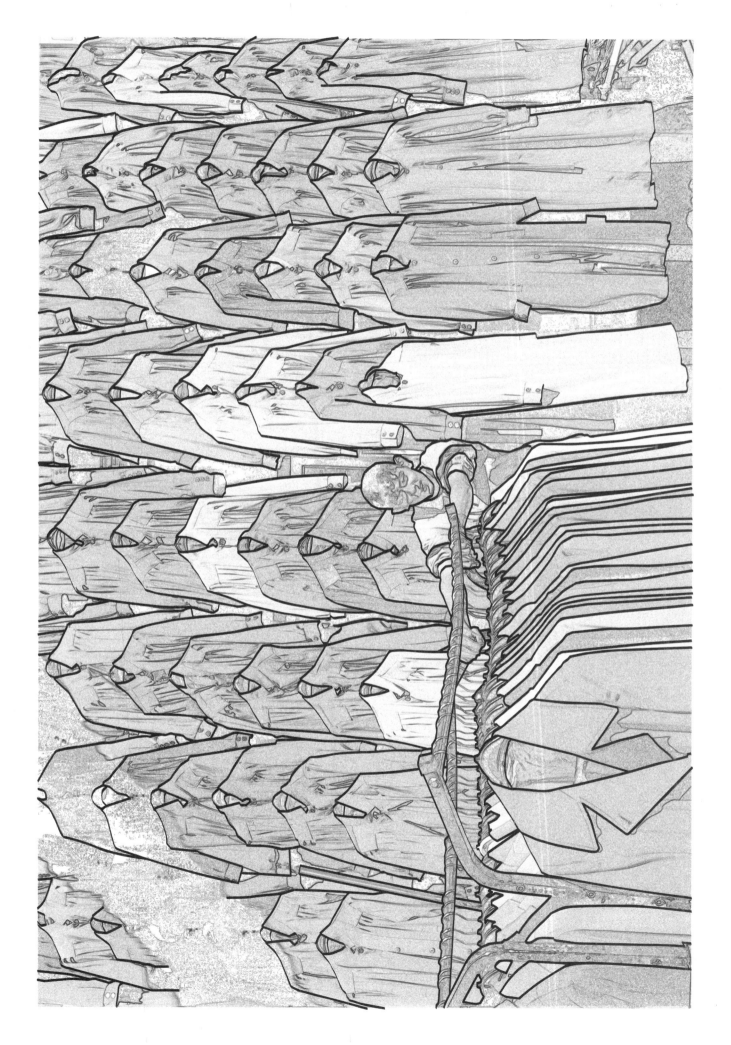

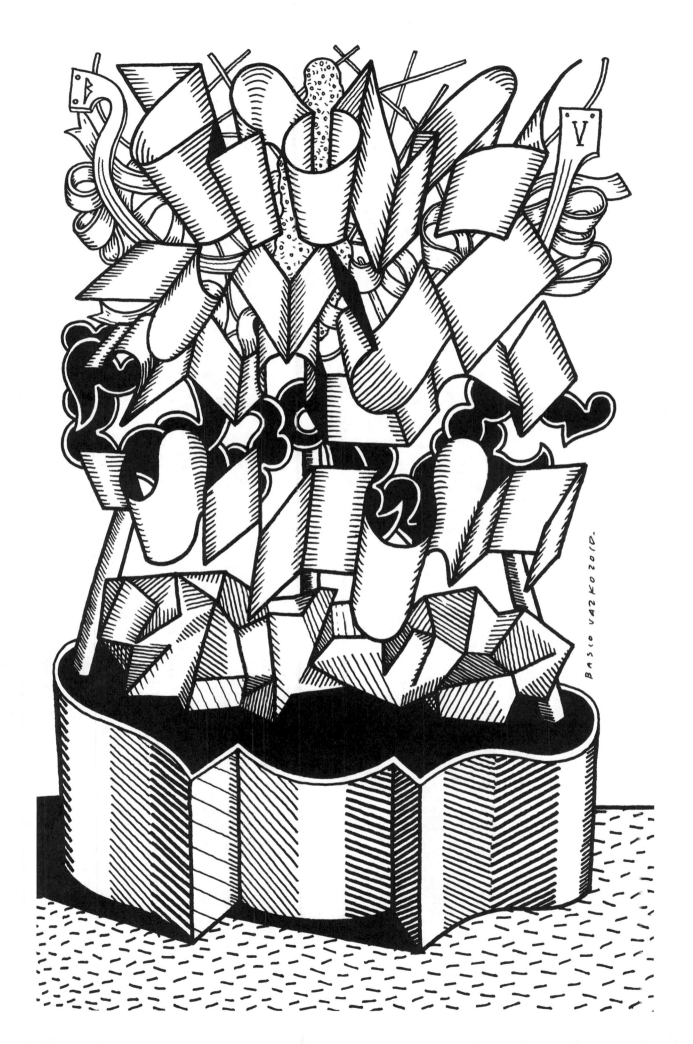

michael C. Bury

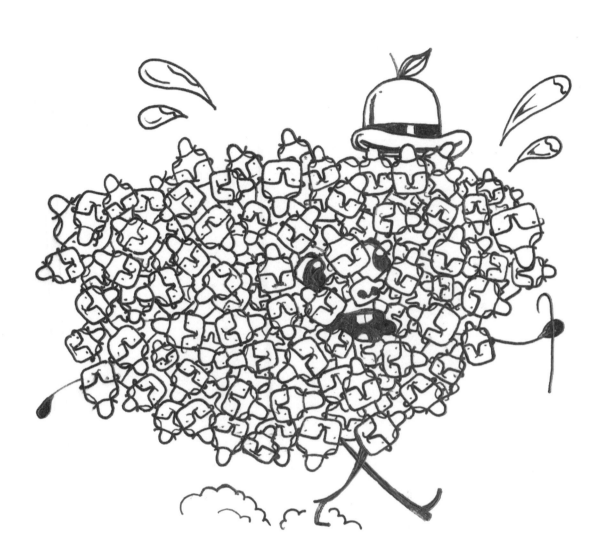

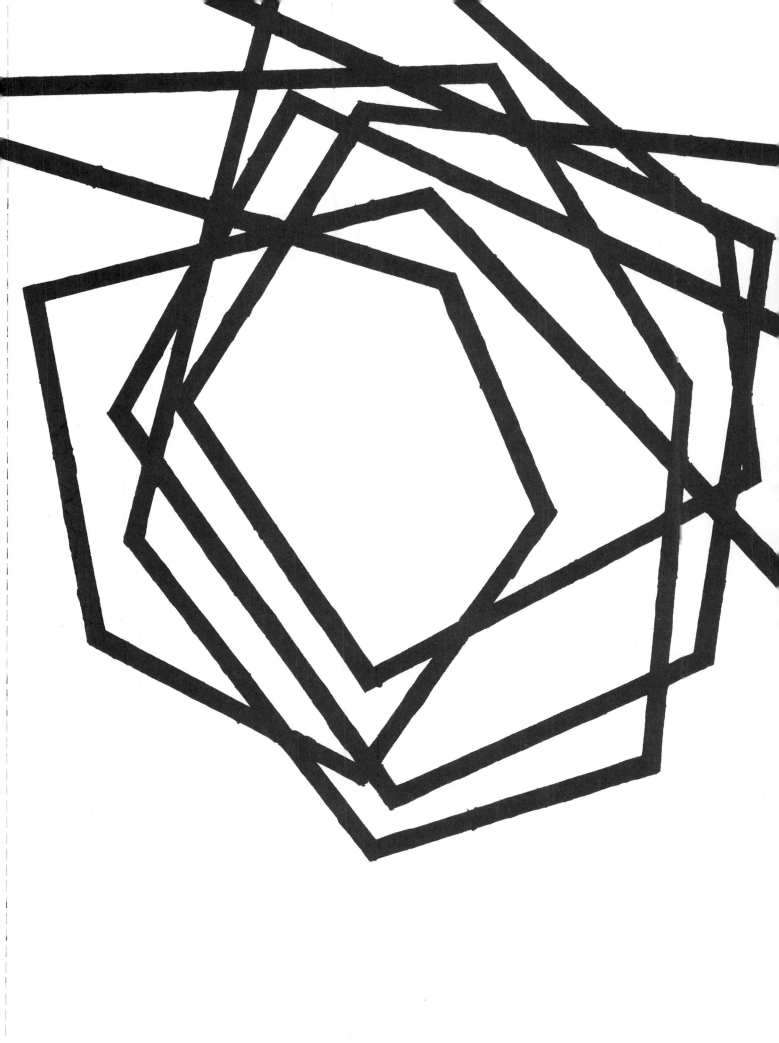

LEARN SOMETHING AND MAKE A NEW FRIEND

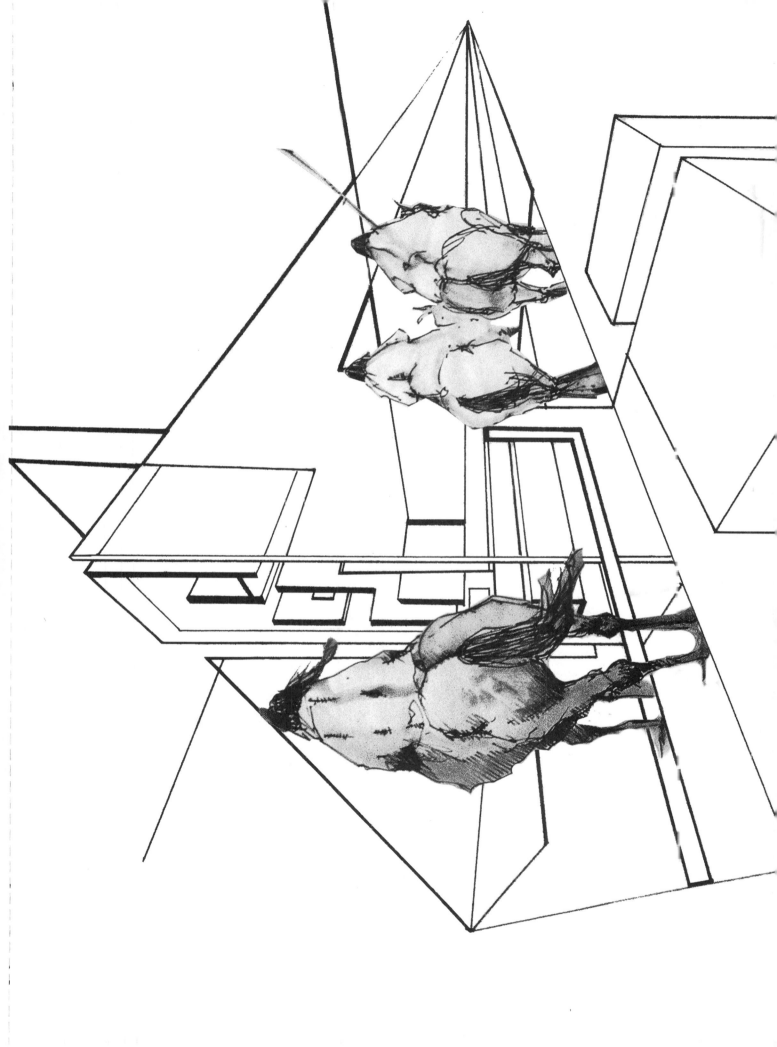

Jean Jullien

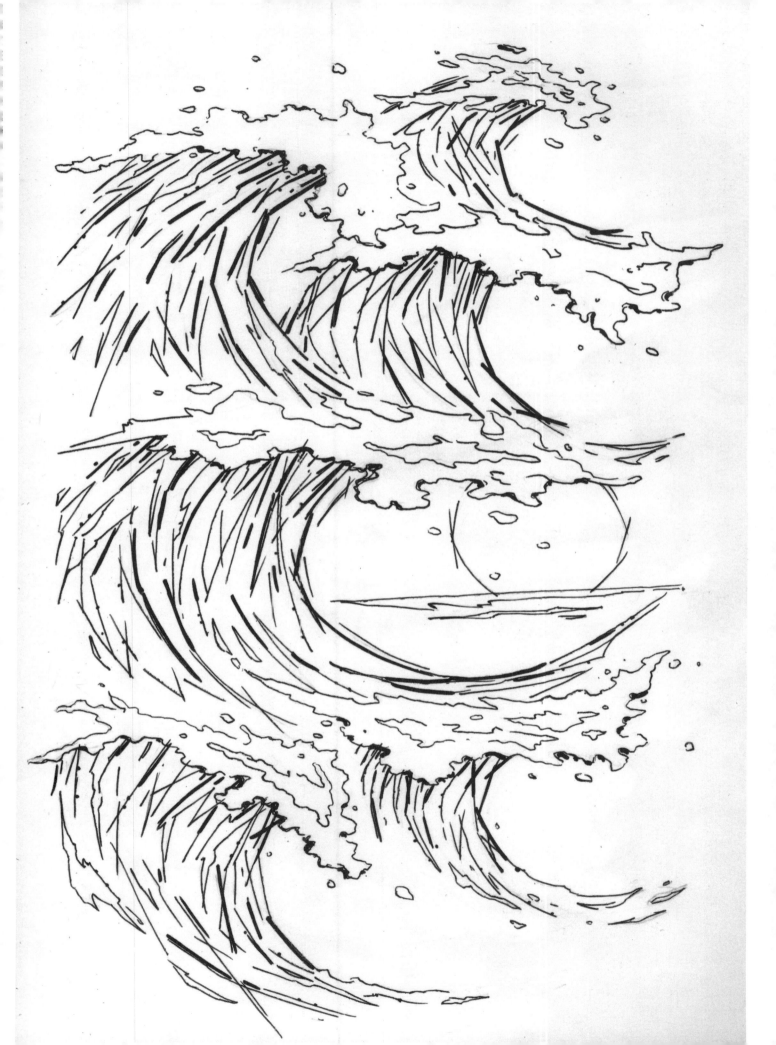

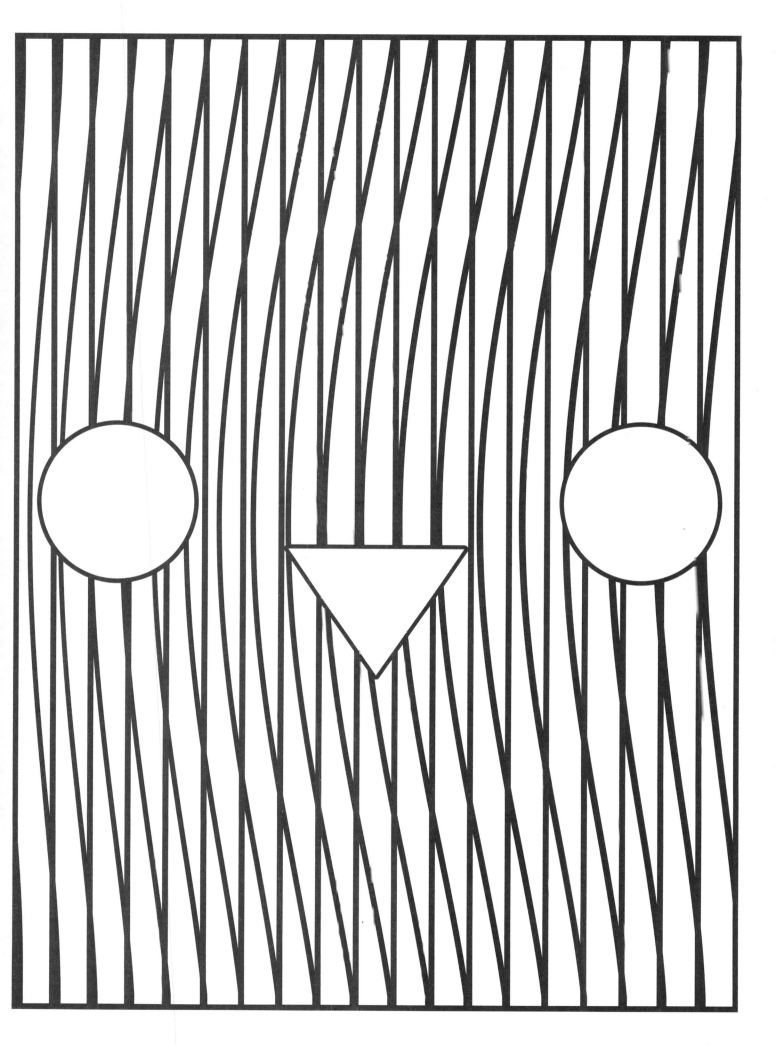

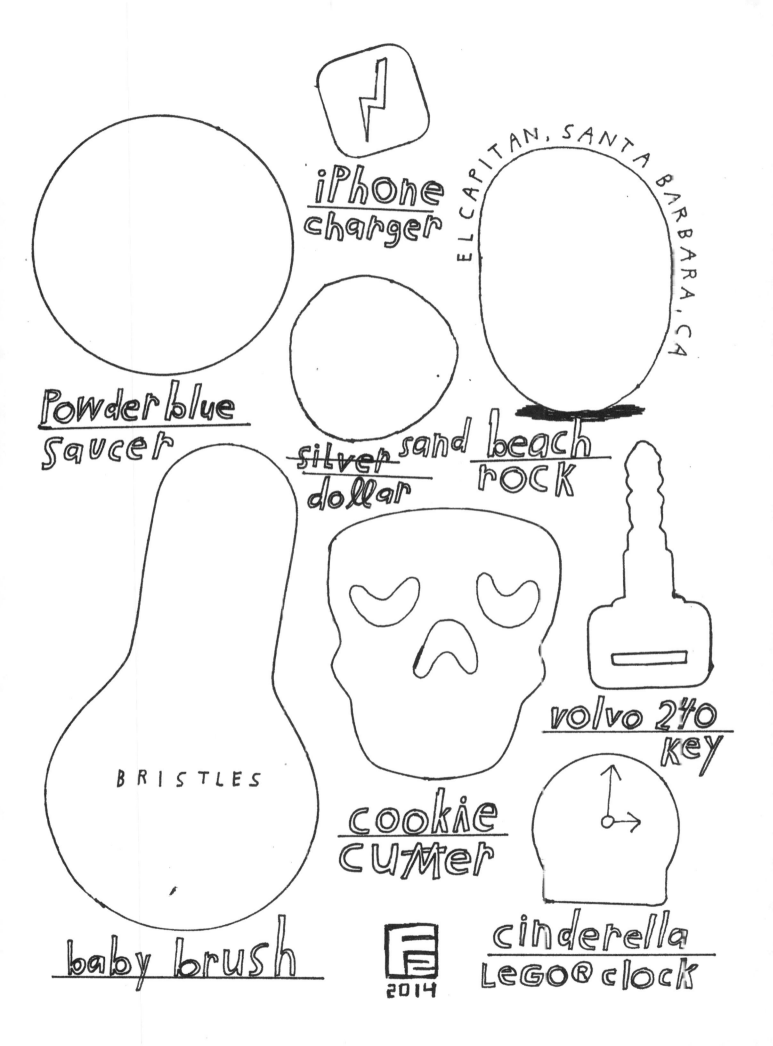

iPhone
charger

EL CAPITAN, SANTA BARBARA, CA

Powder blue
Saucer

silver
dollar

sand beach
rock

BRISTLES

baby brush

cookie
cutter

volvo 240
key

cinderella
LEGO® clock

2014

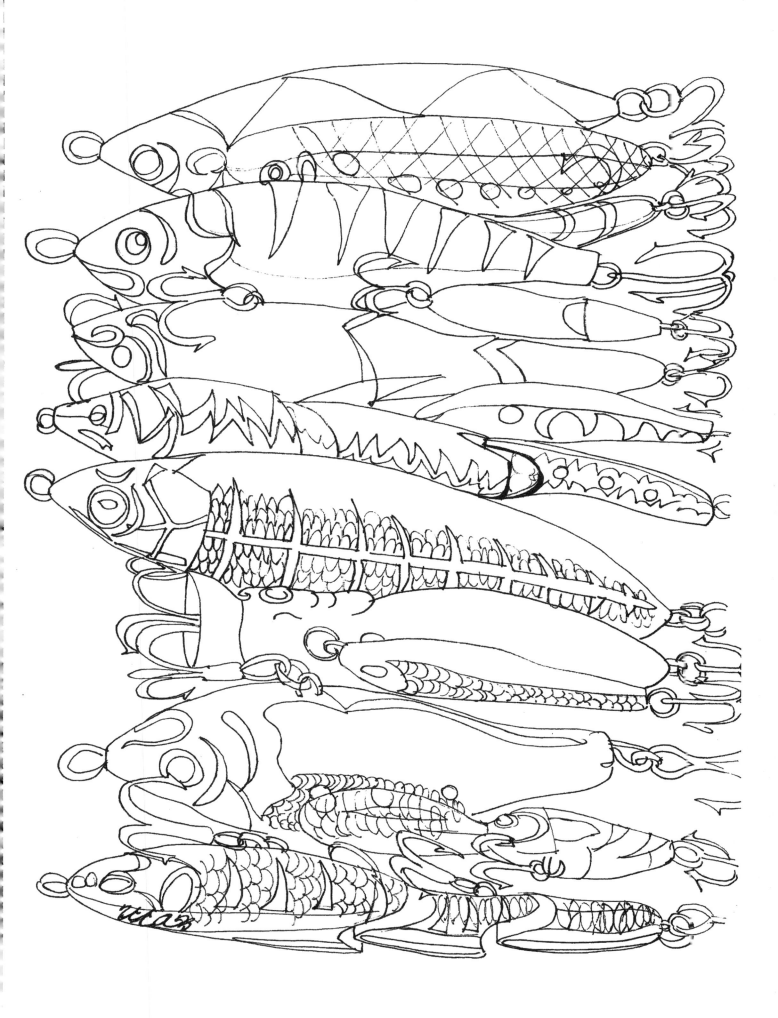

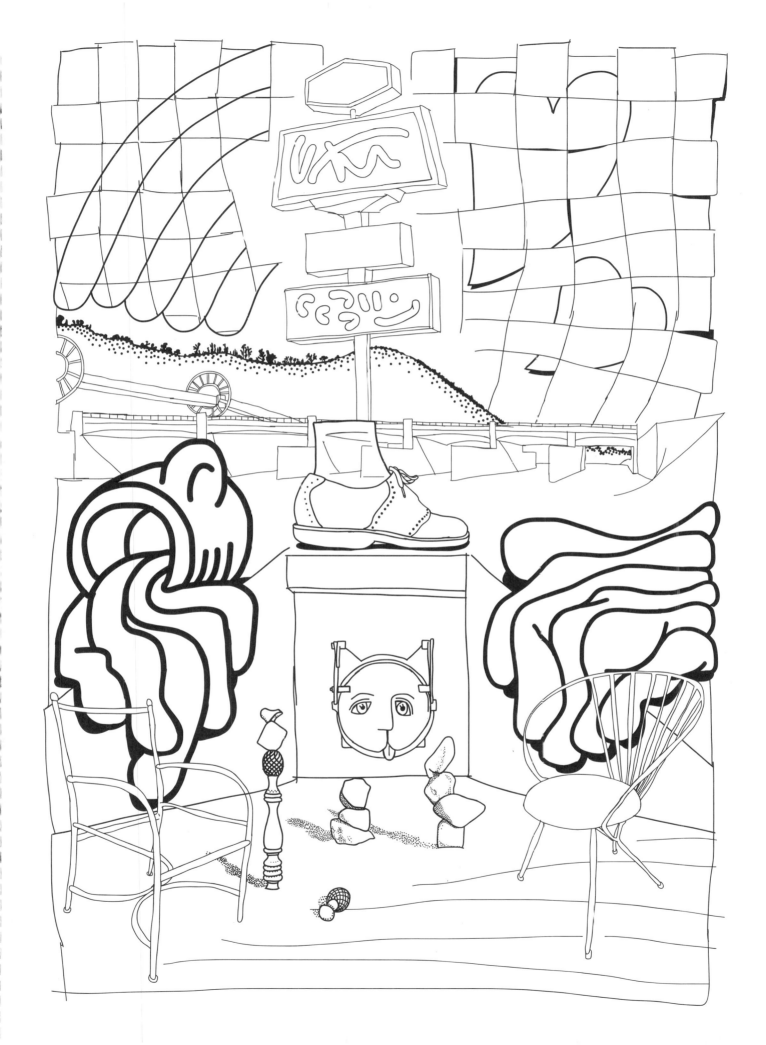

DAVID HORVATH 14

The Ark of Phile

tuesday

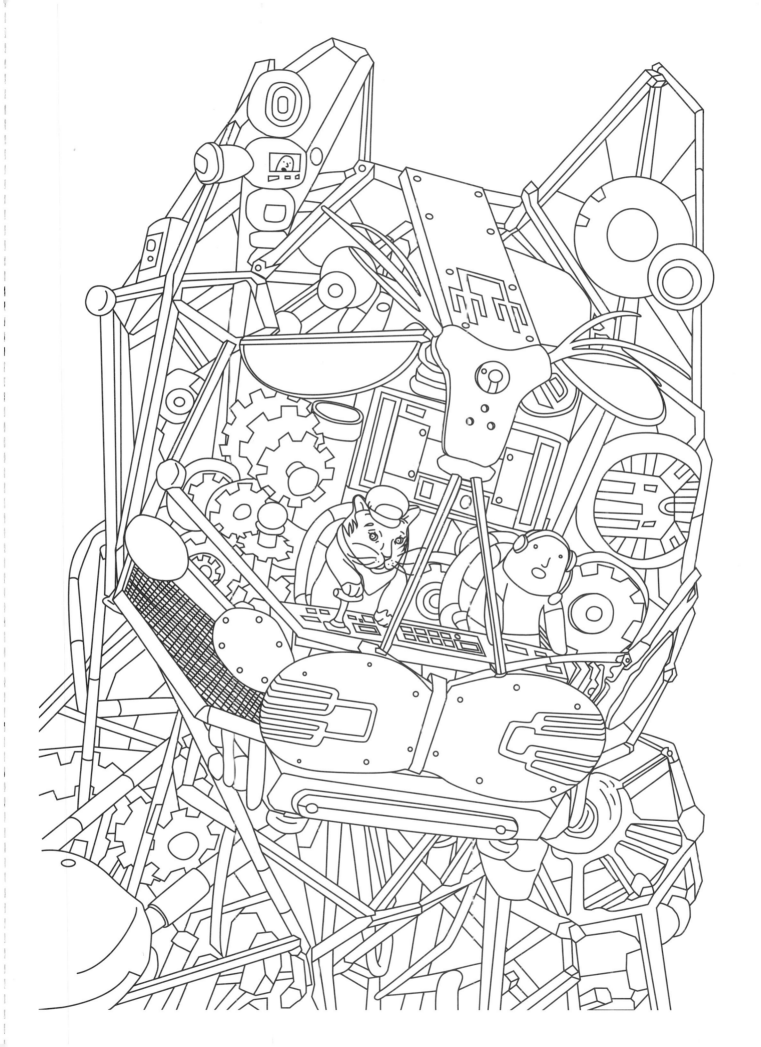

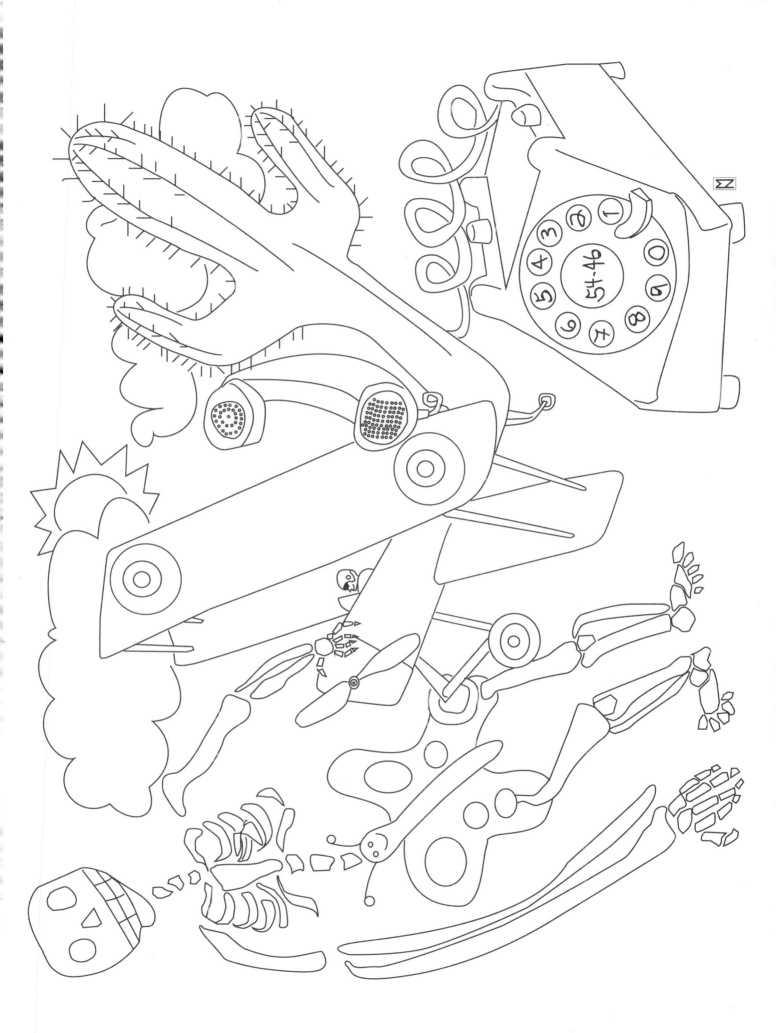

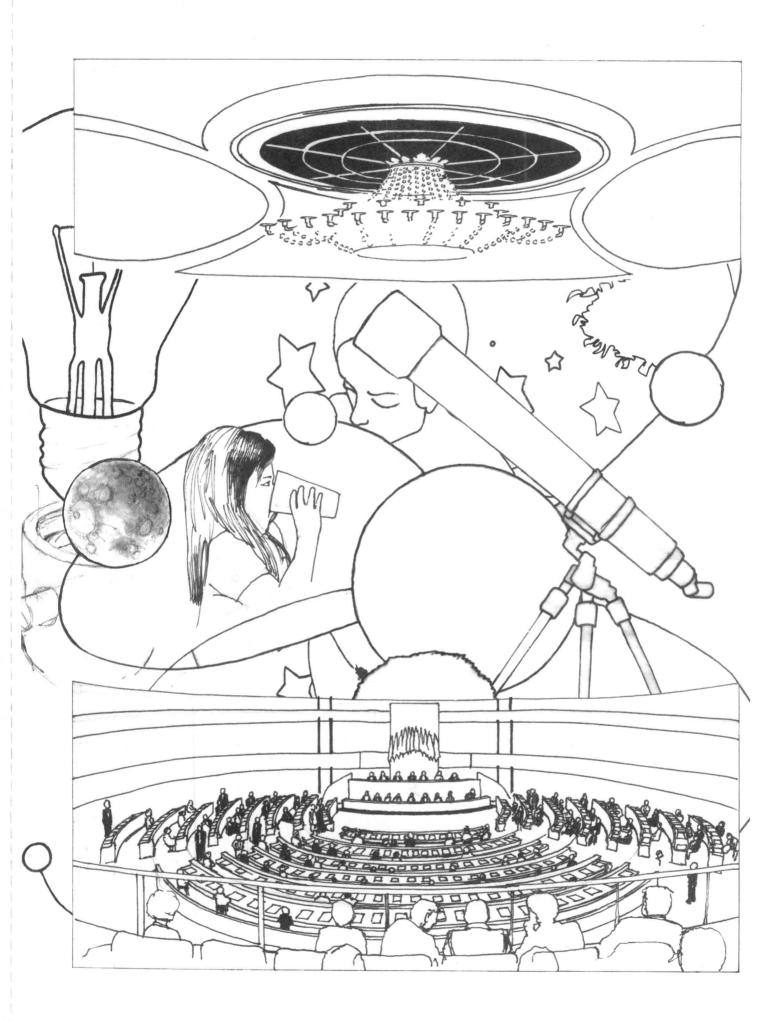

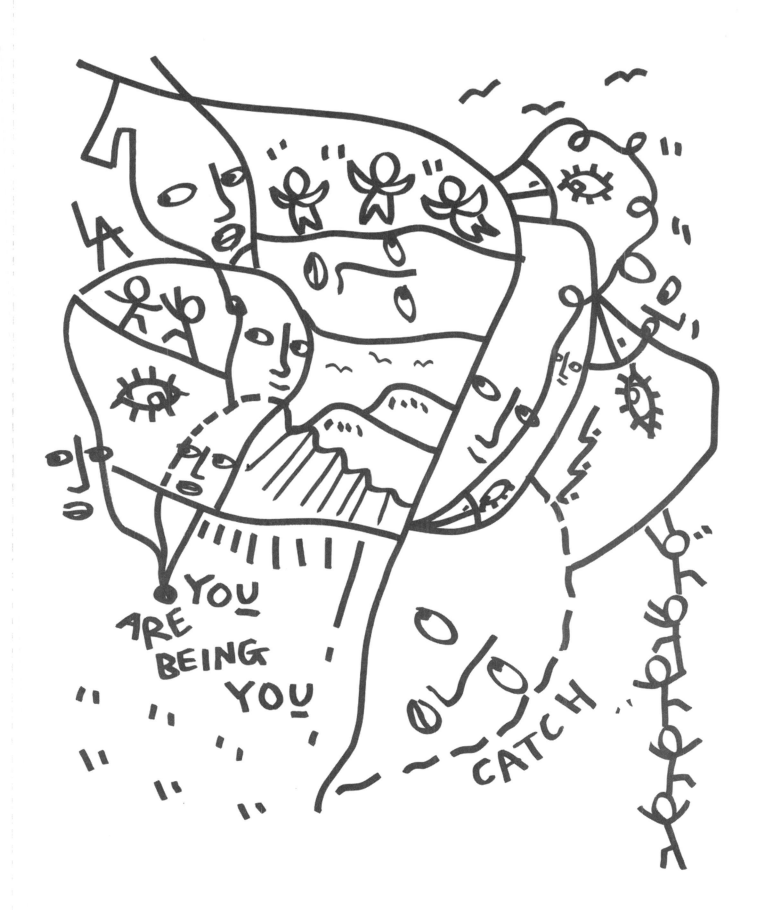

ACKNOWLEDGMENTS

I love art. And I love my creative cabal.

First and foremost, thank you to all the artists who contributed line drawings for this book. Your gusto turned my dream into reality. You inspire me!

Grateful thanks are expressed to my agent, Susanna Einstein; my editors, Amanda Shih and Meg Leder; and my publisher, John Duff, for being rad colleagues and friends.

Help and encouragement came from Dennis Christie, Wendy Dembo, Michelle Borok, Jen Sall, Traci Morlan, MOCA Los Angeles, Monica Roache, Kim O'Grady, Roger Gastman, Todd Roberts, Michele Fleischli, the Windish Agency, Judith Zissman, Rob Maigret, Sunshine Campbell, and frieNDA. Thanks, again.

To all the Smart Girls: Dream bigger!

For my family, who always believes: Ma, Kiki, Emil, Kaly, Hani, Andrew, and Lobo.

For the Nafshun-Bones, Essanee, Le Ba Clan, Dohenys, Hallers, Arnolds, Snyders, and Crystal-Naths, who always cheer me on!

Big love and thanks to my daughter, Lucia Porretta, for reminding me daily to keep it creative. I love this kid!

For all the kindred spirits who color outside the lines, *Outside the Lines, Too* was made for you.

ABOUT THE AUTHOR

Souris Hong is an art enthusiast, idea enabler, and yay-maker. She is co-founder of Creative Cabal, a creative agency headquartered in Los Angeles, California. She lives in an ocean-side community with her daughter and her dog.